Looking Back to See

A Country Music Memoir

MAXINE BROWN

THE UNIVERSITY OF ARKANSAS PRESS • 2005

09   08   07   06   05   5   4   3   2   1

Designed by Liz Lester

∞ The paper used in this publication meets the minimum
requirements of the American National Standard for
Permanence of Paper for Printed Library Materials
Z39.48-1984.

LIBRARY OF CONGRESS
CATALOGING-IN-PUBLICATION DATA

Brown, Maxine, 1931–
      Looking back to see : a country music memoir /
      Maxine Brown.
          p.   cm.
      Discography: p.
      ISBN 1-55728-790-2 (alk. paper)
      1. Browns (Musical group) 2. Country musicians—
United States—Biography. I. Title.
      ML421.B78B76   2005
      782.421642'092'2—dc22
                                            2004025704

*This book is dedicated to the memory
of my mother, Birdie Lee Brown.*

———————

She gave me life, love, courage, and the
strength to face the many problems I've had
during my lifetime. I'm thankful and grateful
to have had her, for she was my greatest
friend who taught me above all things the
power of loving kindness.

CONTENTS

PART 6: The Last Hard Road

FOREWORD

When Maxine was writing this book about her life, her family, her music, and her times, she came by to see me. I had retired to my farm and was always glad to see old friends crop by. As there is no end to things that can be fixed on a farm, we wound up riding around in my pickup truck as we talked and looked for parts and pieces for the things I was "fixing" at the time. What we talked about, of course, was her book. I had written a few and so we supposed I could make intelligent conversation about the project. I knew she was trying to get it right and be fair and accurate. She wanted to leave a record of a very important piece of a remarkable time. I am happy to report now that she has succeeded handsomely.

The book is, by necessity, set in exciting times. The Kennedys, space flight, Elvis, rock and roll, hula hoops, and the Browns.

Ah! The Browns. We heard them everywhere. I heard them first in Germany, where I was with the Army. Ours. Brothers and sisters like the Browns are, as I see it, rare. They not only sang together, they breathed, moved, thought, and listened to the band together. It had to be something in their genes and in their upbringing. It was not at all natural, although they made it sound so. It was more something of a wonder of nature. This is admittedly high praise, but then we have the statistics to back it up. They sold records in the millions.

And so, herein, are the stories of a person (Maxine) and her brother (Jim Ed) and her sister (Bonnie) and all the adventure one could hope to have in three or four lifetimes.

I am happy to have known and worked with this trio and sincerely hope you enjoy the tale. It is told with honesty and humility and in a wonderful American voice.

TOM T. HALL

ACKNOWLEDGMENTS

There are so many people I would like to thank who have helped me during the course of writing this book, but the one person I wish to thank the most is Baxter Clarence Hall. Had it not been for Clarence, this book would have never been seen.

After I finished writing it to the best of my ability, my sister Bonnie insisted that I give it to her friend Clarence Hall to see if it had any potential. Clarence liked it so well that he took it upon himself to put it into book form. He worked hard to improve my efforts, for which I will always be grateful.

It is indeed a great honor to have a man with his credentials help me with my first attempt at writing a book. Some of his accomplishments include being a professor of English at Arkansas Tech University, writer in residence at the University of Arizona, and writer in residence at the University of Houston. He was awarded the Edgar Allan Poe award for nonfiction in 1984 and was elected to the Arkansas Writers hall of Fame in 1997.

I feel very honored and blessed to have had Clarence Hall's guidance and words of encouragement during all the years I felt like giving up.

The people I owe the most besides Clarence Hall are three gentlemen I didn't meet until the latter part of 2001. They are Eric Lensing of Memphis, Tennessee, Edward Morris of Nashville, and Tom Dillard of Little Rock, Arkansas.

Eric Lensing is a freelance writer from Little Rock now living in Memphis. The first time I met Eric was when he came to my home for an interview with my sister Bonnie and myself. He was putting together a story on the Browns for the Memphis newspaper, the *Commercial Appeal*. When he saw I had written a manuscript, he realized how important it was to have it on a computer disk. He went to work editing and transferring my typewritten manuscript to a disk.

Eric worked in Little Rock as a popular deejay for eight years before moving to Dallas, where he wrote and produced nationally syndicated sports programs for radio and television. He is an award-winning author who has had articles published in various periodicals.

It is hard to believe someone would go out on a limb the way he has to help me. He thought I had written a story that needed to be told. I will never be able to thank Eric enough for all he has done for me and for introducing me to his former employer, Tom Dillard.

Tom Dillard was the curator for the Butler Center for Arkansas Studies in Little Rock. We became great friends over the course of a few months while he tried to generate interest in my book. I appreciate Tom's help and his enthusiasm for *Looking Back To See*. Most of all I appreciate him helping me to secure a publishing contract with the University of Arkansas Press. Tom has recently taken a position with the University of Arkansas in Fayetteville as curator for its library system. Good luck, Tom, and thanks a million!

In November 2001, during the Reunion of Professional Entertainers banquet and awards show in Nashville, a friend brought a gentleman to my table and introduced him as Edward Morris. My friend explained that he had given Mr. Morris, a writer, a copy of my manuscript for *Looking Back To See*. The room was so crowded and noisy that we found it difficult to talk, but Mr. Morris did manage to tell me that he had stayed up all night reading my manuscript and thought it was one of the best stories he'd ever read. He said that if I ever needed him to help me get my story published to give him a call. Then he wrote down his phone number, handed it to me and disappeared back into the crowd.

When I asked the people around me who this Edward Morris was, they told me he was the former country music editor of *Billboard* and was currently writing for the Country Music Television Web site CMT.com. I learned later that he had written several books about country music, including a popular one called *Garth Brooks: Platinum Cowboy*. When I returned home to North Little Rock, Arkansas, the first thing I did was give Ed Morris a call. From that moment on, he has been relentless in helping me find a publisher.

Although I had tried years earlier—without success—to interest the University of Arkansas Press in my book, Ed suggested that I try again since the Press now had a new director, Lawrence Malley. Three years after Ed and I first began working together—three years of phone calls, e-mails and reader reports—the Press agreed to publish my manuscript. First, though, I was told, it would need some close editing. All the dates, places, chart positions, and awards I had written about would have to be double-checked and verified. And who better to do this than Ed Morris? He immediately undertook the task as what he called "a labor of love." Ed not only liked my book, I discovered, he also had been one of my biggest fans all those years that the Browns were in show business.

So how do you say thanks to someone like Ed? Well, I guess you do something like this. You let everybody know about him. I will always be grateful for his help, encouragement and friendship, but most of all for this lasting "labor of love."

Over the twelve years it has taken me to write my story, I've tried to convey the difficulties a woman has to face in being a wife, a mother, and a performer, all at the same time. But I'm not sure I've ever gotten my point across. I think I became too emotionally involved in writing some of these painful stories. I don't know how many times the agony of remembering caused me to put the manuscript aside, sometimes for months. When I started writing this, it was for the benefit of my children, who knew very little about some of the bad things that happened between their mom and dad. I had always tried to shield them from those painful times, and I certainly never meant to bare my soul for everyone else to see. But some things need to be told, and I have tried to do that to the best of my knowledge, memory and ability.

MAXINE BROWN
March 2004

INTRODUCTION

Everyone this side of Fabor Robinson's ghost should welcome Maxine Brown's memoir. "Looking Back To See" was the title of the Browns' first hit song (it went to number eight in 1954), and a perfect title for this volume, indicating both retrospective tone and music business focus. What most distinguishes it from other country music autobiographies is its *voice*—strong, consistent, wholly idiosyncratic. From the first pages it's clear that Maxine Brown is now, and was then, a formidable personality—she was the one, after all, who started the whole show by entering her younger brother Jim Ed in a talent contest in 1952—and she comes across here as a woman capable of both enduring rancor and no less enduring gratitude. There's no middle; she almost never says a record is pretty good, or a person just OK. She burns hot, a rhetorical extremist—if she likes you you're a wonderful person, best the world's ever known. If her decision goes the other way you're a snake, a devil in suit and tie. She expresses both feelings fulsomely, and readers will surely be both informed and entertained.

There's a sweeping history here, of the country music business as it boomed from radio into television, flirted with crossover pop success, and dealt with the threat of rock and roll. But the panorama is built with anecdotal blocks, stories told from the perspective of one family group at the heart of these big events, and the anecdotes themselves are vivid and compelling. Sometimes they're hilarious, as when Maxine and Jim Reeves steal a load of Hitler's personal beer steins. Stardom's downtime is a bonegrinding trek, filled with relentless and often dangerous travel, but there are parties aplenty, riotous with booze and sexual escapades.

At other times the anecdotes are petty and sordid—tawdry tales of music industry chicanery starring a huge cast of scumbag promoters, managers, and other company types. Fabor Robinson—a fellow Arkansan, by the way—stars in Maxine Brown's memories as a peculiarly loathsome gargoyle, but he's simply the most prominent of a huge squadron of trolls. (It's reassuring, somehow, when one suspects that Robinson simply couldn't have been THAT bad, to find other accounts confirming her portrait. Colin Escott, for example, interviewed scores of musicians, DJs, and promoters for his 2002 *Roadkill On the Three-Chord Highway.* The summary report on Robinson is a chilling one: "they all came to despise him, and left as soon as they could." Robinson did have one "apologist," a one-time business partner, but the best he could say was that Robinson was "a good man and a Christian man who lost God and became angry and twisted." [1])

At their most harrowing Maxine Brown's stories are simply devastating. Many hard tales are told in *Looking Back To See*—two near rapes, the deaths of beloved parents and siblings, battles with cancer and alcoholism, fires and fatal car wrecks and plane crashes, children left too much alone, parents ravaged by guilt and despair. But these stories, too, for all their horror, are a part of the saga. When Maxine Brown looks back, what she sees is a very mixed scene. At her worst the narrative can almost degenerate into an exhaustive catalogue of unforgotten and unforgiven wrongs. But at her best she manifests a remarkable resilience and generosity of spirit, and surely her narrative gains credibility from its unblinking gaze and unsparing tone.

The story of the Browns has deep ties to Arkansas. From their Sparkman roots to their Little Rock debut on KLRA's *Barnyard Frolic* and later appearances at Robinson Auditorium, to the family restaurant in Pine Bluff, Arkansas places and Arkansas people play central roles in their history. The Browns' sound, featuring smooth close-harmony vocals, appealed across many genres, and was perfect for the great explosion of "crossover" music in the 1950s. Moving outward and upward from their beginnings on the *Barnyard Frolic* and Shreveport's *Louisiana Hayride,* they appeared on *American Bandstand* and the *Ed Sullivan Show* as well as the *Grand Ole Opry,* the *Ozark Jubilee* (in Springfield, Missouri) and the *Town Hall Party* (in Bakersfield, California). They were at the heart of the so-called "Nashville Sound" era, and their biggest hit, 1959's "The Three Bells," is often listed as a "folk revival" piece. Three years after their first record they were singing in Europe (and a Japanese tour was in the future).

Of course their crossover successes were resented by others less capable of them, and the Browns were subjected to sour-grapes accu-

---

[1] Colin Escott, *Roadkill On the Three-Chord Highway* (New York and London: Routledge, 2002), p. 74.

sations of insufficient rusticity. The major anecdote here features a bellicose Little Jimmy Dickens in the purist role, with Maxine as usual counterpunching vigorously. But the whole conflict is baseless— Gene Autry was a telegraph operator, not a cowboy, and Pee Wee King, leader of the Golden West Cowboys, was a polka musician from Milwaukee. The old quarrel is still going strong, too, as if based in reality, with one Nicholas Dawidoff as a contemporary Little Jimmy hammering Garth Brooks at some length in his recent *In The Country of Country.*

A story like this one, then, told in this way by this teller, is at one time an editor's dream and nightmare. The dream is the insider account, the gritty honesty of Maxine Brown's partisan memoir, the detailed eyewitness presence at events long ago turned to legend. Even a glance at the photographs of Elvis Presley, for example, reveals a nascent world, slouching out of Memphis to be born. The nightmare is the sometimes haphazard chronology, the earthy turns of phrase and colloquialisms, the occasional self pity and the more than occasional vituperation.

But in fact something very much like this mix has been present from the beginning, at the very heart of the (generally lame) canon of literature devoted to country music. Here the founding text might be *My Husband Jimmie Rodgers* from 1935, but the field was soon crowded, mostly with losers. Nick Tosches's *Country: The Biggest Music in America* provides a list of low points (many) and high (one, Emma Bell Miles's "Some Real American Music" from 1904, reprinted in her 1905 classic, *The Spirit of the Mountains*). Another obvious high point, though not noted by Tosches, is Alton Delmore's memoir, the wonderfully titled *Truth Is Stranger Than Publicity.*

In her salty indomitability Maxine Brown may at times remind readers of Patsy Cline. Or at her most outrageous she might even come across as a female counterpart of Ronnie Hawkins. But finally all comparisons fail; Maxine Brown is Maxine Brown, and there's nobody else quite like her. The editors at the University of Arkansas Press chose wisely, interposing no editorial extreme makeover and eschewing the full-bore scholarly introduction. What is provided is an appendix, capably compiled by Kelly Owens and John Riley, providing very brief informational entries for many persons and programs whose reputation Maxine Brown takes for granted. But you can't take show business reputations for granted, even for a decade. It's difficult for anyone who lived through their glory days to imagine (let alone accept), but in a class of thirty-eight undergraduate university students in the spring of 2004, only four were familiar with Guy Lombardo and only six could identify Jim Reeves as a country singer. Frank Sinatra was familiar, though not always as a singer, to twenty-nine. Only Elvis Presley was known to all.

Maxine Brown in all her rowdy glory has not only a great Arkansas story, but also a great American story to tell. She was there when great things happened; she shared stages with everybody from Ira Louvin to Ricky Nelson. She saw Elvis at the beginning of his incredible, tragic ride. She's appalling and wonderful. She is, quite simply, the real thing, a brash, ambitious, talented country girl from Arkansas here with the tale of her real-life magic carpet ride, complete with bumps and crashes. *Looking Back To See* is her story, in her words. She does the looking, and we get to see.

ROBERT COCHRAN
Center for Arkansas and Regional Studies
University of Arkansas

PART ONE

Fire and Hunger

Living Lean and Country Values

I was only three years old when I first found out that fire and hunger are sometimes the same thing. That was back in 1934, in a time we now call the Great Depression, and we were a family named the Browns. Like so many poor people who had to endure those hard times, we were more than just a family. We were a strong clan, solid as native stone, living together and laughing and loving and singing as we tried to survive down there in the poor piney woods of south Arkansas.

Uncle Harvey and Daddy hunted and trapped for a living. We ate the wild game and sold the hides for a few dollars a month, and that's all we had to live on. For a mink, they could get two dollars, for a fox, a dollar twenty-five, for a coon, seventy-five cents, and for a big possum twenty-five cents. One year there was no game, and all daddy caught in his traps was a red fox. With the money for its skin, he went into the town of Sparkman and bought a sixty-four-pound sack of flour, a one-pound can of coffee and a bucket of lard, all for a dollar twenty-five. But in all the bad times, I don't think any one of us Browns ever complained or even thought about being unhappy. We didn't know it then, but living off the land must have made us stronger in the long run and given us something special to carry through the years. It's like the time someone asked Hank Williams Jr. what the difference was between his songs and his daddy's music. "What's missing is the poverty," he said. And maybe that's the difference between the music we made and the songs you hear today.

When I was three years old, we were visiting at Uncle Harvey's house. My brother J. E. was just a baby then and asleep in the bedroom; I used to have to take care of him some. When I went in to check on him, I saw fire all around him on the floor and walls. I ran to the kitchen to tell Aunt Ester, who was cooking a big supper of turnip greens, fried potatoes, and cornbread. All I can remember is that they got J. E. and put him out in the middle of the gravel road. I had to stay with him and watch everybody running in and out of the house trying to save a few things. That old house burned to the ground. The smell of that fire lingers in my mind to this day. Aunt Ester's cooking, like my Momma's, had the most delicious aroma in the world, though it somehow gets mixed up in my mind with smoldering timbers and ashes. Of course, no one got to eat any of Aunt Ester's cooking that day.

Uncle Harvey needed sixty dollars to buy fertilizer and seed to plant his next year's crop. He went to the bank, and they wanted to know what he had for collateral. He said, "I've got a horse, a cow, a calf, some one-horse plow tools and, of course, the crop when it's harvested." The bank president told him, "If you will assign us all these assets you just mentioned, and get two upstanding citizens to sign your note, I will let you have the $60." Uncle Harvey told him, "You kiss where I can't and go to hell." He didn't get to plant his crop that year. We were all hungry after that.

• • •

Daddy finally got a job working on a farm for a family called the Butlers for twelve dollars a month. We lived in a dirt-floor shack out in the middle of the farm. Uncle Harvey and Aunt Ester came to live with us after they lost their house. Then, after Grandpa Tuberville died, Grandma Tuberville lived with us too. The house didn't have a single shade tree, and the cracks between the boards on the porch were so wide that if you stuck your toe or hand down there too far, a chicken would peck it. Somehow we all found ways to make it through. I loved sneaking up to the landowner's big house and smelling the aroma of rich food coming out of the kitchen. I'd sometimes peek in the front window at all the pretty things in the house. Now that I think of it, those people might not have been all that rich. But to me it was as bright and beautiful as Aladdin's palace.

After two years of farming for the Butlers, Daddy was offered more money to farm for the Frank Ballard family, who lived only a short distance up the road. Every time Daddy would take a load of cotton into Sparkman, he would go by the local sawmill to inquire about work. Mr. Sam Horn, who owned the mill, assured him that if he ever had an opening he would be sure to let him know. There were two restaurants in town, and when Daddy had to go past them, he would hold his nose and run like hell to get past because the smell of all that food made it unbearable. Although hamburgers cost only ten cents each and a bowl of chili was only fifteen cents, he never had a nickel to buy anything. He knew some of the men from the sawmill ate there and that there had to be something better in life than farming for a living. When he told the Ballards that he was going to work at the mill in Sparkman if and when an opportunity presented itself, they told him we would have to move out of our shack. They said they had to have someone they could depend on for the full season.

So we moved into another house of sorts about a mile behind Herschel Thrower's country store. It was while we lived there that I first remember seeing a hog butchered. Even though it was a horrible experience to watch, I loved the cracklins from the hog's skin that my Momma made in a big old black pot outside the house. My job was stirring those cracklins, and I'd have to stand there and do it all day. When Momma made cornbread from those cracklins, it was the best stuff I had ever tasted.

After rendering all the fat and then storing it in gallon jugs for cooking, we would take the best part of the hog—the hams, shoulders, and backbone—and rub them down real good with salt and sugar. We would then store the meat in salt bins in our smokehouse. We ground up the rest of the hog for sausage. Hog-killing season was a favorite time for country folks, and everyone would share what they had with each other. Nothing in the world tasted as good as sugar-cured ham, red-eye gravy and biscuits. The memory of those country delicacies is still with me to this day.

One day Momma sent me down to the store. I was wearing a red dress. There was a mean old bull in the pasture that hated the color red. Momma kept a watch out for me as I went down the dirt road. It was a good thing she did, because that bull broke through the fence and started after me. I could hear Momma screaming for me to run, which I did, with that bull right on my heels and Momma right on its heels with a big broom. Good old Herschel saw what was happening and ran out to divert the bull's attention. I'm sure I had only a couple of flour-sack dresses, and this red one was my favorite. But Momma would never let me wear that red dress again as long as we lived there.

It was early spring when Daddy got word that Mr. Horn needed someone to help unload logs at the sawmill. This job came along just at the right time. That winter, the only things Daddy caught in his traps were a fox and two minks. Wild game had become very scarce.

By then, though, times were getting much better. Mr. Neal Woods, an independent contractor for Horn's sawmill, came to Daddy and offered him a job hauling logs for two dollars a day. This was more money than he had ever made before. We moved into a rundown shack on the sawmill grounds. The front part of the shack had a wooden floor, but the back part was nothing but packed-down sawdust.

In 1937, the time came for me to start school. My Momma made me wear a pair of old-timey, long brown stockings. From the minute I stepped onto the schoolyard in those tacky stockings, I was the laughing stock. I was also tall for my age, taller than anybody else in first grade. I was always stooping over so I could be on the other kids' level. They teased and taunted me all the more. I failed the first grade. I never could get on their level. I've often wondered, though, just who was passing and who was failing.

• • •

One night Grandma Tuberville saved our lives. Daddy was working out in the logging woods for a little extra money, and we were in the house by ourselves. After we had gone to bed, we heard a loud noise outside and then somebody was pushing against the door. Pretty soon the noise got louder, and the door hinges started cracking.

"Somebody's trying to break in and rob us," Momma said and grabbed J. E. and me up in her arms. The intruder was banging harder on the door. It sounded like a sledgehammer. We were scared to death and didn't know what to do. But Grandma was a tough old lady. Many a time she had told us about living out in the wild country where they had to defend themselves against Indians. What she did next proved that she still had a lot of that old-time spunk left in her.

Grandma got Daddy's shotgun and came to stand in front of us all. She told Momma to hold onto the babies and not let go no matter what happened. Then she hollered out, "Whoever you are out there, if you don't get away from that door, I'll blow a daylight hole right through you!" The intruder didn't heed Grandma's warning. He kept pounding on the door until it sounded like it was going to break in. Grandma didn't give a second warning. She raised the shotgun and let go a blast that blew the whole door off!

We heard a big yelp outside. Our intruder must have been wounded or scared to death because he howled out of there before the smoke cleared. We didn't have a front door anymore, but we did have one brave Grandma. Nobody came bothering us again as long as we lived in that place.

• • •

After making two dollars a day for so long working for someone else, Daddy decided to go into business for himself. He was getting more and more mouths to feed. Our little brother, Raymond, and little sister, Bonnie, were born in 1936 and 1938 while we were living in Sparkman. Mr. Horn knew by now that Daddy was a faithful and hard worker. So he bought Daddy a brand new truck and a team of mules. Mr. Horn allowed Daddy to repay the loan for these things at fifty cents per thousand feet of timber he brought into the sawmill.

There was a big farm for sale near a place called Holly Springs, nine miles out of Sparkman, for one thousand dollars. Daddy thought we'd all be better off living on a farm and that he could make more money by farming his own place. After all, those people he'd farmed for before, such as the Butlers and the Ballards, seemed to be pretty well off. After he got Mr. Horn paid off for the truck and team of mules, he turned around and sold the truck for $1,100 and kept the team of mules. He bought the farm for one thousand dollars and kept the extra hundred dollars to buy seeds and fertilizer. Once we moved to the farm, the mules and a wagon were our only means of transportation. It was a poor but workable farmstead, and our house was big but rickety. Still, it had lots of rooms for Floyd and Birdie Brown's kids to grow up in. With a lot of fixing, we made it a home.

We were kind of stuck, way out there in the country. Our nearest neighbors down the road were black people, and they were as suspicious of us as we were of them, the times being what they were. But there came a time when we had to ask these folks for help. J. E. had a bad habit of getting himself into life-threatening situations. He had already survived being burned up in a house fire. Then, one morning after we'd been living on our farm awhile, he took it upon himself to fall off our big barnyard fence and break his arm.

Daddy had gone to work, and we were all alone. We could see that J. E.'s arm was badly broken. And he was deathly pale. We didn't have any transportation and there was no traffic going up or down our road. It must have been some kind of holiday because even the mail truck didn't run that day. After standing out in the road for what seemed like hours, waiting to flag down a car or truck that never came, I finally ran all the way up the hill to the black people's house. I begged them to come and help us. At first, I think they thought I was trying to play some trick on them. But after a while, they said they would come and take J. E. to town in their pickup. They said they couldn't leave the fields, though, until they finished the day's work.

Poor little J. E. suffered all day with that broken arm all swollen up. We didn't think the black family was even going to come. But along about sundown, here they came in their old rattletrap truck. They took us into Sparkman to the doctor. I was upset that they had taken so long, because I thought my little brother was going to die. Later, however, I grew to understand the reasons for their caution and understood their willingness to help us was an act of kindness. Down in south Arkansas during the Depression, not too much kindness had come our way, and it certainly hadn't come their way either.

Farming wasn't all Daddy thought it would be. After that first year, he still didn't have ten cents in his pocket to buy one of those good smelling hamburgers in Sparkman. So he turned the farming over to his brothers and took a job in Fordyce hauling gravel. Times had gotten so bad that Daddy had to sell his team of mules in order to feed the family. J. E. was only seven years old, but Daddy had him drive that team of mules to their new owner, who lived thirteen miles away. Momma cried and begged Daddy not to have J. E. do this because one of the mules was mean and hard to handle. She was still wringing her hands and praying when J. E. finally made it back home late that night with the money.

Our nearest neighbors, the black family, lived about a mile and a half from our house. They sharecropped for a man named Posey who lived a short distance on up the road toward Holly Springs. Mr.

Posey had been stricken with polio in both legs and was unable to work his farm. But he managed to get around quite well on crutches in his tiny little grocery store, which was about the size of four outdoor johns. He built this tiny store right outside his front door so he wouldn't have too far to walk. He sold only the things that county folks needed, such as flour, salt, sugar, cornmeal, coffee, and lard.

Every so often, Momma would send me to his store for something. On those occasions, Mr. Posey would give me a piece of hardtack candy that he let me choose from his tiny collection of sweets. Sometimes Momma would give me two or three pennies to buy the other kids some candy. You could buy a whole sack full for a nickel.

I'm sure Momma worried about me having to walk that distance by myself. But about the only thing we had to worry about back then were hobos, and they really were harmless. I don't know where they came from or where they were going, but there were a lot of them. Some of them were probably Army deserters. Momma would always fix them a plate of whatever she had to eat, even though we barely had enough to eat ourselves. We all watched and wondered why men would bum their way around the countryside the way they did. I always thought they looked so pitiful. They never talked to us very much. But they always told Momma how much they appreciated her sharing our food with them.

• • •

About a year after we moved in, another white family moved onto a farm about a mile down the road from us. That's how I made my first friend. Her name was Leona Hearne. She was a year older than I was. We became fast friends. And what a treasure it was for a lonely country kid to have a true companion! I was ten years old then, and my Momma gave me my first birthday party. Only two other kids came to the party, Leona and a cute boy named Travis Motes, who lived way up the road. It was a surprise party. I was outside the house sitting on the front steps when Leona and Travis came walking up. Leona was carrying a heart-shaped box of store-bought candy. The box was as red as a Coca-Cola sign and the prettiest thing I had even seen. I treasured it as a keepsake for years and years after. Then I noticed that Travis was carrying a batch of cookies that his mother had sent. "Happy Birthday!" they yelled. It was the greatest moment of my young life.

My Momma had saved up some nickels and dimes and bought me a pair of roller skates. I'd always dreamed of having a pair of skates. Back in those days, even poor country kids wanted skates. Anything that could carry you fast and smooth on the wind was like a fairy tale, especially to those of us who were stuck hard and fast to that old rutted earth.

The first time I tried the skates, I hit a clod of dirt and fell down so hard I was knocked unconscious. I woke up to feel everybody beating on my back trying to start my breathing again. I should have learned a big lesson with those skates. Years later, as I skated my way in and out of the music business, I found life offered many big falls along with the sweet rides.

• • •

Our social life in those days consisted of going to church and visiting Uncle Harvey and his family. When we went to Uncle Harvey's, we also got to go to Thrower's Grocery Store. Thrower's was a little bit of everything to us, our Macy's and Saks, our fashion store and country club and Disney World. A nickel or dime could buy you a jawbreaker or Baby Ruth bliss.

People from miles around would gather at the store. One of the great social activities that took place in that grand old place was the community quilting bee. My Momma always took part in the quilting and was considered a true artist at it. She did so much quilting—along with her fieldwork on the farm—that she developed a bone felon on the tip of her finger. I can remember her crying in pain with this horrible infection. There was no money for a doctor, so she healed herself with an old-time remedy Grandma Tuberville had concocted. When it finally healed, Momma was left with a big knot on her quilting finger. She was unable to wear a thimble, which was a must for pushing the needle through the heavy quilting material. But this didn't stop Momma. She simply put the thimble on her fourth finger and learned to adjust. In no time she was back at Thrower's country store, making those beautiful hand-crafted quilts. They would be called state-of-the-art today, and probably bring hundreds of dollars. Back in those days, we used them for warmth during the raw south Arkansas winters. We never thought we were sleeping under priceless artwork.

While all the ladies of the countryside were quilting, I'd get to visit Grandma Tuberville, who was living then with Uncle Harvey. How I loved listening to her tell us stories of her childhood and how she and her family had fought off the Indians and survived storms and floods. Grandma Tuberville was the best storyteller I've ever heard. She probably would have been a wonderful songwriter if she had had different circumstances. I've always thought that maybe I inherited some of her spirit, for I can still hear her sweet, sad voice talking about the people's troubles and trials and tragedies.

One morning when he was driving the company truck, Daddy dropped us off at Uncle Harvey's on his way to work. That afternoon, a terrible storm came up. Uncle Harvey kept saying, "Floyd had better get back pretty soon or you all will have to stay here for a week. That old Tulip Creek bottom is gonna be rising." The rain turned into real gully washer. Pretty soon, no cars or wagons could get through the bottoms—the fields that lay beside the creek. When Daddy finally showed up, Momma was mad because she thought he had tarried too long and had probably taken a few drinks with the men he logged with.

"Floyd, I can smell it on your breath," Momma accused him.

"That might be creosote too, Birdie, and right now we've got to worry about getting through Tulip Creek."

"We're not taking my babies through high water," Momma said.

Daddy was determined to go home, even though Uncle Harvey was scared about us trying to cross Tulip Creek. Nothing would do for Daddy but to pile all the kids into that old truck and strike out. When we got to the bottom of Peanut Hill, we could see the high water, and it was as scary as the parting of the Red Sea. There stood the man everybody called Peanut, the one the hill was named after.

"Better not try it, Floyd," Peanut yelled, but Daddy drove on down to the bridge. The water was already above the bridge support and rising every minute. Momma kept begging Daddy not to go onto that wobbly old bridge, but he was bullheaded and not afraid of anything. Water was up to the railings as we moved onto the Tulip Creek bridge. Daddy thought he could hold the truck in a straight line but he couldn't. The truck veered to the right and water started running into the floorboard of the truck. All us kids started screaming, and Momma yelled out that we were all going to be drowned.

All of a sudden, the truck slipped into deeper water and the motor died. We were going over the side for sure. Daddy somehow got out his door and pulled J. E. and me out and lifted us into the truck's bed. The truck was leaning halfway over now, and Daddy managed to get Momma and the two babies, Raymond and Bonnie, to the side that was still out of the water. In another minute we would be goners. Even if any of us could swim—and none of us could— we wouldn't survive those rapids. Suddenly, the truck slipped again and began leaning on its side.

"Hold on, I'm coming!" yelled Peanut.

Little Raymond was almost swept away then. Daddy reached and grabbed his foot, the boot came off, and Daddy grabbed him again just before he went under the rapids. The next thing we knew, Peanut was there with his team of mules, pulling us out. Within another minute or less, we would have all drowned. Thank God for Peanut and his great team of mules! When we were back on firm ground again, we sat there and listened to Momma give thanks to the good Lord for sparing us.

The darned old truck was washed out and wouldn't start, of course. But we didn't mind. We were alive. We all started walking home. We were so cold and wet that we must have looked like war refugees. How good it felt to crawl into a feather bed and pull one of Momma's elegant quilts up over us. Years later, whenever I heard Johnny Cash singing, "How high's the water, Momma?" I would always shudder to myself and think about the raging waters of Tulip Creek.

• • •

Grandma Tuberville came to stay with us now and again, and I was always excited to see her. One day she did something so funny that I couldn't stop laughing for hours. She was out in the field helping J. E. and me with our cotton rows, and she needed to pee. The outhouse was too far away, so Grandma just stood straight up, pulled her dress out from her legs and let it fly. Not a drop touched her skin. A few days later I was out in the field and I decided I'd try it. And I peed all over myself.

"Grandma," I asked, "How in the world do you do that?"

"Well, child," she said, "I've only got one pair of britches, and I save them for church. So I don't wear anything under there. That's why I can pee standing up."

Nowadays you hear a lot of talk about adults being role models for children. I'm not sure anyone is good enough to play that kind of role in our times. But I believe if there were more Grandma Tubervilles in the world, we might not have so many confused kids heading in the wrong direction.

* * *

We were all growing up—me and J. E. and Raymond and Bonnie —and getting into the usual cornsilk-smoking mischief and getting the old-fashioned discipline of a leather belt or hickory switch. We still delighted in our family outings to Uncle Harvey's, especially when he was making sorghum molasses (I always felt sorry for that old mule who had to walk in circles all day to power the machine that squeezed the juice out of the sugar cane.) We went to church as often as we could, even though the Sardis Methodist Church was a long way, about seven miles, from our house. One of my biggest thrills was getting to ride in our cotton wagon to the gin in Sparkman whenever we'd picked a bale of cotton. Lord, how we hated to pick cotton. It's the hardest work in the world. I remember putting rocks in my sack to make it weigh more. Country kids just naturally worked more than they ever got to play, and maybe that's why they make better ball players and musicians, poets, comedians, and lawyers.

Another reason I hated to pick cotton was because I was constantly stepping on Devil's Snuff, and I just knew the devil was out to get me. Devil's Snuff was sort of like a big mushroom. When you stepped on it, brown dust would fly out. Our cotton field was full of it. I had always been told that the devil lived in the ground and that if you stepped on his snuff, he'd come up out of the ground to get you. I was so afraid I was going to hell that I had nightmares about it. So finally Momma let me stay home and take care of Bonnie and do chores around the house while she went to the cotton field in my place. This is when I learned how to cook. Daddy always bragged on my old-time butter cake with chocolate icing and often said it was better than Momma's. You can't imagine what this did for my ego back then. For the rest of his life, I took pride in making him his favorite cake.

Every farm family in those days had a dinner bell. When dinner was ready at home, I would go outside and ring the bell to let all the farm hands know it was time to come eat. (We called it breakfast, dinner, and supper. Nowadays it's breakfast, lunch, and dinner.) The dinner bell was also used to sound an alarm if something was wrong around the house. We were always told not to ring it unless something was wrong. One day, J. E. thought it would be funny to ring it as a joke. Everyone out in the field stopped what they were doing and came running. Unlike J. E., they didn't think it was funny at all. He never did it again.

Having treats was a rarity. One day Daddy came home with a truckload of what he called "like bread." (It was lighter and fluffier than homemade bread.) The grocery store owner in Sparkman had thrown it away because it was several days old. We all thought it was the best stuff we had ever tasted. J. E. and I were in hog heaven. Instead of sausage and biscuits in our school lunch pail, we had sausage and "like bread." Another rare treat was ice. Now and then the county ice truck would stop, and we'd get enough ice to make ice cream in a molasses bucket. We kept our milk down in the well to keep it from spoiling and our ice in toe sacks to slow its melting. To make ice cream, we mixed a little sugar with the rich milk we got from our old Jersey cow. Then we put the mixture in a molasses bucket, placed it inside a big old oaken bucket, and surrounded it with chipped ice. We rotated the molasses bucket by its bail—or handle—until the mixture inside froze into ice cream. No other ice cream in the world tasted half as good!

We caught the school bus and rode nine miles to the country school. When we got home, Momma would always have something good for us to eat, whether it was a baked sweet potato with churned butter or sugar cookies. Momma worked in the fields and did all the housework too. But she always managed to have a smile on her face. If she was ever burdened down, she never showed it in front of the kids.

• • •

One day, a carnival came to the big city of Sparkman. We'd never seen anything like it and probably didn't know beforehand that there was such a thing. The carnival didn't have elephants and lions and dancing bears and beautiful trapeze ladies. It was just a plain old carnival with rides, sideshows, and games that beat people out of their money. Mom and Dad loaded up all us children, and we took off to Sparkman. You'd have thought we were going to the World's Fair.

They had this Loop-A-Plane ride that looked totally dangerous but terribly exciting. No one had enough courage to ride it until finally Daddy said he'd take me on it. The Loop-A-Plane went way up in the air, taking my breath away as it spun around like a bullet. All you could hear was yelping and screaming. Then it stopped dead. When it did, we heard a big, fat woman up above us screaming for mercy. All of a sudden, we got a shower, even though the sky was filled with stars and no rain cloud was in sight. The fat woman above us had wet her britches! More such showers were in the forecast, too. We yelled at the top of our lungs for them to stop that infernal contraption and let us off. We were soaking wet and sick to our stomachs.

When we finally did get off, Daddy discovered that he had lost his billfold (it had fallen out of his pocket when they turned us upside down). We looked everywhere but couldn't find it. Since it had all Daddy's money in it, we had to leave the carnival. We didn't get to see very many of the sideshows. The bearded lady, the crocodile man, and the hermaphrodite were part of every country kid's education back then. We couldn't wait until the next year.

•   •   •

Grandpa Brown was almost crushed to death when a load of logs fell on him. He spent months flat on his back, and I remember when we went to see him that he had that stricken look of old people. The doctor wouldn't allow him to eat anything but raw eggs (maybe that was some sort of country cure in those days). We'd gather eggs from the hen house and Daddy would either walk, catch a ride, or hitch up the wagon and go to Grandpa Brown's house so he could have his eggs.

One night my little brother Raymond woke up screaming. He kept yelling, "Paw Paw Brown! Paw Paw Brown!" He got everybody up, and when we gathered around his bed a chill came over us. "Something has happened to Daddy," my Daddy said. Right there, in the middle of the night, Daddy got dressed and walked the nine miles to Grandpa Brown's house in Sparkman. He learned that Grandpa Brown had died at the exact time Raymond had awakened screaming his name. This gave me the strangest feeling I'd ever had. Something or someone higher than this world had let us know through our little brother Raymond that Grandpa had died. I think we always knew that Raymond was a special kid. Just a few years later, when Raymond was taken from us, I got that same strange, mournful feeling that will haunt me all the days of my life. Sweet little Raymond was the love of our lives. I know there is a perfect song somewhere being sung about him.

• • •

Back in those troubled times, poor people like us somehow always managed to "keep on the sunny side," as that great old song says. I can't remember a time when we didn't have some sort of music going. My Daddy's family had always been known for its music. From the time I was a little girl, I remember Daddy and his older brothers singing and playing. Back in those days, we had what were called "country dances." They weren't the hoedowns or barn dances you've seen in movies. My Daddy and uncles played those dances, which always took place in someone's house. Folks would come from miles around and bring all the kids, and the dances would last way into the night. How I loved watching my Momma square dance while Daddy played the guitar! Many a time we'd ride back home in our wagon very late at night because they'd keep playing until everyone left. People always took up a collection for the Brown Band. It wasn't ever much money—a few nickels and dimes—but still the Brown brothers loved playing and singing songs like "Old Joe Tucker" and "Wait For the Wagon." One day while Daddy was chopping wood, the ax flew off the handle and almost cut his finger off. It didn't heal properly, and he was left with a crippled hand, no longer able to chord the guitar. This ended the Brown brothers' music making.

Music was still a part of our everyday lives. Even many families that were poor owned pump organs that had been handed down from generation to generation. When Grandpa Brown died, Grandma Brown came to live next door to us and brought her pump organ. She taught us how to play it, and I guess all of us kids played that grand old thing until it finally wore out. There was no way we could afford to have it fixed. So Uncle Cecil took all the strings out of it and put them on his beat up old Sears and Roebuck guitar. He whittled down the ivory from the keys and made guitar picks. Cecil gave the guitar to J. E. and taught him how to chord. Right then and there, I guess, the Brown Trio was born. J. E. played while he, little brother Raymond, and I started learning how to harmonize. We were just little kids but people all around started coming to hear us and brag on us. We were "those cute little Brown kids who can sing as sweet a harmony as anything you'll ever hear on the *Grand Ole Opry*."

We never took the bragging seriously. We just wanted to sing anytime we could. Singing was always the best feeling you could have. It was better than ice cream, roller skates, or Thrower's country store. Singing was just what we country people did back in those times. We had no thoughts of anything beyond it, no hopes, ambitions, or dreams of glory. But they would come. On Saturday nights, we gathered around our old, bulky battery-powered radio and waited for the "solemn old judge" George D. Hay to toot his familiar steamboat whistle and proclaim: "It's time for the *Grand Ole Opry*! Let 'er go, boyyys!!!"

I don't think we ever missed a single Saturday night listening to Roy Acuff's "Great Speckled Bird" and "Wreck on the Highway." Oh, the mournful, soul-thrilling sound of that dobro! And I remember how my heart would break when I heard Eddy Arnold sing, "Mommy Please Stay Home with Me" and his yodeling theme song, "The Cattle Call." The next minute, though, Minnie Pearl and Rod Brasfield's antics would have us roaring with laughter.

Our radio listening was rationed. We were allowed to listen only to the *Grand Ole Opry* on Saturday nights because we had to save our radio battery—a huge boxy thing almost as big as a table radio that quickly lost its power. This was before we had electricity, of course, so a dead battery meant no radio. I can't remember a time when the battery went dead, however. If it had, I doubt that my folks would have been able to afford a new one.

It's hard now to explain just what the *Grand Ole Opry* meant to people back then. It was more than just a favorite radio show, like the *Jack Benny Show* or *Lux Radio Theater*. It was a very nourishing part of our lives. J. E. and I never thought about growing up and maybe being good enough someday to be a part of the *Opry*. Kids didn't have such dreams in our time. They would have been too far-fetched to live with. The *Grand Ole Opry* was too special to be put on the level of a child's dream. It gave more than simple entertainment, more than songs and laughter and even hope. It carried poor people through troubled times and helped strengthen family bonds when bonds were breaking up everywhere. In a very real way, it made good on the promise of one of its much-played songs. It widened out to all of us that wonderful circle that would always be unbroken.

Raymond's Death and Daddy's Logging Accident

Our little brother Raymond was a free spirit. Even though he was only seven years old, he seemed to me to be wise beyond his years, and he always had a way of cheering us up and making us laugh. I think maybe Momma and Daddy might have favored him a little, too, but that was all right because we all loved him best. J. E. and I were a few years older than Raymond, but his voice was strong and clear when we sang together. We could tell that he was going to be the best singer of all the Browns.

It was Labor Day 1943. The next day we would all start school again. Like so many country kids, myself included, Raymond had failed the first grade and would have to repeat it. How they had managed to fail Raymond in the first grade I'll never know, for he was about the brightest little kid around. I remember clearly Raymond telling me that day, "Sis, I ain't ever going back to that old schoolhouse again."

There was a lot of hardwood timber in old Tulip Creek bottom close by our house. Because Daddy was having a hard time making it on our dirt farm, he had to hire himself out again as a log loader. We were already getting fall rains, and Daddy had left two loads down in the woods until the ground dried out. On that day before school started, all us kids were just hanging around the house looking for something to do. J. E. and Raymond had been begging Daddy to let them go with him down into the logging woods. He had told the boys that if they'd get rid of the possum that had been getting into our chicken house, he'd let them go with him. So they found and killed it. I remember Raymond chasing me all around the house with that dead possum, just dying laughing because he knew I couldn't stand to look at such things. He teased me something awful for being afraid to look at an old dead possum. A little bit later, Raymond and J. E. took off with Daddy in the log wagon.

That was the last time I saw Raymond alive. They hadn't been gone all that long and I was up in the hayloft picking peanuts off the roots in the storage bin. We were going to parch the peanuts, make some popcorn balls and have a little holiday celebration before heading back to school the next day. All of a sudden I heard a commotion down the road. I looked out of the loft and saw the wagon coming.

Daddy was standing up in the wagon, holding Raymond. I had never heard my Daddy scream like that before. Something terrible had happened. J. E. was there in the wagon and holding onto Daddy's legs and crying. One of the men from down in the woods was driving the wagon, and by this time Momma had heard Daddy's screams and was running out into the road. I just stood there frozen, looking down from the loft. Something got hold of me and wouldn't let go. I wanted to explode inside.

They brought Raymond's lifeless body into the front bedroom and put him on the bed. Now my Momma was about to go crazy. She was eight months' pregnant, and the loss of her little boy sent her into shock. I thought surely that she was going to die herself. Finally, one of the men from the logging woods took the wagon to the nearest telephone to call all our relatives and to notify the funeral home. After a while, it got quiet in our house, so quiet you couldn't stand it. J. E. and I went to look at Raymond. My eyes were so full of tears that I couldn't see him. But his voice was ringing in my ears. I can hear it to this very day—his bright, happy, singing voice that, at that moment, made me bitter like bile inside and want to scream out that it was wrong. It was cruel to take him away. He was our brother and he belonged to us. He was meant for us to have and to sing sweet songs with throughout our lives.

It wasn't until a day or two later that I found our what had happened. J. E. had seen it all and finally brought himself to tell me. They were in the logging truck, trying to make it out of the wet woods. Raymond was leaning out the window, watching the tires spin in the mud, when somehow the door flew open and Raymond fell out. The truck slid sideways and ran over him. When the motor died, the truck's tires were resting on his body. Daddy and the other men worked frantically to get the truck off him, but it was too late. Poor J. E. was right there, and it must have been an unbearable sight for his young eyes to see. Years later, I always felt sorry for J. E. over Raymond's death, more so even than I did for Momma. I know that J. E. has carried the horror of watching his little brother die throughout his whole life.

After that, J. E., Bonnie and I were closer than we had been before. We've remained that way ever since. I guess, though, that when a tragedy happens in a family, it brings out some bitterness and guilt and resentments. For a long time after Raymond died, Momma and Daddy went to pieces and started punishing each other for the loss of their little boy. Daddy had once been to a fortuneteller who told him he would have only four children and that if he had more something would happen to one of them. So Daddy used to blame Momma for having another child. Momma in turn blamed Daddy.

We kids heard them fussing late at night. "The Lord took Raymond away because of your drinking and gambling, Floyd," Momma said.

"Shut that up, woman! You're to blame. How do I know that baby you're carrying is even mine?"

The fusses and fights went on until they almost drove us kids crazy, especially J. E. and me. It was a godsend that Bonnie was too young to understand and Norma wasn't even born yet. Our family was going to pieces and I think it was all because of our grieving over the loss of Raymond.

Going to church pulled us back together and saved us. Without the help of the Lord, there was no way we could have ever gotten through the tragedy. It was a trip of several miles, but every Sunday Daddy would hitch up the wagon and we'd drive to Sardis Methodist Church. Slowly the pain began to fade. That little country church and those good people became our salvation. The church even donated a burial space in the cemetery for Raymond since we were too poor to pay for even that. It was during this time that I joined the church. In fact, we all did. We learned the true meaning of that old hymn we sang, "Bless Be the Ties that Bind." And we never forgot it.

• • •

Raymond was killed on Labor Day, September 6, 1943, and Norma was born two months later on November 11. I was twelve years old when all this happened, but I still didn't know where babies came from. Grandma Tuberville came to be with Momma during Norma's delivery (we were all born at home), and they sent me to stay with Uncle Harvey and Aunt Ester. It was while I was there that I discovered the facts of life. I was with some of the older children—teenagers—and they got to talking about stuff, the way kids will when they think it is naughty, and I learned where babies came from.

"No, y'all. Uh huh," I protested. "You're lying!"

How they laughed and mocked me. The awful truth struck me. I felt that the whole innocent world was crashing down on me. God, how I hated my Momma and Daddy after that—not so much because I thought they'd been doing ugly, ugly things, but because they had let me live in blind ignorance. When I got back home, there was a beautiful little baby in the crib, but I wouldn't have anything to do with it. Grandma Tuberville tried to comfort me. She always seemed to have a sixth sense of what was bothering me.

"Maxine, now don't take it that hard," Grandma said to me, "Your Momma needs you to be a big girl. Child, child. Your Momma had a terrible time with the delivery. She almost died. How'd that make you feel? You'd never forgive yourself."

I didn't care! I had lost my little brother and my whole rosy outlook on life had turned as hard and mean as that sorry crust of Arkansas earth we were living on. Life wasn't games and parties and carnivals. It was ugliness, suffering, and dying. For weeks, months, I refused to go near that little baby sister of mine. Somehow I came out of it.

I remember one day after school, when J. E. and I were through with all the chores and he was sitting on the porch steps with the guitar Uncle Cecil had given him. I wasn't paying much attention to his playing, but I did start humming along absent-mindedly to the melody he was picking. It was the song "Wildwood Flower." I knew the words, and pretty soon J. E. and I were singing harmony together. "Wildwood Flower" is a strange and wonderful song. It sounds cheerful until you pay attention to the sad lyrics, then you realize it's about a young girl whose heart has been broken.

That song got me going again. (Years later we would record "Wildwood Flower" on one of our albums.) It took an old, true country song to bring music back into the Brown family. Our voices, J. E.'s and mine, were different without Raymond's. Once we started singing together again, something seemed to make us stronger and better than we'd been before. I was learning my first lesson in life—that, like the girl in "Wildwood Flower," you sometimes have to sing and dance, even in the middle of your sorrows.

• • •

A war was raging in the far-off world and hard times were still holding us in our place. Then it got worse. In April of 1944, Daddy was drafted into the Navy. He and Momma were still grieving over the loss of their son, Norma was just a little bitty baby, and we were all nearly starving. Daddy went to the draft board and told them of our predicament, but it was no use. They drafted him anyway, and we realized that we would just have to do the best we could. Uncle Harvey borrowed Herschel Thrower's pickup truck and took us all to the train station in Fordyce to see Daddy off. As we stood there on the platform, crying and waving goodbye, we thought we'd never see him again.

Times got harder. There were many nights when we went to bed hungry, even though Momma could fix the best water gravy and biscuits and we were never out of Uncle Harvey's sorghum syrup. Grandma Brown lived next door to us then, and the three of her sons who were still at home helped us with the farming. It was a comfort having them close by since it was scary living way out in the country with no way to get around except by a team of mules and a wagon.

As it turned out, Daddy's stint in the Navy was short-lived. By the fall of 1944, he had been in a little less than six months. He wrote to us that he had injured his knee badly while in training in San Diego. Daddy told his commanding officer that if they'd let him go home and take care of his family, he would forfeit all the allotment money coming to him. The Navy made him sign a paper giving up the allotment before they would give him a discharge. On his way home from California on a bus, he developed severe diarrhea and the bus had to make several stops for him right out in the middle of the desert. But his knee finally healed.

Even with Daddy home again, our little farm was just too poor for us to make a go of it. Daddy went to Mr. Lenny Shern, the man he was logging for when Raymond was killed, and asked for a loan to buy his own truck. Mr. Shern knew Daddy to be about the hardest working logger he'd ever hired and took a chance on him.

Daddy took a job working day and night hauling aluminum ore from the bauxite mine near Benton. He worked twenty hours a day. What little sleep he did get was in his truck. He came home only on weekends, mostly late on Saturday nights, and would leave again on Sunday afternoon. Momma sent him off each Sunday with a clean pair of overalls and some clean towels that would have to last him all week. We missed him terribly and would wait up for him every Saturday night. When he came rolling up in that old dump truck, we were so proud to see him that it was always a joyous reunion. We were a happy family once more.

With the money Daddy made hauling aluminum ore, he finally paid off his truck. I think Daddy knew that our old dirt farm held too many bad memories and that's why he worked so hard to get us off that place. No ordinary man could have labored so hard for so long. But Daddy wasn't any ordinary man. He came in one day and told Momma to start packing our belongings.

"We're moving off this sorry clod farm," he said. "We're going to have something better—if I have to die trying."

We were moving once more, and our spirits were higher than they'd been in a long, long time. Our memories of Raymond there on the farm had become more unbearable every day; Momma had gotten to the point that she couldn't stand to look out in the yard where Raymond had played or down that lonesome old dirt road over which his body came back to us. We moved off so quickly that we didn't have time even to put the place up for sale. I don't think we got around to selling it until many years later. Our parents just didn't want to think about that place.

I was in the seventh grade when we moved to Benton, and I found the school there a lot different from the one I'd gone to in Sparkman. Benton was a more progressive place than Sparkman, and the times were changing, too. We still lived a ways out of town and had to walk miles to school. But that was fine because there were several friendly children in our neighborhood to walk with. This kept Momma from worrying so much. She was always afraid now that something would happen to another one of her kids.

At first, we lived in a small cabin behind the Davenport family. I remember having an awful crush on a boy named Pete. He was handsome and athletic-looking but much older than I was. I knew that Pete had a crush on me too, but that nothing could ever come of it. We moved to a bigger house soon after that, so I never really got to know him. Later on, I received a letter from Pete saying he had joined the Army. None of us ever heard from him again. When I grew up, I'd see nice looking young men who reminded me of that handsome boy. I'd be up on stage, singing with J. E. and Bonnie, and I'd pretend that he was in the audience and I was singing just for him. It gave me a funny feeling, exciting and lonely at the same time, and the lines of the "Wildwood Flower" song would go through my mind again. And, oh, it was sweet, because I knew I had all those portions of loving still inside me.

* * *

Daddy was making it a lot better now. He quit hauling ore and got a job with the big Owosso Lumber Company in Benton. For the first time in years, it looked like the family was going to have it a little easier. Then another terrible blow struck. Daddy was working as a logger down in the woods, cutting hardwood timber. Somehow a tree he was cutting fell the wrong way and pinned Daddy beneath it. His leg was crushed. Once again, the Brown household filled up with weeping and moaning.

Daddy lay for days in the hospital in critical condition. We were just about convinced he would die. Gangrene had set in, and the doctor told Momma it was spreading rapidly and that they would have to amputate his leg at the thigh. To make matters worse, Daddy had a rare blood type and unless we could find someone to match it, he would surely die. His brother, Cecil, was the only other one in the family who had Daddy's blood type, and he had already donated all he could. The Owosso Lumber Company paid for radio spots all over Arkansas to locate a donor. Finally they found a man in Springdale and had him flown to Little Rock to give blood. This kind man saved our Daddy's life, and I've often wondered who he was. I'm sure Daddy kept in touch with him, because he was that kind of man. He never forgot those who helped him. No slave ever worked harder than Floyd Brown. He came home from the hospital on crutches, but he was smiling.

"We're still a family, and we're gonna make it," he said. "Not having a leg is not gonna stop me."

The Owosso Lumber Company paid Daddy's hospital and doctor bills and gave him eight hundred dollars to boot. He was an independent contractor, so he never expected anything from them. He had been worried about his hospital bills, and he thought it was great that they gave him eight hundred dollars they didn't have to. He was that kind of man, one who never asked for or expected anything extra.

It was painful to watch him try to walk on his new peg leg. Every day he got up early and practiced, much like a ball player nowadays trying to make an impossible comeback. But come back Floyd Brown did. It seemed like it was no time before he was getting around as well as any man. He went back to work, back to the logging woods. He was determined not to let his handicap interfere with his work. And it didn't. The men who worked with him swore he could do more with that old peg leg than any two normal men. I was never prouder of my Daddy than I was during those days.

Moving on Up—
and Around

Our new house in Benton had indoor plumbing. It was the first indoor toilet we'd ever had. We still didn't have a bath, but how nice it was to be able to use toilet tissue instead of the slick pages of a Sears catalog!

Our next-door neighbors, the Aaron family, were church people. Mr. Aaron was a Pentecostal preacher, and sometimes J. E. and I would go with the Aaron kids to their services. We had always gone to the Methodist church and weren't prepared for the loud way those folks worshipped. There was a lot of shouting and stomping and speaking in tongues. J. E. and I were absolutely scared to death and thought we were going to hell. I'll say one thing: it put the fear of God in both of us. Many years later we ran into Brother Aaron at the racetrack in Hot Springs. He was drunk as a lord and had a floozy on his arm. We found out that he had left his wife and kids for a singer in his church choir. Brother Aaron, whose voice had once made me quake and tremble, was here doing it again as he yelled for his pony to "Run, you son of a bitch, run!"

We had moved "uptown," and we kids were growing up. But we still took our baths in a number two galvanized washtub, just as we'd been doing all our lives. One day we almost had another family tragedy. I was alone with my baby sister, Norma, and had heated a kettle of water for her bath. Just as I started to pour the water from the kettle into the tub, Norma hopped right in. The top of the kettle came off, and I couldn't keep the scalding water from spilling on her. I ran next door to the Aarons', and we rushed Norma to the hospital. She was burned pretty badly. I sat up all night praying for her. I prayed harder than I ever had before in my life. In the back of my mind was the thought of poor little Raymond. I knew Momma would not survive the loss of another child.

This time we were spared. Little Norma came through the ordeal, and soon we had her back at home. I was beginning to wonder if the Brown family hadn't been singled out to suffer the way the Bible says the downtrodden are made to do. One thing for sure, I never gave Norma anything but cold baths after that.

• • •

The war came to an end. I'm sure everyone who was alive in those days still remembers where they were and what they were doing when word came that the fighting was over. What I remember distinctly were the antics of Grandma Brown. All over town, whistles and horns were blowing, and people were out in the middle of the street jumping up and down and hollering. Grandma Brown was leading the pack. She was a big, fat woman, and I was totally shocked and a little embarrassed to see her carrying on so. I didn't know she knew how to do such things. She was the center of attention. Everybody else stopped celebrating and watched the show she was putting on. She didn't care, even as all of us kids hid our faces. She was overjoyed, and she was jumping and shouting to let the whole world know.

Daddy was doing all right financially down in the logging woods, but he got an opportunity to go into business for himself. He bought a grocery store back down in Fordyce and put the Brown family on the move once more. The store was across from the sawmill where Daddy had once worked. Our living quarters were in the back of the store. It was pretty cramped, but we were used to makeshift living by then. Momma took it all in stride.

On my first day at a new school in Fordyce, I caught the "itch" and brought it home to infect the whole family. Momma used an old-time remedy of sulphur and grease to cure us. The smell was God awful, so unbelievably bad that people quit coming into the store to buy anything. Maybe they feared catching the "itch" too, but I think it was more likely that they just couldn't stand how the place smelled. It took days to get rid of the odor and lure all our customers back.

While we lived in Fordyce, I learned how to skate for the first time. My teacher was a special person; a young man named Houston Nutt. Lord, I had a bad crush on him—and what young girl wouldn't! He was tall and handsome and about as nice a person as I'd ever known. All his folks were deaf and mute, but Houston could talk. He later went on to become a great basketball player and coach and is today one of the county's leading educators of the handicapped. When I think of that young man teaching me to skate (the one dream of my early life), I understand why I'm writing this story in the first place. The reason is that when lives cross and touch each other, even briefly, the encounters can give us strength and make us more than we knew we could be. That's the gift of loving kindness.

• • •

Despite his trying, Daddy's heart just wasn't in the grocery store business. He ached to be out in rough open spaces. His heart was always down in the logging woods. So once again we moved. We were becoming regular vagabonds. This time we moved to a shack on the sawmill grounds near Pine Bluff. And it was here, on these shoddy mill grounds, that I first learned to drive a car. I was almost sixteen, old enough to get a driver's license.

It all happened quite by accident. I was always after Daddy to teach me to drive, and he always kept putting it off. There was an old jeep that had been left on the sawmill grounds. So one day I decided to teach myself to drive. I got it started and rolling along OK, but I didn't know anything about the clutch and brakes. I ran over logs and junk every way I turned and I screamed out for help. A whole bunch of men from the sawmill came running, and there was Momma right behind them. I led them on a bumpy, bulldozing chase. Finally I figured out where the danged brake was and got the jeep stopped. It was scarier than I thought, but I learned to drive. It wasn't the first time I had learned at the school of hard knocks—and it was certainly not the last.

We went to school at Watson Chapel, near Pine Bluff. Again, we wouldn't get to finish out a whole year in one school. The one thing I remember from that time was eating lunch at a café across from the school. Every single day I ordered a grilled pimento cheese sandwich, potato chips, and a coke, all for twenty-five cents. The pimento cheese sandwich was a big favorite with everyone back in those days, bigger almost than Big Macs are today.

A few months later we moved to the little town of Redfield to be closer to Daddy's work. By now, we were all used to moving away and leaving our newly-made friends behind. I think this made all of us kids a little insulated from the outside world and therefore closer to each other. A "friend" was someone you met, played with awhile, and then waved goodbye to.

We didn't live at Redfield long either, about six months. But while we were there, an incident happened between my Momma and Daddy that put a mark on our family for a long time. It wasn't really a fuss, I don't think, not like the ones they'd had after Raymond died. And I don't think they knew we were listening. I overheard them talking, and although I didn't fully understand it all, it was dreadful to my ears. They were talking about another woman. Momma was saying jealous things and making accusations. Daddy wasn't saying much of anything. The more he kept quiet, the more Momma accused him. She was jealous of this woman for sure and maybe she had a right to be. It was a taint on our family that each of us would have to come to terms with later.

That bad time faded soon enough, and we all went on with the business of living. Daddy had saved up some money and bought a piece of land on Highway 65, north of Pine Bluff. An old rundown house came with the property. We moved into it and started fixing it up. Since the land was on a major highway, Daddy decided it was a good location for a business. He had tried the grocery business before and thought that he'd give it one more shot. This time, though, he was smart enough to add an extra feature, a restaurant right next door. How proud they were of their business. They called it the Dollarway Restaurant and Grocery Store.

Soon the business was doing well, and we all started believing we were heading for better times. The kids were all growing up. It seemed like no time until we were ready for high school. J. E. and Bonnie went to school in Pine Bluff, but I couldn't stand the thought of leaving my friends at Watson Chapel. It was the first school I really ever loved and felt at ease in, and for the first time I had made a lot of friends. After begging and pleading all summer, I finally convinced Daddy to let me stay at Watson Chapel. He even bought me an old junker Model A Ford to drive to school. I was absolutely in hog heaven!

Daddy still worked down in the logging woods to help ends meet. Momma ran the restaurant and oversaw the grocery store. It just about worked her to death, but I think she enjoyed it. After a while, she and Daddy decided that the grocery store side of the business wasn't making nearly as much money as the restaurant. So they closed the store, got a beer permit, and expanded the restaurant. It was wonderful to see Momma and Daddy with a little money in their pockets.

Birdie Brown was always about the best cook in the world. Now other people besides her family were finding this out. In later years, the restaurant's face would change drastically—yet another catastrophe would strike the Browns—but Momma's special dishes and pastries would keep on gaining a wider reputation. When J. E., Bonnie, and I started making it in the music industry, a lot of our new friends would go out of their way to have some of Momma's cooking. When we were on the road with Elvis Presley, he always came home with us and was the first one in the door yelling "Momma!"

The restaurant was better than going to any carnival. I was too young to serve beer, so I kept house and looked after Norma. After I'd cleaned the house and done the laundry, I'd run as fast as I could over to the restaurant. The Pine Bluff Arsenal was nearby, and a lot of the soldiers from there used to hang out in our restaurant. Lord, I thought they were the handsomest things in those uniforms!

The greatest surprise of my life came when I went to the assembly program one day at Watson Chapel High School and the principal stood up to announce who was to be Homecoming Queen. When he called my name, I couldn't believe it. I just sat there shaking all over until my best friend, Delores Smith, pulled me up out of my chair.

"It's you, girl!" Delores screamed. "Maxine, you got Homecoming Queen!"

I was so shocked and thrilled that I don't think I came down out of the clouds for all those days before the Homecoming dance. It is almost unbelievable to think that this little, ratty, backward kid who had failed the first grade had been chosen Homecoming Queen of the whole school!

There was one drawback. Momma was working so hard getting the restaurant started that I knew she didn't have the money or the time to make me a formal dress. I guess word of my problem got out among those soldier boys who came into the restaurant. One day when I came in from school, they were waiting for me. They had taken up a collection to buy me a dress. I was so overcome by their kindness that I couldn't keep from crying. I still think they were the sweetest boys who ever lived.

• • •

My friend Delores and I did everything together. We flirted with boys, went to the movies and spent hours listening to country music on the radio. A local heartthrob in those days was a singer named Dick Hart. He had his own radio show on a Little Rock station. We'd see pictures of him in newspaper ads for Sunway B-Vitamins and developed hard schoolgirl crushes on him. We used to sit and scheme ways we could meet him. Finally we got up the nerve to play hooky and go see him in person. I wished a thousand times that we hadn't done it because of what happened afterward.

I got permission from Momma to spend the night with Delores and go from her house to school the next day. But we really didn't plan to go to school. Instead, we were going to take my Model A and drive to Little Rock to see the famous Dick Hart. We had to leave early the next morning because Hart's show came on at six o'clock. We were both scared to death that we'd get caught, but we were excited too as we drove the forty-five miles to Little Rock. The old car was hissing and steaming as we pulled up to station KLRA, got out and peered through the window like two star-struck groupies (or "snuff queens," as they were called back then). This was the supreme moment of our lives. There Dick Hart stood, strumming his guitar, smiling a slick smile, and winking right at us!

We hung around the studio half the morning. Then someone told us Dick Hart was married and had kids. That exploded our bubble. I looked at Dick Hart strutting around and leering at us, and I saw him in a new light. I saw he was just a fair-to-middling country singer, not nearly as good as my brother, J. E. We drove back home feeling down-hearted and wishing we hadn't cut school that day. All of a sudden, the car's radiator seemed to blow up. It spewed out an awful smoke, and the motor roared like it was going to take off and fly.

By the time we got half way between Little Rock and Pine Bluff, that old Model A was smoking so bad I just knew it was on fire. The radiator was completely dry now, and we had to stop in front of a grocery store. I didn't want to stop at this place, but we didn't have any choice. The store was owned by the woman that I had heard Momma and Daddy fussing over. I hadn't wanted to believe any of that talk and had tried to blot it out of my mind. But there was Daddy's truck parked beside the store. When I saw it, I just froze. But it was too late to turn around and run away.

Daddy was inside. He saw us coming and ran outside to meet us. He looked furious and he started yelling at me, accusing me of playing hooky from school and meeting some boys on the sly. My heart was running away. He was one to talk! I don't know if I hated him or was just scared to death. I simply stood there as he bawled me out. I was in such a daze I didn't even notice him putting water in the radiator and getting the old car started again. He even took out his billfold and offered me some money. "Go on now," was all he said.

Our day had been a romantic adventure. all right. Delores and I didn't say a word to each other all the rest of the way home.

. . .

After that episode, I always thought of myself as on my own. I graduated from Watson Chapel High School in May of 1950. I was nineteen years old. I put all thought of going to college out of my mind. My folks didn't have the money to send me, and I wouldn't have asked them for it even if they did. I wanted to be my own person and make my own way. I took a job with the local telephone company, saved money and enrolled in a business course at Draughon's Business School.

It seems that trouble was destined to follow my family every turn we took. My Momma had worked her fingers to the bone getting that restaurant started, and just about the time it started paying off, the place burned to the ground. We all stood around the rubble and ashes and just stared. It was like a curse had been put on the family.

"There's no use in hanging our heads,' Momma said and gave a little laugh. "We'll just start over again, that's all."

Daddy moved the family again, this time to Star City, where he could get steady work with the May Lumber Company. I didn't move with the family this time. I stayed with my Uncle Bo and Aunt Willie in Little Rock until I finished business school. I rode the bus home on weekends to be with the family.

During this time, a coldness developed between my Daddy and me. It gave me a strange feeling because we had been so close while I was growing up. Daddy didn't like me being on my own. He still thought of me as a little girl he had to protect. One time when I was home, he ordered me not to go out with boys.

"You son of a bitch!" I yelled at him.

I can still see his eyes as he glared at me. Then he slapped me back into my place. I wouldn't have minded a thousand whippings if I could have changed that look in his eyes. I just stood there with my eyes closed, holding back the tears. I have been sorry about it all my life. I knew what I'd said was wrong, just as I knew I couldn't keep from loving him.

Later Daddy moved the family back to Pine Bluff, and he started making pretty good money again. Things began to look up for the family. He even bought me a new yellow Chevy to drive back and forth on weekends. A man had been following me on the bus. We soon learned that the guy was a convicted rapist who had escaped from a penitentiary in another state. This scared my folks so bad that Daddy wouldn't hear of anything but that I have my own car.

After graduating from business school, I got a job with the Arkansas State Police. I loved every minute I was there. I made a lot of great friends that I've kept over the years. My boss was Capt. Frank McGibbony. A finer man has never lived.

After I had been working with the State Police for almost two years, a series of events took place that would change my whole life. Soon I would enter a glittering world of spotlights and cheering crowds and rub elbows with the biggest stars and celebrities of the entertainment world. For the rest of my life, I would be pulled in opposite directions by the attraction of the "high life" and the comfort and security of home.

PART TWO

The
Other Side

Now We're in Show Business

It started for us in the spring of 1952. The whole country seemed to be living on boogie-woogie and swing music, television, horror movies, and nickel Cokes. We didn't have rock 'n' roll, school integration, air conditioning, a polio vaccine, or the pill, but all those things were just around the corner. It seemed hardly any time until everything turned upside down in my life. It was like one of those patchwork quilts my Momma made—gaudy and wild and kind of wonderful. We singing Brown kids were going to get to be a part of it although I have never been sure just how we fit into the crazy quilt pattern of it all.

I was still working at the State Police, J. E. was going to college at Arkansas A&M in Monticello (now University of Arkansas–Monticello) and Bonnie was still in high school. Radio station KLRA in Little Rock had started a big country music show, the *Barnyard Frolic*. It was held every Saturday night in Robinson Auditorium. Crowds packed the place like they do country and rock concerts today. The station conducted an amateur contest on Saturday nights that drew contestants from all over the country. I went with my friends to the *Frolic* almost every weekend, and I began to think that J. E. could sing better than most of the contestants who were winning. For one thing, J. E. had practiced imitating the best *Grand Ole Opry* singers. He could do Hank Snow so well that you actually couldn't tell the difference. So, on my own, without another soul knowing about it, I entered J. E. in the *Frolic* contest.

A few weeks later, the radio station sent him a letter. I was home for the weekend and so was J. E. I never will forget the look on his face when he opened the letter and read that he was invited to appear on the *Barnyard Frolic* the following Saturday night. He looked straight at me, and I couldn't hide my excitement.

"You did it, didn't you!" he said. "I ought to wring your neck."

But he was more excited than I was. For the next few days, he couldn't eat or sleep. But when it came time for him to be on the *Frolic*, he lost all his butterflies. And I have to say that he sang better that night than he'd ever done before. A whole pack of the Brown clan turned out to whistle, cheer and clap for Jim Edward Brown (that's what the MC called him.) After he finished his song, the crowd really went wild. He had to come out and take extra bows. No other contestant that night got half the applause J. E. did. We just knew he was going to win.

He didn't win. I was so angry I wanted to explode. We all knew who the best contestant was that night. I was just about ready to give Jim Stuart, the man ramrodding the *Frolic*, a solid piece of my mind. He came through he crowd and up to J. E. as we were leaving, and he had a twinkle in his eye. Before I could lash out at him, he told J. E. that he thought he was the best one on the show. We knew he wasn't just trying to be nice, either. Before we left the auditorium, he took J. E. to one side and asked him to come back next week and sing again. "The crowd loved you, and we want you to be a regular on the show," Mr. Stuart said.

So that was the start. We went home higher than kites that night. A lot of the contest winners were never heard from again. But from that moment on, I knew that my little brother was going to be a star.

• • •

Jim Edward Brown sang every Saturday night on the *Barnyard Frolic*. There wasn't any money in it at first, but that didn't seem to matter in the least. After all, J. E. was getting more and more popular. The *Frolic* soon progressed to the point that it was taking in a lot of money at the door. A few months later, a promoter named Dutch O'Neil took over the show and started upgrading the talent. He put J. E. in a featured spot the very first night and paid him. Paid him! There it was, a check from the *Barnyard Frolic* made out to Jim Edward Brown. Ten whole dollars—real money for just singing. J. E. has never cashed that check. Dated August 15, 1952, it now resides in the Browns' scrapbook.

More excitement came soon. The first television station in Arkansas, KRTV, had recently been built in Pine Bluff. In those days, TV stations did a lot of live studio shows. We had made friends at the *Frolic* with a couple of country singers, Shelby and Sarah Jane Cooper, who had a regular thirty-minute show on KRTV. Shelby played the guitar and Sarah Jane the fiddle. They both sang, but their playing was better than their singing. They knew they needed a strong singer for their show, and they had heard J. E. sing several times on the *Frolic*. One night they asked him to join them. He agreed. It wasn't long until J. E. had all the girls in Pine Bluff and Little Rock watching him roll those big brown eyes and sing his great imitations of Hank Snow, Ernest Tubb, and just about any other star you could mention. He had a way of singing right through the cameras to the audience at home. The fan mail started pouring in.

J. E. still continued to sing on the *Barnyard Frolic* every Saturday night, sometimes with Shelby and Sarah Jane. The crowds just ate him up, especially the young girls. They flooded into the auditorium to see and hear this new heartthrob. I remember sitting in the audience one night and holding my ears while the teenagers yelled and whistled for Jim Edward Brown. Then it happened. I saw J. E. looking down into the crowd directly at me and motioning for me to stand up. I was really embarrassed. Then, J. E. announced over the microphone: "Now, ladies and gentlemen, I want to call my sister Maxine up on stage to sing a song with me."

I was so nervous I don't know how I ever made it up the aisle and onto the stage. With Shelby and Sarah Jane playing in the background, J. E. and I harmonized on a song we'd worked on maybe two or three times. It was a song made popular by Jim and Jesse and the Virginia Boys called "Are You Missing Me?" It's a sweet, hurting song that calls for pure harmonies. I guess we did OK with it, even with my nervousness, because the crowd gave us several rounds of applause and even yelled for us to do an encore.

Being on a stage and singing in front of a crowd was something I had only dreamed about since the hard old days of south Arkansas. Now that it was happening to me, I don't think I felt anything but the music itself. When J. E. and I came off stage, everyone was buzzing with talk about how well we could harmonize. That night Shelby and Sarah Jane came over to us just beaming.

"You kids sure do get a great sound together," Shelby said. "I think you ought to keep it up. Why don't you join our band and sing duets? Y'all are just naturals."

Before we left for home, it was settled. I was going to get to sing with J. E. in a band on a real stage and maybe on television. The feeling I took home with me that night was way above anything I'd ever felt before and maybe since. It wasn't real to me. It was a movie, and everything was in shadows on a white, blinding screen. All my life, it seemed, I had been standing on one side looking over to the better side, and that night for few brief minutes I had stepped across the line. All of a sudden I was on the "other side," and all I knew was that I wanted to stay there.

• • •

So Shelby and Sarah Jane made us a part of their show. It wasn't anything like instant success because we weren't making but a few dollars each night. I kept on working with the State Police, and J. E. went back to A&M and tried to keep up with his studies in forestry. We rehearsed our duets when we could and managed to work up a good show. The crowds kept giving us big applause and calling for encores.

J. E. had been playing the guitar since he was a little boy, but I had never learned to play any instrument. Oh, I could play the piano by ear—Grandma Brown had taught me that—but I wasn't great at it. So we decided that I'd take up the accordion. A lot of country acts back then had "cowgirls" with accordions. If we were going to take this business seriously, we thought we'd better pretend to do it right.

My folks were almost as thrilled as we were over our breakthrough. They always encouraged and supported us. Daddy went with us to Hot Springs to buy two Martin guitars (both model D-28s and very valuable today). While we were in the music store Daddy saw this beautiful red and white pearl accordion. Without saying a word, he took out his billfold and counted out the money for it and the two guitars. We knew it almost broke him to pay all that money, but he wouldn't listen to us when we argued that we could get by with cheaper instruments.

"No you can't," he said. "If you're gonna do this picking and singing, you're gonna get the chance to do it right."

Momma and Daddy never missed a Saturday night when we were singing at the *Frolic*. At that time, Daddy was trying to keep his logging business afloat, and Momma was running the café. She was the most remarkable woman in the world. She took care of the house and family, ran the restaurant, kept all the books, ordered the supplies, and supervised all the hired help. Still, she found time to make me beautiful costumes to wear on stage. She designed and made me a red-and-white cowgirl outfit to match my new accordion and made J. E. a shirt to match. I wore white cowgirl boots and a white cowgirl hat, just like all the stars on TV and the *Grand Ole Opry*. She made sure we looked good in the spotlight. Hardly a week went by that she didn't come up with a new and prettier outfit. Without a doubt, there was love in every stitch she sewed.

Weeks passed by like lightning bugs. We were happy just being part of the local show. I'm sure neither J. E. nor I ever thought it would go much beyond that—just as I never dreamed that I'd write songs. In a way, I was still standing looking over to the other side.

One day when she was about nine my little sister Norma came home from school mad as a hornet. She ran to her room and didn't come out until supper. Momma and I could see she was still very upset. All at once, she broke out crying. Norma was always a spirited little girl, and Momma was about the only one who could calm her down. Finally, Momma got her to stop crying and tell her why she was so upset.

"I got into trouble with the teacher," Norma said. "And for no reason at all. There was this cute boy, and all I was doing was looking back to see if he was looking back to see if I was looking back to see if he was looking at me." Momma and I just died laughing at the cute story.

"Come on, say that again, Norma," I asked her, but by then we were laughing so hard she refused. I thought about what she had said for a long time. I even wrote it down and began to wonder how it would sound as a song. It really was catchy and clever. And it really did make sense because that's how all kids thought. The more I fooled with the words and phrases, the more fun it became.

I could play the guitar well enough, now that I knew my chords. So putting a tune to the chorus was no problem. Then I had to think of some verses. Pretty soon they started to flow. I thought of J. E. and how he was always wishing he had a Cadillac to show off and drive his girlfriends around in. So I wrote the first verse with that in mind; the next verse came to me just as quickly. Since I had put the song in a boy's voice, it naturally called for a girl's answer, which focused on the boy's cuteness, not the kind of car he was driving.

After I finished the song, I just sat there humming it, singing it under my breath and giggling to myself. To tell the truth, I was self-conscious that I'd written a song at all and even a little embarrassed to show it to anybody. But I did want J. E. to have a song all his own. He dreamed of making it big. For myself, I never had any illusions about a life in show business. I was quite content with my job and my life. People at the *Barnyard Frolic* were always telling J. E. that he had the voice to make it big time but that he needed his own material. That was the formula for getting a record contract. Maybe, just maybe, "Looking Back To See" could open a door.

Each time we sang at the *Frolic*, we met big time singers who were there making guest appearances. Known across the country, they were snappily dressed, drove expensive cars and seemed so wealthy that J. E. thought it looked downright easy. Were we ever naïve! If only we had known it was all like it says in Tom T. Hall's great song "Homecoming" —that fancy cars, clothes, and diamond rings are just a scared picker's way of "putting up a front."

When I showed "Looking Back To See" to J. E., he grabbed his guitar and started working on it right away. Later we sang it for Shelby and Sarah Jane, and they absolutely flipped over it. "You have gone and written yourself a hit," Shelby said in that sweet old drawl of his. They started rehearsing it for the *Frolic*. Shelby helped arrange it, and it was his arrangement we used later when we recorded the song.

Our First Recording Session

As the *Barnyard Frolic* kept growing in popularity, so did J. E. He sang a real crowd-pleaser called "Hey Joe," and the girls yelled and screamed for him so much that sometimes he'd have to encore with the same songs. To tell the truth, I think he was more popular with the *Frolic* crowd than most of the big-name guest stars. We got encore after encore when we sang, "Looking Back To See."

In those days, I never gave a thought to trying to make a living by singing. But more and more it was getting to be J. E.'s dream. My folks were doing well with their businesses now. Our restaurant and house became a "must stop" for just about all the stars that came to perform at the *Frolic*. I still worked with the State Police, and J. E. was still in college. But getting popular at the *Frolic* and meeting all those established performers did put some stars in our eyes.

Two country artists we grew especially close to were Skeeter and Bee Jay, the Davis Sisters. (Although they billed themselves as "the Davis Sisters," they were not related.) At this time, the girls had a number one record called "I Forgot More Than You'll Ever Know" that would evolve into a country music classic as the years went on. It certainly made Skeeter and Bee Jay famous almost overnight. They were as nice and sweet as young girls could be—and their harmony was even sweeter. My Momma took them under her wing and treated them like her own kids. Every time they came to the *Frolic*, they made a point to visit our house and get some of Momma's home cooking. They were terribly homesick out there on the road, but Momma knew just what to do to cheer them up.

After one appearance on the *Frolic* in 1953, Skeeter and Bee Jay came to our house for supper. They were very excited because they were finishing up their tour and would be getting to spend some time at home. Two weeks later, on their way to Wheeling, West Virginia, they were in a horrible car accident and Bee Jay was killed. Even before J. E., Bonnie, and I went on the road ourselves, we learned the bitter lesson that the path to the top is often paved with pain and tragedy. It was a lesson we would learn again and again.

• • •

While it was fun writing "Looking Back To See," I never got worked up over the song's prospects like Shelby and Sarah Jane did. I actually thought it was too simple and—to tell the truth—silly. I was certain I could write something better. Shelby kept encouraging us for the next year or so to keep writing. He was determined that we should come up with some more original material so we could make some "demos" (demonstration recordings) of what we sounded like. The goal in doing this, of course, was to land a recording contract. Our first attempt was a dismal failure.

At that time, Wayne Raney was another big-name artist who appeared occasionally on the *Frolic*. He listened to J. E. and me sing and took a liking to us right away. He also liked the way Shelby and Sarah played. He invited us to come up to his place near Rose Bud, Arkansas, so he could help us find another original song or two.

We all drove up to Wayne's place one Sunday. I remember thinking on the way to his house that ol' Wayne was probably a very rich man. After all, I'd been hearing his records on the radio since I was a kid. I expected we'd arrive at a mansion with a swimming pool, tennis courts, and servants. When we got there, I had the shock of my life. He lived way out in the country in a shabby old farmhouse where a bunch of kids were playing in the dirt. Why, he didn't have any more than we did! We felt right at home.

While we were there, Wayne hired Sarah and Shelby to play on his next recording session, which was coming up right away. He told J. E. and me that if we came along with them he would get us an audition. "Maybe," he said, "I can get you on the *Grand Ole Opry* on your way back home." Not the *Opry*! My heavenly days, not us! Not where Eddy Arnold and Hank Snow and Roy Acuff were appearing in person! That was a dream that passed over country kid's heads like tiny, distant clouds.

Wayne recorded for King Records in Cincinnati, and his producer was Sid Nathan, who also owned the label He was a real brute! Wayne took us into the studio and right away Nathan told him he didn't have time to listen to a couple of country kids. But Wayne finally persuaded him to give us a chance to sing.

"I'll listen to them for three minutes," Nathan said. "But they'll have to do it on their own No backup or nothing."

"At least let Shelby and Sarah play them some accompaniment," Wayne said. But it was no use. We'd have to go it alone. We got up and started without so much as a warm-up. There we were, two scared kids who'd never been in a recording studio, trying to impress a gruff old buzzard who wasn't even bothering to pay attention. Our voices quivered a lot, and we didn't come across with any of our natural style. Nathan just shook his head and walked out on us.

There were some well-known artists on King, but it certainly wasn't the label for us. On the way home, J. E. and I told each other we'd just have to forget the idea of recording. I'd go back to the State Police and he'd go back to college. To hell with show business if it meant dealing with people as mean as old Sid Nathan.

• • •

Wayne didn't get us on the *Grand Ole Opry*, and we didn't really expect him to. We pretty much knew that you had to have a record out to get near that famous place. But Wayne did manage to get us on the *Ernest Tubb Midnight Jamboree*. To us, that was almost as big a thrill as getting on the *Opry*.

All the way to Nashville, we were as nervous as kittens in a kennel. If a nobody like Sid Nathan could be that hateful, what would a big star like Ernest Tubb be like? He'd probably just laugh in our faces. We tried to rehearse a little bit on the long drive to Nashville, but we just couldn't get the sound we wanted. I recall dozing off once and dreaming that I heard Ernest Tubb ask Wayne, "Is this some kind of joke, Raney? These dumb Arkansas kids can't even carry a tune."

Started as a radio show in 1947 to promote Ernest Tubb's new mail-order record store, the *Midnight Jamboree* was nearly as popular as the *Grand Ole Opry*, which it immediately followed on the air. We didn't meet Mr. Tubb until it was our time to go on. I wasn't just shaking, I was rattling as bad as that old Model A Ford I used to drive.

Shelby and Sarah hadn't come with us, so we didn't have anybody to play accompaniment. When some of the musicians there learned we didn't have our own band, they volunteered to play for us. No problem, they said. We didn't learn until later that they were Mr. Tubb's own band, the Texas Troubadours, and probably the best musicians in the business.

When it came our time to go on, Mr. Tubb gave us a really great introduction to warm up the audience. Just as we were about to start, one of the young musicians behind us leaned up to me and said, "Knock 'em dead." He gave me a warm, encouraging smile, and all of a sudden I was completely at ease. We sang "Looking Back To See" and put everything we had into it. We cut up and capered around. J. E. was a really good-looking boy, and he had all the girls in the audience jumping and squealing. At the end, the audience gave us a big hand.

Mr. Tubb had a big smile. He put his arms around both of us and praised us to the big crowd. "We're going to be hearing a lot more from these youngsters in the future," he announced. And as we were leaving the stage, the young musician behind me leaned up again and said, "Attaboy, girl." I have never forgotten those words and the sweet smile he gave me. A few years later, when we became members of the *Grand Ole Opry*, I heard that same voice and those same words. I learned the musician's name was Lightnin' Chance. He was a phenomenal player and a legend in Nashville. He never failed to make a singer feel good on stage. He remains one of the unsung heroes of country music. Without Ernest Tubb's willingness to give us a chance and Lightnin's genuine encouragement, I don't think we would have ever gone beyond the *Barnyard Frolic*.

• • •

We came back home all pumped up. Momma and Dad were excited about our success on the *Midnight Jamboree*. But all we really had to show for it was the honor of appearing on the same stage with Ernest Tubb. After a week or two, we came down out of the clouds and tried to face reality. Shelby and Sarah were still very high on us. They weren't going to give up on us, and they never did.

Shelby got us to take a big step. He booked a recording session at Steve Jaggers's studio in Little Rock. A kind and helpful man who knew his business, Mr. Jaggers set up a good session for us to record

"Looking Back To See" for the very first time. The demo turned out to be a good one.

When I think back on the way that song came about and what happened to it later, I have to think crude thoughts and smoke unfiltered cigarettes to keep from crying. "Looking Back To See" would become one of the biggest country hits of the 1950s and be recorded by dozens of country and pop artists, including Ray Charles, Rusty Draper, Buck Owens, and even bandleader Guy Lombardo. Our own recording of the song went Top Ten on the country charts, where it stayed for weeks.

I suppose it's an honor to have written a big hit and hear people talk about "Looking Back To See" as a true country classic. Listening to a "goldie oldies" station the other day, I heard a deejay refer to "Looking Back To See" as a "unique song in the highest realm of the country's native music." Oh, the song made a lot of money, too. But not for us, the ones who wrote and sang it. We never made a dime on that song from record royalties—not one dime.

The music industry, whether it's country, rock, pop, or punk, has some fine, upstanding people in it. However, it also crawls with shysters, crooks, and con artists. On our rocky road to the big time, we had yet to meet up with probably the sorriest bastard then infesting the industry. His name was Fabor Robinson.

A few days after we recorded the demo, Wayne Raney came through on his way to Dallas. He listened to the demo and liked it a lot. He was heading to a recording session with Lefty Frizzell, who was a red-hot recording star at that time. He said he'd love for us to ride down to Dallas with him and meet Lefty. "Don Law is going to be there, too, and I'll get him to listen to your demo."

"Who is Don Law?" I asked, innocent as a baby.

"Don Law is with Columbia Records. He's a big-time record producer, and he's made a lot of people famous," Wayne said.

So we were off on another adventure. Since we were just tagging along, J. E. and I weren't too nervous this time. This was back before the interstate highway system was constructed, so the trip was long and weary. When we finally got to the recording studio in Dallas, we were worn out. Wayne introduced us to Lefty. I'd always loved his records, but meeting him was another story. He was kind of bean-poled and loop-legged and pretty stuck on himself. He would hardly say hello. After all, we were nobodies.

Don Law was different. He was nice and kind and seemed to take an interest in us right away. He took time to listen to our demo of "Looking Back To See." He sat there listening to it, thinking, and playing it back again. "Maybe," he said. "Yes, I think it's got a good chance. But we'll have to wait and see what the big dogs at Columbia say."

We came back home feeling that we were on the verge of a breakthrough. Don Law of Columbia Records had accepted our demo. We had a foot in the door. All we had to do was wait for the good news. We waited and waited while weeks and months went by. Pretty soon we made up our minds that we'd never hear from Don Law or Columbia, and there we were again on "this" side gazing over at the "other."

In the meantime, we made several copies of the demo and sent them to anybody who advertised in the trade magazines that they were looking for new talent. Shelby and Sarah Cooper kept giving us pep talks and staying on top of everything. I was still with the State Police, getting some raises and as content as I could make myself. J. E. stayed in college another semester. He continued to appear regularly on the *Frolic* and was a big star on Channel 7, the up-and-coming local television station.

Wayne Raney came through again and picked up another copy of the demo. He had heard of a new producer in California who was supposedly lining up all kinds of new talent for his own record label. That producer was Fabor Robinson. He had already produced "Mexican Joe" for Jim Reeves, and it was climbing the charts. In addition, we read in the trades that Robinson's label had another hit, "I Love You, You, You," a duet by Reeves and Ginny Wright. Since "Looking Back To See" was also a duet, maybe we'd attract Robinson's interest. Shelby had noticed all this too and insisted that we give this new label a try.

"What have you got to lose?" Shelby said. "After all, it's been months, and you haven't heard a word from Columbia."

The next day we dropped a demo in the mail to Fabor Robinson. In less than a week we got a cheerful reply. Fabor loved "Looking Back To See." He sent us contracts offering to sign us to Fabor Records.

You would have thought we had just been named top recording

artists of the year! We had finally made our breakthrough, and every-body we knew just went crazy. We knew it was only a matter of time until we had our own big-time recording sessions. After that, we'd be touring the country and on our way to stardom and the *Grand Ole Opry!*

J. E. was walking in the clouds. I think that Shelby, our most ardent supporter, was just as thrilled as we were. We signed the con-tracts and fired them back to Fabor. And then, just two days later, another fat envelope arrived from Don Law at Columbia Records. He apologized for taking so long but said he was happy to offer us a recording contract. Everybody at Columbia was enthusiastic over "Looking Back To See," he assured us, and he was confident it would become a big seller. "Please sign the contract," he concluded, "and we will make arrangements very soon for a recording session."

Just two days too late. Our haste and Columbia's tardiness affected our lives and careers for years to come.

• • •

On March 15, 1954, we had our first recording session. It look place in the studios of radio station KWKH in Shreveport, home of the *Louisiana Hayride*. We were in a daze as we got ready to make our first record. We couldn't begin recording until midnight, when KWKH went off the air. It took about an hour to set up and make sure every-thing was balanced on one mike. We had only about three hours recording time because the station went back on the air at 5 a.m. We had to be completely cleared out of the studio by then so the disc jockey could start his newscast. The studio was so full of musicians and technicians that we were almost lost in the shuffle. A couple of people walked by talking.

"Boy, you sure wouldn't know that's Jim Reeves over there," said one.

"Yeah," said the other, "and who'd believe that feller at the piano is Floyd Cramer?"

My eyes bugged out. Jim Reeves? Floyd Cramer? You mean those guys wearing work shirts and old, worn-out hats? I just couldn't believe that these two big artists would be playing on our session. They laughed and kidded around and were very friendly. They must have known we were really nervous because they went out of their way to put us at ease. Jim and Floyd both had more than one big hit out already. They recorded on the Abbot Label, which Fabor Robinson also owned. We were soon to learn that when it came to recording sessions, the country music business acted like one big family.

We cut "Looking Back To See" without any difficulty, and all those who took part thought it was a fine little duet. However, we later learned that Jim Reeves had told Fabor that if "Looking Back To See" was a hit, he was going to quit the business. He thought it was the worst song he'd ever heard! It then came time for J. E. to solo on a song called "Rio De Janeiro" for our flip side. That was the side I was hoping would be a hit for J. E. All this contract and recording stuff was fun for me, but I continued to think of myself as a support for J. E. until he found a hit to make it big with.

That first recording session took everything out of us. We were completely exhausted. That night we stayed at the famous old Caddo Hotel in Shreveport. Since we couldn't afford two rooms, we got one room with two beds. We thought nothing of it. After all, we'd slept crowded together in shacks without floors when we were kids. The only other time we had ever stayed in a hotel was at the Jefferson Davis in Nashville, when we sang on *Ernest Tubb's Midnight Jamboree*. That time, Wayne Raney had paid for separate rooms for us.

We hadn't been in our hotel room ten minutes when there was a knock on our door and Floyd Cramer walked in. "I just came by for a minute to visit with some good old Arkansas folks," he explained.

Floyd, the smooth piano stylist who could have passed himself off as a New Yorker, was a native of Arkansas. He wanted to talk about good old times in our home state. Floyd was entertaining and funny. He stayed on. And on. And on. Finally, at about 6 a.m., I ran out of things to talk about. I was so exhausted from all the session work that I curled up on one of the beds and dozed off. I woke up an hour or so later and there was ol' Floyd was, still jawing away at J. E. It all seemed a little odd, even suspicious, to me. He seemed to be searching for things to talk about. It wasn't until about daybreak that he left our room.

Later on, we found out that his visit was all a put-on. It seems that he and Jim Reeves had a bet going about J. E. and me. People in the recording session kept looking at us. They were convinced that we were not brother and sister, but man and wife. I think it was because of the way we sang "Looking Back To See." We had convinced everybody that we were flirting back and forth and wanting to, as the song says, "spend some time in each other's company." I guess we should have taken it as a compliment, and I often wondered who won that bet.

• - •

Sure as the world, we had a hit on our hands. The song started getting big play by deejays all across the country almost as soon as Fabor Records released it. In a few weeks, it climbed up into the Top Ten and from there to a solid number eight in the almighty *Billboard* charts. Not a bad start for two little kids from the poor, piney woods of south Arkansas.

You turned on the radio and heard "Looking Back To See." You flipped the dial and you heard it again. This was true only if you were listening to stations *outside* of Arkansas. As was the custom in those days, other singers rushed to record their versions of our hit, and strange to say, those versions were the ones that most Arkansas radio stations chose to play. It was almost as though they were boycotting us, and for no reason we could figure. This phenomenon would also happen to us with our other hits. I've heard other artists and writers from Arkansas say that the same has happened to them. Wiser minds than mine will have to explain why. Maybe the words of Saint Matthew best explain it: "A prophet is not without honor, save in his own country, and in his own house."

Perils of the Road and That Old Devil Robinson

"Looking Back To See" was such a big hit that J. E. and I were in demand. I quit my job with the State Police and J. E. dropped out of college. The first date we ever played after the song hit was in Cleveland, Ohio. Up until the time J. E. and I started trying to get a recording contract, we had never been out of Arkansas. Our show in Cleveland was being sponsored by radio station WERE and the disc jockey Tom Edwards. We were supposed to go to the radio station for an interview with Tom prior to the show. When we got into Cleveland, I was asleep in the back seat. J. E. drove all over town looking for the station. Finally he stopped the car and reached back to shake me. "Sis, wake up, this is the biggest damn town I've ever seen in my life, and we're lost!"

I watched for street signs while he kept his eye out for those big city drivers. We stopped and asked directions several times, but we still couldn't find the place. After a while we decided the best thing we could do was call and cancel the interview because it was getting late by now and they'd probably given up on us anyway.

"Better still," J. E. said, "lets get a cab to take us there." He went up to the taxi stand and told the cab driver we wanted him to take us to WERE and asked where we could park our car. The cab driver looked at us like we were idiots. Then he said, "I need the money young man, and I could drive you all over this city. But then I'd bring you right back to this same spot. WERE is right across the street."

One of the major Saturday night live country music shows at this time was the *Louisiana Hayride* on KWKH in Shreveport. It had become a steppingstone to the *Grand Ole Opry*. A lot of stars got their start on the *Hayride*. It was a big thrill for us when Horace Logan, the show's producer and MC, asked us to become regular members. To us, that meant we were getting one step closer to the *Grand Ole Opry*.

We got our first booking agent, Pappy Covington, who also booked most of the other singers and pickers on the *Hayride*. Though we had a hit, our first show dates were few and far between. We were sometimes being booked so far from home that it took all the money we made just to pay for gas, food, and lodging. We played the *Hayride* almost every Saturday night. Then we'd hit the road. What time we had off we spent rehearsing new songs. I also helped out in Momma's restaurant, while J. E. worked with Daddy down in the log woods or at his sawmill.

The road will kill you. Every time we took off for Amarillo, Lubbock, and points west, the grind took just a little more out of us. We were still kids and discovering the road wasn't at all what we thought it would be. Somehow or other, though, we learned to take it. We would spend the next fifteen years or so watching the countryside from the window of a moving vehicle. Some pickers love it, some tolerate it, and some let it drive them crazy. Perhaps it was Tom T. Hall, the Storyteller himself, who summed it up best: "Taking pills and drinking whiskey, pickin' can be mighty risky."

After several grueling weeks on the road, we finally told Horace and Pappy that we'd just have to have more dates between those long hauls. So Pappy lined us up a tour with Slim Whitman. Slim was pretty popular in those days (although not nearly as popular as he became much later through the marketing of his golden oldies on television). We traveled with Slim and his band all over the Southwest and wound up the tour in Roswell, New Mexico. It was the longest tour we'd been on, and we made some money for the first time—a total of $1,700. That was big money to us, and though we hadn't received any royalties from "Looking Back To See" yet, we just knew we were going to make it.

We'd had a good time with Slim. Now it was time to drive back and play the *Hayride* and then go on home for a few days. We felt good about the money we'd made and planned to save up to buy a Cadillac. It seemed like everybody on the *Hayride* drove a Cad. So we thought we had to have one too. After all, putting up that almighty front of wealth and style was part of the business.

On the tour with Slim, we drove my yellow Chevy. We were heading home when we noticed a car that seemed to be following us. As we got over into Texas from New Mexico, we saw the same car about a mile behind us. This made us a little nervous. Every once in a while, we pulled off into a roadside park, thinking that car would go on by and that maybe we'd get a license number. But each time we stopped, the car would stop too. It never got close enough for us to see the driver. Convinced now that we were being followed, we got really scared, too scared to stop and eat or sleep. Finally we talked to some truck drivers at a rest stop, and they said they'd keep an eye out for that car. We felt a little better as we got closer to Shreveport.

When we got there—completely exhausted—we checked into the old Caddo Hotel. It was in the afternoon, and we were due to sing on the *Hayride* that night. We just had to get a few hours of sleep. Once again, we took only one room with two beds, and when we hit those beds, we just died away. When we got up at six o'clock that evening, we had a terrible surprise. We had been cleaned out. All our clothes were gone: J. E.'s pants and shirt, my dress, J. E.'s billfold, the car keys, everything! We were almost hysterical. How in the world could anyone get into our room and rob us blind in broad daylight?

Finally we called the hotel manager and the police. We also called our musician friend, Jerry Rowley, to come help us. Luckily my old Chevy hadn't been stolen. We must have made a peculiar sight, J. E. and me, wrapped in sheets and standing in the parking lot while Jerry broke into the car to get our suitcases. We've always been grateful to Jerry. A fine fiddle player on the *Hayride*, he and his wife, Evelyn, who played piano, and his sister, Dido, who sang, never failed to make us welcome.

Somehow we got through our appearance on the *Hayride* that night. Pappy loaned us some money so we could go home the next day. The robbery was never solved, and we never got our clothes or $1,700 back. We drove all the way to Pine Bluff with hardly a word spoken between us. Here we were, coming back home broke again, our Cadillac dreams nothing but a shooting star that died out before it got halfway down the sky.

"I don't know about you," J. E. said as we drove up to our folks' place, "but I'm not going back. I'm gonna quit this damn sorry business."

• • •

We didn't quit. We went back to the *Hayride* the very next week and took some show dates down in Texas, which made us nothing to speak of. In Little Rock, the *Barnyard Frolic* was still going strong. They booked us every other week or so. It was a good feeling to get back with Shelby and Sarah and not have to make that long drive down to Shreveport. I began to wish I hadn't quit my job with the State Police.

I was in my twenties, but I found I had little time for the things other young girls took for granted, things like dating and parties and other normal activities. I did meet a young man that I developed a hard crush on. His name was Fuzzy Owen. He was from Conway, Arkansas, and was just about the cutest guy I'd ever seen. Fuzzy played steel guitar with the *Frolic* band and was a fine musician. He never suspected that I had a bad crush on him. Oh, he'd tell me how nice I looked in my new outfits, and he'd cheer me up a little when I was blue, just enough to keep me swooning. I think he was going to ask me for a date, and who knows what might have happened from then on. I faced a real dilemma: I wanted to date, but my father wouldn't let me go out with a boy, even though I was grown now and making my own way. Young girls in those days, especially those of us brought up out in the country with rigid parents, had it so much harder than girls do now. Boys could run around and raise hell all they liked, but girls had to live under an iron rule, right up to the day they got married.

I've often wondered what would have happened if that sweet, good-looking Owen boy had had half as much a crush on me as I did on him. It kind of reminds me of that great Tom T. Hall song of love averted, "Pamela Brown." Anyway, Fuzzy left the *Frolic* and went out to California to see if he couldn't make it in the big time—and he did. After playing for years in the big recording studios there, he went on to manage Merle Haggard. One of these days, I'm going to write a sweet song about lost love, Fuzzy, my Daddy and all the other things that keep me looking back to see.

Along about the middle of December 1954, Fabor Robinson started calling us up. He said he loved the way "Looking Back To See" had climbed the charts and wanted us to come to California for another recording session. It was close to Christmas, though, and we certainly didn't want to miss the holiday with all the Brown clan.

"No problem about missing Christmas, kids," Fabor assured us.

"Just hop a plane and come on out." Of course, J. E. and I had never flown before and were scared to death at the thought of flying. But Daddy talked us into it. He even bought roundtrip tickets for us, just so we'd be sure to make it back for Christmas. Fabor never reimbursed him for those tickets.

The lights of Los Angeles were a dazzling sight to behold the night we flew in. They looked like all the stars of heaven and half the Milky Way thrown in for special effect. I started staring at them a hundred miles before we got to the airport, leaning over the man seated next to me. When he realized it was my first flight, he got up and let me sit by the window. I could tell he was getting a big kick out of watching me, but I didn't care. This, to me, was the eighth wonder of the world, and I wasn't going to miss a minute of it.

J. E. and I stayed in a motel near the Burbank Recording Studios where we were to do our session. Once again, we shared the same room. After our terrifying experience in Shreveport, I was too scared to stay by myself, especially way out there in the crazy world of California a million miles from home.

We recorded a song called "Draggin' Main Street" that I had written a few weeks before. It was about teen life—and boredom—in our hometown of Pine Bluff. Fabor liked it: he said it had a new and unique quality. The session musicians seemed to like the song too. Two of them—Speedy West on steel guitar and Billy Strange on electric—were especially nice to us. We took their encouragement as a compliment. They were such great session players, among the very best musicians in the country. With their help, maybe we'd have us another hit.

Before we flew back, Fabor took us out to dinner at a nice L.A. restaurant. He was one stylish-acting guy, and he told us to get used to this high style because he was personally going to see to it that we became big stars. Uh huh! Throw another shrimp on the barbie, 1954 style. At dinner that night, though, I did get to see my first movie star up close. The heartthrob of that era was Jeff Chandler, and there he sat with his two children not five feet away from me.

"I'm going to get his autograph!" I said.

"Don't you dare," Fabor stopped me. "A lot of stars come to this place to get away from nosy people."

Nosy people, like me. I sat and stared and stared. How I wanted

Jeff Chandler's autograph to show the folks back home. But Fabor shook his head scornfully at me. Handsome, strong, soul-killing Jeff Chandler. Years later, when I heard that he had died, I thought of my first starry-eyed trip to Hollywood and of that night in the restaurant. And I couldn't stop thinking about that most handsome man in the world.

• • •

"Draggin' Main Street" was released in January 1955. It received little fanfare at first. But it got some attention from deejays. And it caused a terrible row in our hometown. It seems that the locals, particularly the town's most upstanding citizens, were taking the song as an insult. The local newspaper even ran an editorial that was very critical of the song—and of J. E. and me. The last thing in my mind when I wrote the song was to demean my hometown; I was just putting into words what most young kids had always felt, whether they lived in Pine Bluff or Milwaukee or Reno, Nevada.

The local folks didn't have to worry very long. The sound quality of the record was poor because the studio Fabor used was far inferior to the one we had used in Shreveport. "Draggin' Main" stalled low on the charts and soon died there. Another cloud drifted by.

Fabor called us again to say that he was putting together a big tour of the Pacific Northwest and ask if we'd like to be a part of it. "The tour will last six weeks," he said, "and, kids, I'm telling you, after you're through with this tour, you'll have enough money to buy two Cadillacs."

We took the bait. Jim Reeves, our new friend from the *Hayride*, was designated to headline the show. Others who would be on the bill were Tom Tall and Ginny Wright, Jerry Rowley, Evelyn, and Dido, Alva Deane and Sandy Coker, Shirley Bates, and the Jim Reeves Band. Right before we left for the tour, Daddy came in and told us he had a surprise for us. He led us outside and there sat a shiny new Lincoln. For the first time, we were hitting the road in style.

The tour was enjoyable but exhausting for all. We played stage shows, big ballrooms, dances, and even some Army bases. Jim Reeves's wife, Mary, was a godsend. She helped sell tickets, counted heads in the crowd to make sure we got our fair percentage of ticket sales and generally kept our spirits up. She suffered right beside Jim through those long and lean first years, and I don't think anyone ever heard her complain. If there is a synonym for courage, it surely is Mary Reeves.

On this first big tour, we were supposed to make big names for ourselves as well as big money. Well, J. E. and I missed the first show. That old Brown bad luck caught us again. There we were, tooling across Texas in our brand new Lincoln, when the damn car started smoking and caught fire. Talk about your sudden panic! J. E. and I jumped out of that thing and began screaming and hollering. When the thing finally cooled down, we flagged down a trucker and had a tow truck pull us in. It turned out that the car had never been serviced and was running on maybe a pint of oil. It was a total loss. (Daddy was so mad I thought he was going to explode. He raised so much hell with the car dealer that we got a replacement.)

Singers and pickers back in those days caravanned in their own cars. There were no big tour buses or smooth four-lane highways. As soon as we caught up with the tour, we found out quickly that there wasn't going to be much glamour or glory in it. We didn't finish up our show until late in the night. Then we had to drive on to the next date, which was sometimes twelve or fourteen hours away. We got tired early, and we stayed tired. The only good times we had were on the stage in front of people.

Since it was on his side of the continent, Fabor came along to manage everything—and collect all the money. He met with everybody on the tour and told us he would pay for our road expenses. When the tour was over, he continued, he would pay us the money we had coming from the dates. We should have smelled a rat right then. But J. E. and I figured we might save more by not drawing any of the money coming to us. We were certain we'd collect several thousand dollars, enough to pay for the car Daddy had bought us. That was our dream, to walk into our folks' house with big wads of money to show that we really had made it big.

So we scrimped and saved, went without proper food, slept in the car instead of getting rest in hotel rooms. Many a night I'd curl up in the backseat, under a pile of dirty clothes, while J. E. drove until morning. He was pushing himself so hard I was afraid he'd get sick. Pretty soon my fears became a reality. No, a nightmare.

Way up in the Northwest, the countryside was rugged and the

little towns few and far between. We had only a little gas in the tank, and it was close to midnight. We passed one closed filling station after another. Finally, the car started sputtering and then stopped. Thank God Jim and Mary were following close behind us. We waved them down.

"We're out of gas," J. E. yelled out.

"We're running on empty, too," Jim said. "I'll try to make it on down this mountain and bring some gas back."

So there J. E. and I were, stuck on the top of a mountain in cold, cold Washington. A cold front had come through, bringing a snowstorm with it. It kept getting thicker and thicker. The hours dragged on as we waited for Jim and Mary to come back. The snow was so heavy we couldn't see out the windows. In all my life, I've never been any colder or more scared than I was that night. We worried that something bad had happened to Jim and Mary, and we didn't see another car pass all that night. We were stranded, snowbound, and about to freeze to death.

As we were soon to learn, Jim and Mary had made it down the mountain and had run out of gas right in front of a closed service station. Jim told us he went next door to the owner's house, woke him up, and tried to get him to sell some gas. But the guy absolutely refused to open up until morning, even though Mary kept pleading to him that we were stuck back on the mountain and might freeze to death.

The only thing that kept us from freezing was a bunch of comic books that Leo Jackson, Jim's guitar picker, had left in our car. We burned them a page at a time to warm our hands and feet. Thank God for Superman and Wonder Woman, not to mention Captain Marvel and the Phantom!

Just after daylight the next morning, we saw Jim and Mary coming back. We were never so happy to see anyone in our lives. But we soon found that our troubles were just beginning. We put some gas in our car, got it started and were ready to take off down the mountain when we saw that Jim was having a problem getting his car turned back around on the narrow road. The more he tried to turn, the more his car slipped over toward a steep ravine. Pretty soon, his tires started spinning and buried the car in three feet of snow.

It must have been ten degrees below zero that day, and there we were, all stranded. We all shoved and pushed, trying to get the car straightened out. But we couldn't. More hours passed as the weather over the mountain became even more threatening. J. E. and Jim tried everything. They scraped snow from under the car, broke tree branches and stuck them under the tires, heaved, and cussed. J. E.'s eyes were watering and he was not looking well at all, but he kept at it. He didn't have a cap or hat of any kind, so I got a pillowcase out of the car and he wrapped it around his head. He crawled under the car as he dug away at the snow. All that morning, not another single vehicle came along the road.

At last, with all of us shoving and pushing, we got the car to budge a little and then to roll free. When J. E. got back into our car, he was almost dizzy and I could tell he was running a high fever. Sure enough, a few hours later, he came down with pneumonia.

* * *

There was no dignity in the way Fabor conducted our shows. His rule was that all the performers had to remain on stage for the whole show, which ran for hours. After we sang our songs, we had to stand on stage and smile and act like we were enjoying ourselves. It was so ridiculous that even the crowds knew it. Instead of "The Fabor Robinson String Music Show," which was its formal name, we started calling it the "Strange Music Show."

Fabor had hard and fast rules of conduct for us and easy ones for himself. He forbade any of the single girls on the tour to dance with our fans or to date them on our days off. Yet Fabor, a married man himself, was traveling with a little road honey that he shacked up with every night in some fancy hotel or motel.

Some of our crowds were good and some only middling. One night, Fabor called a meeting of all the members of the tour in his motel suite. Word had already gotten around that Fabor was upset and was going to lay down the law. I went to the meeting alone because J. E. was still recuperating from pneumonia. Besides that, the hours of standing on the stage had just worn him down.

As soon as we got there, Fabor lit in on us. He said we were lazy, ungrateful, and undeserving of what he was paying us. He accused us of doing all sorts of nasty things behind his back. Then he noticed that J. E. wasn't there in the room. I told Fabor that J. E. was sick, and he accused me of lying.

"He's out with some tramp," Fabor said. "Well, he can just stay out. You're fired, the both of you!"

"Wait a minute, Fabor," Jim Reeves protested. "You can't fire these kids. You drug them halfway across the country, and you treat them worse than dirt."

"It's all right with me!" I yelled at Fabor. "I don't want on your damn stupid tour anyway! Just pay us the money you owe us and we'll leave right now!"

"Pay you? That'll be the day, lady."

A lot of yelling and accusing went on after that, but in the end Fabor had his way. As usual. He refused to pay us a single dime of the money we had coming, and there was nothing we could do about it. We left in the middle of the night, mad but still scared babes in the woods. We didn't know what in the world we were going to do.

Without a bit of money, we were stranded way out in the middle of Idaho. Jim and Mary came to our room as we were packing to leave. They were broke too, but they'd collected a few dollars from the guys in the band, enough at least to get us to the nearest town where we could wire home for money.

"I'm not asking Daddy for money," J. E. said. "I just can't do it. I don't care if we have to walk back home."

As we drove along, we hit upon an idea. We'd sell our autographed pictures at restaurants along the way. After all, we reasoned, we had had a big hit. So our pictures ought to sell pretty good. Knowing nothing else to do, we began bumming across the country, peddling our pictures at cafes and truck stops. Some truckers were very nice. They bought pictures, gave us extra tips and even spread the word about us to other truck stops along the way. Then, somewhere out of Boise, we got stranded again. Almost out of the dimes and quarters we'd collected, we stopped in front of this nice looking restaurant. J. E. went inside and asked the manager if we could sell some pictures because we were broke and hungry. The folks in that place were very nice. They even displayed our pictures and tried to help us sell some. But we stayed there until it closed and didn't sell a single picture.

We had just enough money for burgers, and I remember having chili on mine. I was starved and the chiliburger was delicious. We were sleeping in the car that night when I woke up with a raging case of food poisoning. There was no bathroom anywhere around, nothing to clean myself with. All I could do was retch and vomit and let the diarrhea flow.

By morning, I was a little better. J. E. just sat looking at me, crying and saying that all this trouble was his fault. It took a great deal of courage for him to make a telephone call to Jim Reeves back on the tour. When J. E. came back from the phone booth, he sat in the car a long time before he looked at me. Then he said, "We're going back on the tour."

"No," I said. "I'm not going to be around that Fabor Robinson ever again."

"It'll be all right this time. Jim said that he'd been waiting for us to call. He said that Fabor would take us back—or every single person on the tour would quit on the spot."

"You mean they'd all quit because of us?"

At first I was shocked, then moved. We found out something about the real people of the country music industry. The fact that Jim and the others would pull out of the tour on our account (and maybe lose a lot of money) proved that there were some great people in the business, a lesson we would learn time and again over the years. People get into the music business out of love for the music itself. But they stay and endure, I think, out of love for each other.

Raymond when he was a baby. He is being held up by
Momma in front of one of her beautiful quilts, which she
made at the Herschel Thrower Country Store. Maxine was
about four and J. E. was probably two. *From the collection of
Maxine Brown.*

Herschel Thrower's store. He sold it to Frank and Pearl
Williams about 1946. *From the collection of Maxine Brown.*

Bonnie and Maxine. This was taken outside our farmhouse
after we had it painted white (we were coming up in the
world!). I would guess that we were about five and eleven.
From the collection of Maxine Brown.

J. E., Maxine, and Raymond, at the ages of about four, six, and two. *From the collection of Maxine Brown.*

The Browns' first place of business, The Dollarway Restaurant and Grocery, in 1949. Mom, Dad, Norma, and Maxine are behind the counter. *From the collection of Maxine Brown.*

J. E. and Maxine on top of Daddy's truck with the biggest load
of logs ever brought into the paper mill in Pine Bluff, Arkansas,
about 1950. *From the collection of Maxine Brown.*

J. E. and Maxine singing on mike at the very first TV station in Arkansas, KRTV, in 1952. *From the collection of Maxine Brown.*

Maxine and Jim Edward Brown's first publicity picture, taken while on the *Barnyard Frolic* in Little Rock in 1953. We used to sell these pictures on the shows we worked with Shelby and Sarah Jane Cooper. Maxine and Jim Ed were billed as "The Western Sweethearts." *From the collection of Maxine Brown.*

Red and white costumes made by Momma and worn on the *Barnyard Frolic*. The costumes matched a red and white pearl accordion that Maxine played on stage. *From the collection of Maxine Brown.*

This was the first publicity picture that our good friend Jim Reeves made under Abbott Records. He used to sell it on show dates. He autographed the back of it. It reads: "Maxine, may you live as long as you want and never want as long as you live. I mean it, Jim Reeves." It meant a lot!!! *Courtesy of Ed Gregory, Nashville, Tennessee.*

Maxine on stage at the Barnyard Frolic. In the background are
Shelby and Sarah Jane Cooper, Old Cyclone (on bass) and J. E.
(on the left, though you can only see about half of him). *From
the collection of Maxine Brown.*

Maxine Brown's first publicity picture, from 1954. *From the collection of Maxine Brown.*

Jim Ed and Maxine Brown. *From the collection of Maxine Brown.*

One of the first pictures of Maxine, Bonnie, and J. E. taken
when Bonnie first started to perform on the *Louisiana Hayride*.
From the collection of Bonnie Brown.

The first publicity picture of Bonnie and Maxine together
with J. E., from 1955. Bonnie later had a dress made to match
Maxine's, by California costume designer Nudie Cohn. *From
the collection of Maxine Brown.*

We Get Screwed

When we returned to the tour in Boise, Fabor acted as though nothing had happened. J. E. kept blaming himself for everything, all our troubles and my getting food poisoning. I blamed that devil Fabor. God, how we hated that SOB. We stayed pretty much to ourselves for the rest of the tour, except for traveling and sightseeing with Jim and Mary when we had a few hours off.

One day, Fabor came to us and said he had something to discuss. He had his official face on, and I knew from experience that he was fixing to unload some bad business on us. Sure enough, I was right. He'd been in touch with his business office in California, he said, and there was some trouble over our song, "Looking Back To See." The song was still on the charts after having stayed near the top for a long time. We weren't so green that we didn't know we had some royalties coming.

"I'm afraid the royalties on that song will be tied up for a long time," Fabor said. "There's a lawsuit against you."

"Lawsuit?" J. E. and I said at the same time. "What are you talking about?"

Fabor had a shit-eating look on his face. "Do you know somebody named Charles Davidson?" he inquired.

"Why, yes, we do." I said. "Charles is the manager of the *Barnyard Frolic* back in Little Rock."

The thought that Charles was in any position to take credit for our music just about floored me. He had never written a song in his life. He had weaseled his way into the *Frolic*, where he mostly just got in people's way.

"Did you ever get the song copyrighted?" Fabor asked.

No, we hadn't, we admitted. I guess Charles knew that and saw his chance to jump a claim. We argued with Fabor a long time. There would never be a problem of proving the song was ours, because Shelby and Sarah Jane Cooper could verify everything we said. At that moment we were so mad that if we'd been around Charles Davidson we would have given him the going-over he deserved.

"Now, don't you kids worry," Fabor went on, getting that sickening "father" tone in his voice. "You'll get your royalties. I guarantee it. But you'll have to get yourselves a lawyer."

So we called home and told Daddy the whole sorry story. At first he was going to go and take care of Charles himself, but we convinced him that would only complicate our rightful claim. So Daddy hired the best—and most expensive—lawyer in Pine Bluff. We'd have to wait until we got home to settle the stupid claim. For the rest of the tour we were down and blue.

At last, the long tour was over. We all met at Jim and Mary Reeves's house in Shreveport to settle up. Everybody was just about worn out, relieved to have the hard journey completed and feeling pretty good about the big money we'd all be getting. When Fabor walked in, looking as serious as the chairman of the Edsel Company, we knew something bad was on us again.

"Well, first of all," Fabor started, "you people didn't draw a fraction of the crowds you should have. My God, the expenses you ran up."

"Cut the crap, Fabor," Jim Reeves said. "Get to the money."

But Fabor wouldn't discuss the money, not at first. He wanted to criticize each and every one of us first. He started in on J. E. and me, bringing up the fact that we had missed a lot of shows, hadn't pulled our weight and had even walked out on the tour. I thought J. E. was going to tear into him right then and there. I noticed, too, that Fabor's little sweetie was nowhere to be seen. He probably had her holed up in some plush suite to spare her this ordeal.

Finally, Fabor said he'd give us all the money we had coming. I've never forgotten the mad and sullen look he kept on his face. He missed his calling in California. He should have been one of those nasty producers with a casting couch. He handed J. E. some folded money. When J. E. counted it, it came to only $234. Not twenty thousand or even ten thousand—just a little over two hundred dollars. I couldn't help myself. I began whimpering like a tortured dog.

All around the Reeveses' living room, the same scenes of disbelief were taking place. Instead of apologizing, Fabor was getting meaner and madder, as if we were the lowest scum he'd ever come across. At last Jim Reeves stood up, holding the paltry bills in his clenched fist, and called Fabor a lowdown sneak and cheater. They got into a cussing match and pretty soon some punches were flying. Jim went into his bedroom, got his gun and pointed it right at Fabor. We just knew he was gonna kill him. Mary knew it too, but she was able to convince Jim that the sorry SOB wasn't worth it—but not until he fired one shot at Fabor and missed. We were all wishing he'd go ahead and kill the bastard.

Finally, Jim picked Fabor up off the floor by the seat of his pants and literally threw him out of the house. He told him he would never record for him again.

"I've got a contract with you buddy, and you'll have to do what I say," Fabor yelled. "I'll see you in court!"

"Damn right you will!" Jim yelled back "You'll lose and you'll not swindle anybody else. I'll see to that!"

After Fabor left, we all sat around stunned, mad, and crying. Everybody had gotten a couple hundred dollars from Fabor. We'd been stiffed by one of the worst con men in the business. It was the bitterest of lessons to learn. But in the end, Fabor conned only himself. For a few thousand dollars, he had pissed off recording artists who would go on to make millions for other record companies.

• • •

We limped back home. All during the long drive back to Pine Bluff, J. E. and I talked and cried and took turns feeling sorry for ourselves.

"I'm quitting this business," J. E. said. "I'll go back to work for Daddy in the log woods. I don't want to record another song for that SOB."

"You don't mean that," I said to my little brother. "All you've ever wanted to do is sing and make records. You can't give up. You'll find another record label."

"We can't, Maxine. We just can't. Fabor's still got us under contract, and we don't have the money to fight him in court."

"We'll find a way."

We were booked to end the tour on the *Louisiana Hayride*, but we skipped it to head home. How in the world could we tell our folks that after all our ordeals—the car blowing up, J. E.'s pneumonia, my food poisoning—that we had only $234 to show for our troubles? We knew we couldn't tell Daddy all the mean things Fabor had said to us. He would have been a dead man. So we crawled on home, tired, broke, and disgusted with the world. Sometimes I wonder if we did the right thing by keeping the worst of it from Daddy. Down South, daddies are a different breed. Girls in my day didn't ever have to worry about being roughed up or mistreated, for their daddies were always there to offer a final reckoning. It was not a question of law or courts or anything like that. It was a pure and simple form of rough justice that always worked.

When we got home, our folks welcomed us like long lost prodigals. Everyone was so happy to see us and we were just as glad to see them. All the mean things that happened on the tour suddenly seemed to fade away. Nothing mattered as much as it recently seemed. We were back in the safety of our home and the love of our parents.

We had a surprise waiting for us too. Our little sister Bonnie had been growing up right before our eyes. She was out of high school now and a freshman at Arkansas A&M down in Monticello. When she was younger, Bonnie had had trouble controlling her weight. But she has always been a beautiful girl, with raven black hair and the darkest eyes this side of a gypsy song, not to mention all the other physical endowments that drove the boys crazy. She hadn't greeted us with the other members of the family when we walked in. But now the door to her room opened and out stepped this dazzling young debutante, the belle of the ball.

"Well, whatta ya think?" she said, putting on her best imitation of Mae West. My goodness, Bonnie had lost so much weight that she looked almost slinky, like one of those fashion models. She told us she had been rehearsing for hours every day with some of our tapes we'd left at home. "Here, I'll show you," she said, and turned on one of the tapes. She started singing harmony with our voices, and J. E. and I both raised our eyebrows. She added an ingredient that really gave the Browns a full sound.

"I'm ready to go with you on the next tour," she said. "We'll be the Brown Trio and we'll knock 'em dead."

How could we tell her that there wasn't going to be a next tour?

We didn't have the heart to mention all the ugly things that happened to us out west. But we started encouraging her not to be too hasty about getting into the music business. She needed to stay in college, we argued. Just look at us. We hadn't made one red cent, and there was no way we could ever repay Momma and Daddy for their support. Unable to hold back any longer, we broke down and told Bonnie all the bad things that had just happened to us.

"You don't want to quit school," I told her.

"Not for a life like that," J. E. added, sadly.

Bonnie didn't say anything. So we thought it was all settled. We'd all stay home. J. E. would go back to college and complete his degree in forestry, I'd try to get my job back with the State Police, and we'd all be much better off.

We sat around the house a couple of days, and before long we ran out of things to say and do. J. E. picked up his guitar and started strumming some chords. Pretty soon, he struck up a song and I joined in singing. Then here came Bonnie to add that new layer of harmony. The more we sang, the more we never wanted to stop. J. E. and I had been pretty good at singing duets, but Bonnie gave our sound a special quality, the best we would ever have. Right then and there we knew that we had to go on.

■   •   •

We took Bonnie back with us to the *Louisiana Hayride* the next time we went. You'd have thought some sort of miracle had occurred. Everybody at the *Hayride* thought they'd seen the last of us. But here we were, three crazy Arkansas kids, singing better than we ever had before. We got several encores and left the stage with the crowd wanting more.

"What the dickens happened to y'all?" asked Pappy Covington, the *Hayride* booking agent. "You've got a brand new sound. If you keep this up, I'll be able to get you a lot of bookings."

Pappy was as good as his word. Before we left the *Hayride* that weekend he had lined us up some one-night stands with several of the *Hayride* regulars. Mostly they were in school auditoriums in and around Texas and Louisiana. We talked with Jim Reeves at length about the prospect of having to record again for Fabor. We didn't want anything else to do with him.

"As long as you're under contract, you have no choice," Jim said. "He'll sue you like he has me."

Like it or not, we were still in the business. Back home, we had a little score to settle, and its name was Charles Davidson. Daddy had hired us a lawyer to look into Charles's claim against "Looking Back To See." Back in California, Fabor's lawyer kept calling us for depositions to prove I had actually written the song. Hendrix Rowell, our sharp Pine Bluff lawyer, had been working on it for us. One day, Hendrix came to our house and said to me, "Let's just go and look this Davidson person up and put him on the spot."

We drove together to Little Rock to snoop around for Charles. I knew him only by sight. He managed the *Barnyard Frolic*, but that wasn't much of a job. It just involved making sure the stage was set up and the mics worked. It took us the better part of a day to track him down. We discovered he had a day job clerking at a grocery store in Oak Grove, a little town outside of North Little Rock.

When we drove up to the Blue Hill Grocery in Oak Grove, I spotted Charles behind the checkout counter right away. As we walked in, we saw that he recognized me. He shot from behind that counter and ran like hell for the back door. But I managed to catch up with him before he could get away. The fact that he ran like a scared dog was all the proof of his guilt anybody needed.

Hendrix and I had him cornered. He stood there turning every color. "I want you to look me in the eye, Charles Davidson," I said, "and tell this lawyer here who wrote that song."

He dropped his head, stared at his toes and sputtered out something about how he was sorry for what he'd done and that someone else had put him up to claiming "Looking Back To See." When Hendrix asked him who that someone was, Charles just turned real pale and lost his voice.

Word soon got around to all the regulars on the *Frolic* of what Charles Davidson was trying to pull. All the singers and pickers got together and decided that they would quit the show in protest. A few days later, the station that sponsored the *Frolic* announced that Charles Davidson would no longer be the show's manager. Everybody was coming forward to say that I had written the song and had performed it many times in the past two or three years.

I have never been to court regarding my song, and although

Fabor Robinson and his lawyers kept insisting that it was tied up in litigation, I know in my own mind that it never was. Something even more upsetting concerning that song would happen when next we met up with Fabor.

. . .

Even though we were a trio, the Browns didn't skyrocket to the top overnight. It seldom happened like that way back in those hard days of country music. We sang on the *Louisiana Hayride* every weekend and played some dates around Texas and Louisiana. The money was OK, but we had run up so many debts that it all seemed a losing battle. The showcase for our new sound and look came when my folks opened up a new supper club.

While Daddy was building up his lumber business, Momma was busy managing our restaurant. The place had grown so popular that people were standing in line to get in. My folks decided they'd have to expand. It was a big venture involving big bank loans, but we all were giddy as the new building went up.

When the club opened, it had a big sign hanging over it flashing "The Trio Restaurant and Supper Club." As the crowd came in that first night, they saw a picture of J.E., Bonnie, and me over the entrance. The opening was a grand success. Within the next few weeks, people from all over were coming to the Trio.

Three months later the old rotten Brown luck struck again. The club somehow caught on fire. It didn't burn to the ground, but the fire caused damage in the thousands. The insurance company didn't pay a fraction of the cost. True to their undeniable spirit, my folks wouldn't let this disaster beat them. They scraped up all the money they could beg and borrow and completely rebuilt the Trio. When it was finished, it was even more beautiful than before.

To prove that they wouldn't be whipped, Momma and Daddy planned the biggest grand opening the state of Arkansas had ever seen. Many of the artists we'd gotten to know on the road called to say they were coming to sing at the event. When the big night finally arrived, the Trio Club featured a star-studded playbill that would have rivaled that of any state fair or grand tour. Appearing that night were Jim Reeves, Porter Wagoner, the Louvin Brothers, David Houston, Bobby Lord, and Werly Fairburn, all top recording artists then.

It was such a big show that you'd have thought we had won every top musical award of the year. KRTV-TV did an hour-long live special from the club that night, and many state dignitaries and politicians were in the overflow crowd. It was the first high point in the new Brown Trio's career. Later we would have many hit songs, appear many times on the most popular national television shows and tour the world with the best in the business. But that night, when J. E., Bonnie, and I sang in front of that big home audience, I felt we had won a major victory.

PART THREE

Here Today and Gone Tomorrow

Screwed Again

After the reopening of the Trio Club, we stayed busy with show dates in and around the region. As regulars on the *Louisiana Hayride*, we journeyed down to Shreveport nearly every weekend. One Saturday night while we were waiting our turn to go on stage, we ran into Fabor. He smiled that broad, sneaky smile of his and greeted us like long lost orphans.

"Hi, kids," he chirped. "Guess what I'm releasing on your next record?"

We couldn't believe what he said next. Back when we had recorded "Looking Back To See," we had also knocked out a pretty dreadful song called "Itsy Witsy Bitsy Me." We never thought it would be released. It didn't fit our style, and we couldn't get a decent cut on it since we had run out of studio time. The other side was one we had cut at Fabor's studio when we cut "Draggin' Main" and "Your Love Is Wild As The West Wind." Everyone connected with recording "Itsy Witsy Bitsy Me" knew it was all messed up and would need some special work before it could be made halfway decent. Now here stood Fabor with that diabolical smirk, boasting that he was going to release it anyway.

"You're kidding," J. E. said to him.

"Not a bit," Fabor said. "You kids tried to get a little too big for your britches. I'm going to release that turkey of a song just to put you in your place."

We were so shocked that we didn't know what to say. If nothing else proved that man was evil, surely this stunt was the one to do it. "Itsy Witsy Bitsy Me" was written by Gene Davis of Pine Bluff, who was a good friend of Shelby and Sarah Jane Cooper. The song itself wasn't a great one, but it wasn't all that bad. It was just the awful way it was set up and recorded that bothered us. For one thing, the cut had a bad piano note right in the break. Floyd Cramer had hit the wrong note because he had been playing for hours and was worn out. The mistake was as obvious as a two-headed calf.

A few weeks later the song came out. All the deejays around the country played the song. Once. They must have thought that Fabor had sure enough lost his marbles. Later, when people started putting him on the spot about the record, he was heard to say, "Oh, my wife released the wrong cut while I was on the road." We told people the real truth whenever we got the chance, not that it helped.

In years to come, we could all share a bitter laugh over the "Itsy Bitsy" incident. Floyd Cramer would cringe when the subject came up and say, "Oh Lord, don't ever let anyone know I played on that record." In the long run it didn't hurt us nearly as badly as it did Fabor. We were still young enough and new enough to the industry to live it down. Fabor not only hurt himself by releasing a single that didn't sell, his action also caused a lot of people in the business to view him in a new light.

• • •

We were playing shows all over the region, so I had no time to think about my own personal life. Naturally, I chose this time to fall in love. One night we were booked to play at a baseball game in our hometown. Pine Bluff was a member of old Cotton States League and had a very good team that year. It drew big crowds for the minor leagues. While we were singing that night, I caught sight of a good-looking young player. After the game, he came up to me and started chatting. His name was Merrill Smith. Not only was he cute, he was a nice boy.

Smitty and I made a date to meet the next week. I still had to dodge around my Daddy, who watched me like a hawk. It was easy enough to meet Smitty because he was in town for two or three weeks at a time. He didn't have a car, so I'd pick him up after a game and we'd ride around or go park and smooch. In no time at all, we were desperately in love. When Smitty left on a road trip, my heart would just break. I guess I sensed very early that our love wasn't going to make it. We were from two different walks of life, ones that seemed designed to keep us away from each other too much.

And, sure enough, we did begin to grow apart. I kept telling myself, "He's just here today and gone tomorrow and I get so lonesome for someone's company when he's gone." One night I sat down and wrote a song about Smitty and called it "Here Today and Gone Tomorrow." I was crying my eyes out as I wrote it. I guess I learned one of the most valuable lessons of my life during this period: after the pain of love dies, you've still got the music to sustain you. While I thought my song was beautiful, I wouldn't show it to anyone for a long time. It was too special and too painful.

We were getting some good show dates but not enough to support us. Bonnie and I helped at the restaurant and J. E. worked with Daddy's lumber business. One day J. E. came in from work and heard me singing my song.

"Is that a new song?" he asked.

"No, it's just something I made up for myself."

"How long did it take you to write it?" he asked.

"Not very long, a few minutes. It's nothing . . ."

"You're wrong. It's good. It's another hit."

He made me sing it all the way through. Then he picked up his guitar and joined in. In just a few minutes Bonnie walked in. She listened while we ran through it and then added her voice. While we were singing, a lot of folks had come into the Trio Club and were listening to us. When we finished, they all gathered around and applauded us. I guess I turned red all over. I know that I got a special feeling that's hard to ever get back. I knew it was a special song, even more so than "Looking Back To See," and I felt that one day it would be a big song that many people would like.

As I said before, we had worked a few shows with the great Louvin Brothers, Ira and Charlie. In my mind, Ira was about the greatest songwriter who ever lived, right up there with Hank Williams. A few days after we put "Here Today and Gone Tomorrow" together, Ira came by our house on his way down to Mississippi. J. E. told him we had a new song, and Ira asked us to sing it. After we were through, he got up and stared us right in the eye and said, "If you ever thought of quitting the business, you can't now. It'll be a smash hit."

Right away, Ira got busy writing another song to go along with "Here Today." Not just anybody could get an Ira Louvin song to record, and we started getting excited all over again. We called up our booking agent and got him to get us some dates down in Mississippi so we could work with the Louvins. It was down in that crazy state that I was to have another one of my comedy-of-errors adventures.

We were somewhere in Mississippi playing with the Louvins when I went to Ira's motel room to work on the new song. It was late at night, and the motel manager saw me going into a man's room. This guy must have had some trouble before with shady business, for he jumped to the conclusion that I was a hooker. He came to Ira's room a few minutes later, barged right in and cussed us out good. Believe you me, I told him off good—and so did Ira. We cleared out of that place fast.

We were to work many more dates with Ira and Charlie, and I guess we recorded as many of their songs as anybody else in the business. They were beautiful songs too, as clean and as sweet as fresh honey. Many years later, in 1975, Emmylou Harris scored her first top five hit with one of Ira's songs, "If I Could Only Win Your Love." Whenever I heard it, I would just break down and cry. You see, Ira was killed in an automobile accident in 1965, and we just about all died from grief ourselves.

• • •

You'd think people would learn. There's an old southern saying that a scalded cat fears cold water. After what happened to us just a few weeks after we got back from that tour with the Louvins, we should have learned some cold-water truth about appearance versus reality. But we didn't. We were playing a few dates around home, but we had refused to consider any more recording sessions because Fabor had burned us so badly on "Looking Back To See." Ira had bragged on my new song but nothing had seemed to come of it. Then one day the great singer Johnny Horton came knocking on our door.

Johnny was a tall, good-looking man with a full head of wavy hair. On stage, that is. In real life he was bald as a coot. Now, Momma had been down to the *Louisiana Hayride* a couple of times to see us perform, and I remember her marveling at how handsome Johnny Horton was. Well, there he stood in person, but he was dressed in ordinary clothes and his bald head was shining.

"Howdy, Miz Brown," he said. "I'm Johnny Horton. I wonder if I can come in and get a bite to eat?"

Momma didn't recognize him as a big country star and almost ran him off like a hobo. But Johnny kept telling her that he was a good friend of J. E.'s and mine. At last, she called over to the Trio Club and asked me about this slouchy ' impostor." I ran right home, took one look and told her that this honestly and truly was the big star Johnny Horton. Momma was so embarrassed then that she could hardly look his way.

Johnny was by no means the first country performer who came by to partake of Momma's hospitality. I think every singer we got to know on the road sooner or later came to our house. Word spread from Nashville all the way to Motor City that Momma Brown had a heart of gold and put out the best spread in the whole country.

Johnny was a little short on money and spent the night with us. We sat up almost all night singing every song we knew. Bonnie, J. E. and I sang him the new song, ' Here Today and Gone Tomorrow," and we could tell he liked it.

"Y'all, that gives me goosebumps," he said. "If you're not going to record it, I will. You can have a hit there, and I mean a big one."

Johnny agreed with us that Fabor Robinson was crazy and probably a crook, but there he was, still putting out big hits by artists all over the country.

"I've been in this business a lot longer than you kids," Johnny told us that night. "Lord, it's hard for a singer to make it. You have to have courage and never give up. Never."

I think Johnny had everybody at our house convinced, except for Daddy and me. I still felt the scars of that Great Northwest Tour and the way Fabor was holding out on the royalties we should be getting for "Looking Back To See." This talk of going back to a recording studio—whether it was with Fabor Robinson or anybody else—made me feel like I was caught in a rat trap.

But it had to happen. Bonnie was home by herself one day when Fabor called. Since she hadn't had any dealings with him, it was only natural that she would succumb to his charm. He could sell dead skunks to a buzzard. When we came home that night, Bonnie was bubbling over with enthusiasm. She told us she had talked long distance for hours to Mr. Robinson and had even played a tape of our new song to him over the phone. J. E. and I were dumbstruck. We had never told her the whole truth about what Fabor had put us through.

"He's coming here to see us tomorrow!" Bonnie squealed. "Isn't that great?"

J. E. and I just looked at each other and hid our true feelings. Surely that man wouldn't have the nerve to come to our very own home and look us in the eye. But sure enough, he showed up. When I came home from the Trio Club the next night, Fabor was sitting on the floor in our living room and acting like he was some sort of deity. Momma had already filled him up with chicken and dumplings and peach cobbler. He was as sassy as an old settin' hen. Our house was small to begin with and now the walls seemed to really close in on me. I nodded but didn't even speak to him. Then I ran into the kitchen and washed every plate, glass, pot, and pan at least twice. I tried to avoid going near him but I could hear him talking incessantly.

"I've made many a star out of a nobody," he told my folks. "I've made Jim Reeves what he is today and Floyd Cramer and a dozen others too. I can make the Brown Trio one of the biggest acts in the whole music industry. That's why I'm here." He droned on and on. He attacked Jim, accusing him of getting "sassy" when he hit the big time. If it hadn't been for Fabor, he boasted, Jim Reeves would still be a nobody. He spewed out the same stuff we'd heard a hundred times before when we were on that god awful tour with him. But as well as I knew the bastard, there was no way I could stop him from buttering up my family.

When it became clear that nothing else would shut Fabor up, J. E., Bonnie, and I sang him our new song, "Here Today and Gone Tomorrow." As we finished, he jumped up and clapped and made for the phone. Right there in front of Momma and Daddy, he called his studio in Malibu, California, and scheduled us a recording session. Daddy, who did know something about Fabor's shady ways, began arguing with him. He told him he wasn't going to allow us to record with him again because we hadn't got a dime out of our first song, even though it was a hit.

We knew that if Fabor could win Daddy over, he could win over the devil himself. Before he was through that night, he not only convinced Daddy we should record for him again. he even convinced J. E., Bonnie, and me. I guess we just fell under his spell after he promised that we'd get paid every cent that was coming to us and more.

"And I'm sure you kids would rather have a good deal like this than have to go through court trying to break our contract," he said, sugar dripping off every word. He was stressing that he still had us under contract and would see to it that we'd never sign to another label. Of course, he had to soften the threat in front of Daddy.

Pretty soon the phone rang. It was Fabor's wife, calling back to say that the recording session was booked and inviting us to stay at their place in Malibu Canyon while we were out there. She insisted that we keep receipts of all our expenses for the session so she could reimburse us. It was a hopeless situation; we had been flattered into submission and backed into a corner. We also feared that "Here Today and Gone Tomorrow" would never see the light of day unless we gave in to old Fabor one more time. So in the end that's what we did.

• ▪ •

Fabor, of course, didn't give us any advance money. But committed now to another trek out west, we had our booking agent line us up a few shows along the way. It was summer, and Bonnie was home from college. I thought, well, she'd get to see what it's like in California and maybe she'd see for herself what a rotten scene the recording business really was. J. E. and I were still suspicious. We talked between ourselves and decided that we'd stay only long enough to record the song. Even at that young age, we'd learned the bitter lesson that show business wasn't what it was cracked up to be. Bonnie was soon to learn her lesson the hard way.

We journeyed west, stopping here and there for one-night stands along the way, and finally found our way to Fabor's fancy spread in Malibu Canyon. Oh, it was grand. He seemed to have the whole canyon to himself, not a house around for miles. His house was a big ranch-style mansion. He and his wife lived upstairs, and the recording studio occupied the whole bottom floor. An adjacent building housed Fabor's distribution center and held what appeared to be millions of records. A nice fellow named Del Roy ran the center. Fabor was constantly giving him orders. From the moment we walked in, we were shocked at the way Fabor ordered his wife and poor old Del around. I believe Fabor's wife would have jumped into fire if Fabor had told her to. It certainly was a strange and strained situation.

Fabor was acting peculiar. Even before we got set up in his studio, he could talk about nothing except sex. He kept eyeing Bonnie and said, "If a girl hasn't slept with a man, she can't really sing." It was so sickening that we didn't to know to react to this carrying on. We weren't used to such language. I saw that Bonnie was getting nervous. Fabor wouldn't let her out of his sight. He followed her around wherever she went. Once or twice he tried to hug her, but she shucked him off with a laugh. I managed to keep myself between them after that. Bonnie was just seventeen and had never so much as gone out on a real date. I could tell Fabor was getting irritated at us for not letting him have his way.

But at least our recording session went well. First we did "Here Today and Gone Tomorrow." The session musicians all complimented us and said they knew the song would be a hit. Ira Louvin had written us a song called "You Thought, I Thought," a novelty number to serve as a follow-up to "Looking Back To See." Just as we started rehearsing it, Fabor came in and stopped us cold. He didn't like it at all, said it was stupid. He gave us a song his own company held the publishing rights to.

"We're doing this song for the B-side," he said flatly.

"Wait a minute," J. E. argued. "You promised us we could choose any song we wanted for the flip side."

"Yes, sir," I insisted. "You promised us that right in our house in Pine Bluff. You call my Daddy if you don't remember."

Fabor relented. But he huffed and fumed all the time we were getting ready to record "You Thought, I Thought." He stood over in the corner of the studio, almost drooling over Bonnie. As we began to record, he snapped, "Well, just go ahead with that pile of shit, Maxine. You and J. E. can do it by yourselves. It's not good enough for Sister Bonnie."

Although the conditions were strained, we had rehearsed the song all the way out to California. So it was easy to do. Since the song called for a duet, Bonnie wasn't needed for any of the verses. I could see Fabor was making the most of the opportunity while J. E. and I were distracted. He kept trying to get her off to herself, and I heard him suggest that she leave the studio with him. She must have said something negative to him, because right in the middle of the session he blurted out, "Maxine can't sing! She's never slept with a man. That's why she can't sing."

I was so hurt by his remark that I burst into tears. The session musicians were very nice and tried to calm me down. "Don't pay any attention to that turd. We don't," one of them said. "That's the way he treats all his girl singers. He thinks he's got to be the big cocksman." We got through recording the B-side somehow. J. E. was putting his guitar away as Fabor came up and wrapped his arms around Bonnie. He gave her a wink. "Your sister can't sing," he repeated, "but I'm going to make a singer out of you. Tonight."

Bonnie was scared to death by then. A little later, when we were by ourselves, I whispered to J. E. to put his guitar in the car and told him I would get the rest of our stuff together. "We may have to leave this place in a hurry," I explained. J. E. had already been thinking the same thing.

We ate supper with the Robinsons in their big dining room. As scared as we were, we still had enough spunk to ask for the expense money Fabor had promised. His wife got up and brought us the money in folding cash. I could tell Fabor was upset with her for paying us off. But he had other things on his mind. During dinner he carried on a one-way conversation about his favorite subject, perverted sex. I couldn't believe some of the things that came out of that nasty man's mouth. You must remember that this was back in the 1950s before the idea of free love and sexual permissiveness ever struck the country. Bonnie and I were as sheltered as innocent ducklings. Fabor carried on about "love" and "open marriage" and said he could make out with any woman he liked because he and his wife had an agreement. She could do as she pleased, too. We were amazed to see her nodding in agreement.

"Everything should be free," Fabor said.

And that's why you don't pay anybody, I thought, wishing I had enough courage to say it out loud. It was getting late, and we finally got away from Fabor. We went to the rooms he had assigned us. I noticed that Bonnie's room was way down at the end of the long hallway. I went over to her and whispered for her to come sleep in the room with me. Still not quite convinced that Fabor was danger-ous, she declined, saying she didn't want to make a scene. She'd lock her door, she said, and told me not to worry. I did worry. I went to bed and lay there for the longest time, determined to stay awake. J. E. and I both left our doors open; I knew Fabor wasn't interested in me because we had argued too many times before.

It wasn't long before I heard the telltale noise of a key turning in a lock. I sneaked to the door and peeked down the hall—just in time to see Fabor going into Bonnie's room. About three seconds later, Bonnie began yelling, "Maxine!"

J. E. and I rushed out at the same time. We hit Bonnie's room like a couple of razorbacks plowing through the brush. There stood old Fabor with fire in his eyes, gaping at our sister like a wild man. He screamed at us to get out, but we managed to yank Bonnie out of the room and run like hell. Fabor was right behind us. He jumped at J. E. and drew back like he was going to hit J. E. But we were too fast. We threw all our stuff in our car and jumped in. Fabor followed us out. "I dare you to say anything to the police!" he shouted. But our only inter-est was in getting away from that hateful place. "Who's gonna believe a bunch of punk kids?" he continued. "Who's gonna be a witness for you? It sure won't be my wife. She'd lie for me any time."

J. E. pulled the car out and we whizzed right by the maniac. It was two o'clock in the morning. We had been suckered again. Now we were having to run away. Fabor had the last word. "You're still under contract to me," he yelled. "I still own you!"

Putting on That Almighty Front

I should have written a song about Fabor. I should have written a song about dumb kids with pipe dreams and California promises. That song would have been right up there with "There's No Business like Show Business" and "Hooray for Hollywood."

We weren't thinking about recording sessions or hit records as we bolted out of that maddening world. Once we were out of L.A., we stopped and called our booking agent and luckily got some show dates along our way back. We made it into Hobbs, New Mexico, and stopped in on George and Lucky Brazill, good country music lovers Jim and Mary Reeves had introduced us to. George and Lucky were great folks. They took us in, fed us, offered to loan us money to get home, and treated us like long-lost prodigals. In the years to come George and Lucky would become our very close friends. When their daughter got married and had a baby, she named it Bonnie Maxine and her second child was named James Edward. We have always had a special place in our hearts for those sweet children.

Daddy sensed something was bad, bad wrong as soon as we got home. When we told him what happened in California, he was mad enough to go out there and strangle Fabor with his bare hands. But we assured him that we would never go back and record another song with that man. Our biggest problem was finding some way to be released from that stupid contract we had signed. We kept telling Daddy that we were going to get Jim Reeves to help us because Jim had gotten free of old Fabor. But Daddy wouldn't wait. He got on the phone, called up Fabor and gave him the cussing of his life. I still remember very distinctly the words Daddy used: "You better not ever show yourself anywhere near the state of Arkansas, you California goon! There's a lawsuit waiting for you, and if that don't get you, I'll stomp a mud puddle in your sorry ass!"

Evidently, Fabor believed Daddy because we heard through the grapevine over the years that Fabor Robinson was mortally afraid of coming within a hundred miles of Arkansas and didn't even want to fly over it.

• • •

"Here Today and Gone Tomorrow" was released in August 1955, and before the month was out, it was close to the top of the charts. Deejays everywhere were playing it. Everywhere we went, people were talking about what a smash hit it was. The simple little song, born out of the hurt of lost love, seemed to touch everyone the same way. To have such a song is the dream of every songwriter, but it's not something you can just sit down and make up. The people, the listeners, have the uncanny ability to see through the formula of phony songs. I've talked with a lot of young songwriters in Nashville, and we all agreed that the best way to write songs is to tell the honest truth: write from the heart even if that heart has been broken.

"Here Today and Gone Tomorrow" stayed near the top for weeks and weeks and remained on the charts throughout the rest of the year and into the next. I guess I always knew the song would be a good one because of what it said and the way we put the harmony to it. Even after the song became a hit, we didn't hear a word from Fabor about it. No congratulations, no talk of royalties, nothing. And as with "Looking Back To See," we would never receive a cent from Fabor on it.

Still, we were a hit trio now, known throughout the country and greatly in demand for personal appearances. Bonnie dropped out of college that fall and we hit the road. When we first started recording, we were billed as "Jim Edward and Maxine Brown," and when Bonnie started singing with us we were "Jim Edward and Maxine Brown with Bonnie." T. Tommy Cutrer, a well-known deejay in Shreveport, began referring to Bonnie as "with Bonnie," and for a long period of time that was her nickname. People would come up to us and say, "Hello, with Bonnie," or "Where's with Bonnie?" Pretty soon, though, she became a full member, and we started being known as the Browns, Jim Ed, Maxine, and Bonnie.

Again, things were looking up for us. We started making some good money because we were doing so many shows. Of course, having a hit song didn't hurt us at all. On each date we played, we got to meet many wonderful recording artists, and I can say without exception that they were all more than nice to us. I think most of those singers and pickers had come up from poverty the way we had, the way country music itself had. We all had a hunger inside to make it big. I know that the Browns were now determined to make it, by hook or crook. Somehow, though, we had to get us a new recording company.

Now that we were making some money, we decided to spruce up our act. Momma was way too busy running the Trio Club to sew us new costumes. Besides that, her eyes were getting bad. Several artists who sang on the *Louisiana Hayride* were getting their outfits made by a family of two sisters and a brother. We contacted them and put in an order for three outfits each, a sizable job. When we picked up the costumes, we paid for them in cash. Wouldn't you know it, here came another con job! About a year later, the costumers sued us for nonpayment. I was never so upset in my life. We had always paid our bills. After a big and very public to-do, the court threw out the lawsuit. Still, it was terribly embarrassing. The sewing sisters had spread the vicious gossip all around the *Hayride* that we had cheated them. I was beginning to believe that country singers existed only for people to take advantage of.

• • •

"Here Today and Gone Tomorrow" became far more popular than "Looking Back To See." We were showered with offers to perform. Jim Reeves came to us with the idea of putting together another tour. He said we would go back to the places we had pioneered in that first horrible tour. But this time we would do it right. It would be great fun without Fabor around to torment us. Jim promised that we'd never have to worry about getting paid and that we'd get our money after each date—and there was never a better man than Jim Reeves at keeping his word. At that time, Jim was still under Fabor's boot. His songs were getting released, but he still had to assign the rights to Fabor. It seemed liked we'd all be trapped for life and that the tour would be the only way to get enough money to fight Fabor. So we set out on another swing through the Great Northwest. And this time, we were going to do it in style.

Costumes were our biggest problem. Back then big hoop skirts and crinolines were in style. My Lord, we had more slips than we did clothes! How in the world were we going to carry our instruments and clothes and still be able to sleep in the car as we traveled along? Jim Reeves had had a trailer on the other tour, so J. E. got the bright idea of designing a trailer to pull behind our car. This he did, and it was the most hideous contraption you ever saw going down the highway. It was too tall, too narrow and too long, but at least he painted it to match our car.

This tour was Bonnie's first. I was thankful she wouldn't suffer the hardships we did on our first one. Since we'd been getting good money for our shows, we decided, almost at the last minute, to put up the ultimate front. We traded in the Lincoln on a new Cadillac. Talk about streamlined, uptown living!

So there we went out across the west Texas plains in our spanking new Cad, pulling that tacky trailer. We were within a mile of where our other car had caught fire when we started smelling smoke. For a few minutes, we kept driving and tried to ignore it. But pretty soon smoke started pouring out from under the hood. Our new Cadillac was on fire! It made you just want to get out and scream to the heavens, "Too much. Lord, too much!"

This time, the damage to the car wasn't as severe, although it would take a few hours for repair. The hideous trailer had caused the problem. It hadn't been wired properly and was so out of balance that it would weave back and forth on the road like a drunk. This had put a strain on the car's motor. After the repairs were made, we got back on the road, played a date in Albuquerque and then headed straight for George and Lucky Brazill's place for their wonderful hospitality. Bonnie had now been introduced to the perils of the road.

Most of the time, we had to drive all night and most of the following day to reach our next show. Once when we opened the trailer to get our costumes, we discovered a mother cat and her nine kittens lounging on top of our clothes. A lot of those fancy duds that we'd paid a pretty penny for were almost ruined. Jim and Mary Reeves came along and saw our mess. "I've seen that cat before," Mary said. "I shooed her out of our trailer back in Albuquerque."

As often happens on the road, a good Samaritan came forward to help. In this case, a woman who was a big Jim Reeves fan took our messy costumes to her house and cleaned them. When she came back, she gave us a big sack of freshly baked cornbread. She told us she was also from Arkansas and knew we liked cornbread. She had worked on the costumes for so long that she missed our show. We gave the dear lady a dozen autographed pictures and wrote her notes expressing our gratitude for saving our necks I think she exemplified what country music fans are all about. They are not just the most loyal supporters a picker can have, they are actually part of the music itself. Without them, we'd have no music.

On that tour, we came to be known as "The Cornbread Kids." I guess the word must have spread about the cat mess and the cornbread lady because at our very next show some fans showed up with cornbread for us. Folks would meet our little caravan when we came into their town, ask us if they could do anything for us and invariably bring a heaping platter of rich cornbread. We'd always let these folks into the show free. I've always thought you could tell if people were true country music fans by the cornbread they made. We tasted some of the best way out there in Idaho and Oregon.

I was proud we had a chance to go back to the Pacific Northwest and proud that Bonnie got to see the mountains, deserts, Indian reservations, and other far-off places we'd all read about. We took a lot of pictures so Momma, Daddy, and Norma could see the beautiful world that God had created. (I've wished a thousand times over the years, though, that I had taken more pictures of people we worked with and fewer of the scenery.)

As the tour was winding down and we were working our way back home, Jim Reeves decided to get rid of his battered trailer once and for all. It wasn't easy pulling those hideous things over the Rocky Mountains and across the rugged terrain we traveled. When we reached the highest point of Pike's Peak, Jim pulled over to the side of the road. He had Mary and the band take everything out of his trailer and put it into ours. Then he unhooked the trailer hitch. We stood there in disbelief as he slowly pushed his trailer over the side of the damn mountain. It rolled and tumbled into what seemed like a bottomless pit. You could hear the echo of Jim's laughter all the way down the mountain. I've often wondered if anyone ever found the remains of that contraption and if they could ever figure out what in the world it was used for.

• • •

Bonnie turned out to be a real road trooper. She was young, just seventeen, but she never complained. In fact, she would always try to cheer J. E. and me on when we got discouraged. The tour was a big success. We all made some good money. Better still, we got ourselves a lot of exposure. Jim held the tour together and made sure everybody was happy. At the end, we held a big party. Amid all the celebration, I kept recalling how terribly that first tour had ended, with Fabor cutting everybody down and cheating us out of what we had coming. "Class will tell and shit will smell," my Daddy always said.

The Brown Trio was greeted royally when we returned to the *Louisiana Hayride*. We found a lot of new fans waiting for us and so many new booking offers that our old agent couldn't handle them. At the *Hayride* this time, Jim Reeves introduced us to a tall, skinny fellow named Tom Perryman. He was so friendly and funny and genuine that you couldn't help but love him immediately. Tom must have sensed that we needed some personal attention. He invited us home to meet his wife, Billie, and his kids, Vicky, Marilyn, and King (who everybody called Stud). Pretty soon, the Perrymans became our family away from family. Tom booked a lot of the *Hayride* artists all over East Texas. He was also a deejay in Gladewater, Texas, (on station KSIJ) and the funniest one you've ever heard.

Right away Tom started lining us up some good shows, such as the Reo Palm Isle in Longview, which was a great place to play. Tom had such a special knack and cared so much about performers that we asked him to become our agent and personal manager. It was a big step for us and for him too. He had it made as a deejay, and taking us on involved some risk. But he agreed to do it. From that moment on, Tom looked out for our best interests, took care of all the minute details and set us on the right course.

• • •

Some big things were starting to happen for the Browns. The first large function we were ever invited to play was the Jimmie Rodgers Memorial Celebration in Meridian, Mississippi, in 1954. We were on the verge of making it as artists, and that event was to make a big impression on our music and on us. Not only did we get to meet most of the top artists in the business, we were accepted as a part of it all. We knew we had been accepted by the way the deejays treated us. And they welcomed the Browns with open arms. Just as important to us was the fact that we were in Jimmie Rodgers's territory. After all, Rodgers had more influence in creating country music than just about anyone except the Carter Family. His achievements had given us our dream. A native of Meridian, Rodgers died of tuberculosis when he was only 36 years old. Still, he gave us such classic songs as "Mule Skinner Blues," "T for Texas," and "In the Jailhouse Now." If you're a singer or a picker, just thinking about Jimmie the Kid is a humbling experience. If Hank Williams was the heart of this country's unique music, Jimmie Rodgers was its soul.

• • •

As hard as we worked, we still had fun. And sometimes we got into a little mischief. While we were in Mississippi, I met a good-looking disc jockey named Fred Winter. He was one of those crazy, impetuous fellers, and I couldn't stop myself from flirting with him. He was driving me back to my room one night when he pulled the car over and started smooching on me. I didn't know what to do. He was so damn persistent, but I did manage to hold him off. Oh my, Freddie was a good kisser. When I came in that night, Tom Perryman looked at me and laughed and kidded me unmercifully because I was so flustered. But I found out that Freddie was married, and I made sure we weren't alone together after that. A single girl on the road always looks like fair game, and I always seemed to attract the married men.

Our next big event was the Disc Jockey Convention in Nashville that same year. J. E. and I won our first award there as Up and Coming Vocal Group. We had been to Nashville once before—when we played Ernest Tubb's show—but we were so young and green then that it didn't seem to make an impression on us.

With "Here Today and Gone Tomorrow" still riding high on the charts in 1955, we were up for several awards in the trade magazines. J. E. was nominated for Most Promising Male Singer, I for Most Promising Female, and the three of us for Most Promising Vocal Group. For a bunch of bean-fed Arkansas kids, we thought we were doing all right, and we couldn't help but wish spitefully that Fabor was there to witness it all.

During the convention, I met a handsome deejay from station WAGS in Bishopville, South Carolina. His name was Joe. I developed a big crush on him. He was single, too, or so he said. Most of the dee-jays who attended those conventions were married until they regis-tered at the Andrew Jackson Hotel, where all the festivities were held. The lobby was always full of snuff queens (country music's version of groupies) and hookers who came from all over the country. Billie Perryman said she would never trust her husband Tom to attend one of those conventions without her. She was smart. Anyway, Joe sent me flowers and cards all the time, but somehow we got to see each other only once a year. Here today and gone tomorrow all over again.

The Disc Jockey Convention became an annual awards show for us. In 1956, we were invited to sing as part of the program, along with the great Webb Pierce. We went in on a cloud of publicity. People knew who we were, and we were going to be part of the big show. We were invited to join The Country Music Disc Jockey Association. (Our membership numbers are seventy-nine, eighty, and eighty-one, though there are thousands of members now).

The show that year was held at the famous Plantation Club. We were awfully nervous because all the great *Opry* stars were there—Roy Acuff, Eddy Arnold, the Carters, Marty Robbins, you name them. And, of course, there were the deejays who could make or break you. The thing that got us through it all with flying colors was the presence and encouragement of Dee Kilpatrick, then an execu-tive with Mercury Records, who sat on the front row and never stopped smiling and applauding. He seemed to love everything we did and made me feel so good about myself that I've had a special love for him ever since. The big crowd must have thought we were all right too, because they gave us a standing ovation, our very first one. It looked like the Browns had finally arrived in Nashville!

But then it was back to the road and the grind of driving all night, sleeping in a cramped car, and having to look your best in front of a new crowd every night. None of us could ever quite get used to those long trips on two-lane highways. We always had trouble find-ing our way in and around big cities. One time Bonnie was driving us to some little town in the Midwest. We had just played Detroit and knew we had to push hard to get to the next show. J. E. woke up every few minutes and asked Bonnie if she needed him to drive. But Bonnie, the toughest one of us, said she couldn't sleep in the car and liked to drive. Several hours went by, and when J. E. woke up again and asked where we were, Bonnie pulled the car over and started crying. There was a road sign right in front of us that read "Detroit. City Limits." Bonnie had been driving around in circles. It was easy enough to do that back in the days before interstates and expressways. We still had all those miles to go and knew we'd never make it. But we burned up those state roads, sometimes at one hundred miles an hour, and got to the show when it was almost over. Although we were dead tired, we put on the show of our lives. I cringe now when I think of that insane rollercoaster ride. It's no wonder that so many pickers and singers met their Maker on those mean old roads.

·   ·   ·

We were working dates every night now, living on spotlights and coffee and the next kind-hearted fan with a cornbread handout. We made it into Wheeling, West Virginia, for the big Jamboree there, a show every country artist got to eventually. While we were in Wheeling, we met Patsy Cline. She was pretty, bright-eyed, earthy, and about as wonderful a singer as anyone had a right to be. She was also one of the nicest people we'd ever met. Patsy took us under her wing, showed us all around and made sure we got to know everybody on the show. Then she took us home to meet her folks, which, to us, was like coming home to Momma Brown's kitchen. Talk about your basic southern comfort and your sweet dreams! We sat up all night, telling jokes and singing songs. Patsy was the ultimate singer, equally at home on the *Opry* or at Carnegie Hall. In 1957, she married Charlie A. Dick, one of the most entertaining people I've ever met. He always referred to himself as Charlie A. and always had a practical joke to pull. During one Disc Jockey Convention, we all got together and had a blast. Charlie went around passing out his calling card, which read: "Come C. A. Dick . . . Room 407, Andrew Jackson Hotel."

Finally we got to go home for a few days to rest our weary bodies and souls. Now that we were a busy country music act, the idea of home became more and more precious to us. Momma was always there to feed us, comfort us, and soothe our rattled nerves. Even more than we did, Momma kept up with everything going on in show business. She could tell if a record was going to be a hit or a flop the first time she heard it. We should have put her in charge of picking our material.

Coming home meant we could work in the Trio Club, and J. E. could go back and help Daddy in the logging woods. We were content to do the home things and keep our minds off the road. We didn't even listen to the radio very much except when we were in the car. One night at supper Momma told us about a song she'd heard on the radio.

"There's a new boy coming on the scene," she said. "His name is Elvis Presley, and I think he's from over in Memphis. He's got a song out called 'Blue Moon of Kentucky,' and it's good. He's going to be a big star."

"You really think so, Momma?" Bonnie asked. "How could anyone named 'Elvis' be a big star?"

"He will be," Momma insisted. "You wait and see."

Elvis Presley

He wasn't any better looking than a dozen other young studs on the music scene. He was slender and walked with a sexy hitch to his hips. He wore his hair full and wavy, with a teasy strand on his high forehead, and long sideburns, which were just becoming the smoky fashion for the cool cats of those days. But it was those deep-staring eyes that mesmerized all the girls—that and those sexy lips and hips.

Elvis Aaron Presley. It was our manager, good ol' Tom Perryman, who introduced Elvis to us one night. "I'm so happy to meet y'all," Elvis said. "I've been listening to the Browns since y'all started."

A few months after his first single from Sun Records came out, Elvis made a guest appearance on the *Grand Ole Opry*. But he didn't go over to well with the audience. When he tried getting on the second time, the *Opry*'s manager, Jim Denny, wouldn't hear of it. He was very ugly and cruel to Elvis. "Go back to Memphis," he told him. "We don't allow no Negro music on the *Opry*."

We went to Horace Logan of the *Louisiana Hayride* and put in a good word for Elvis and asked if they would please give him a chance. The rest, of course, is history. Tom sort of took Elvis under wing—until that carnival man, Col. Tom Parker, came along. Elvis looked so young and sweet that you wouldn't have thought he could produce such a big sound. He had two very good musicians backing him in those days, Scotty Moore on guitar and Bill Black on bass fiddle. They were all good-looking boys and had no trouble getting attention from all the young things around the *Hayride*.

The first time I met Elvis, I told him my mother had predicted he'd be a big star. He just laughed shyly. In those days, he truly had no idea of how big he would become. I don't think he ever had a big head or even gave fame a second thought. He was too busy having fun and being young. I believe he would have been content to sing the way he did on the *Hayride*. His favorite music, by far, was old-time gospel. Many a night, we'd all sit up late and sing the old hymns. Elvis was the last to want to quit. He often said that his big dream was to make it as a gospel artist. That's what his mother wanted for him, too. Who knows, that might have been best for him in the long run.

Few know this, but there were actually two Elvises inside the one. As we traveled the road with him, we came to see both sides. He could be very, very shy, the sensitive momma's boy, and he could be as wild as a joker in a game of spit in the ocean. I know that others who call themselves biographers and scholars have written exhaustive books about Elvis. But all their pronouncements about him still come down to guesswork. They weren't there. You had to be with him day to day, facing the grind of the road, to really understand him.

It's a little strange now to look back and remember when the Brown Trio got top billing over Elvis Presley. Tom Perryman thought the three of us and Elvis and his group would make a good package. So he arranged us a tour together all over Texas.

On January 26, 1955, the Browns stole the show from Elvis in Gilmer at the Rural Electric Association building. Then we did it again two days later at the high school in Gaston. I'm sure that few stole shows from him after that. I know for sure that the Browns didn't.

We worked fifteen straight days with Elvis. Our common band consisted of Scotty, Bill, and J. E. That was it, but we put on great shows. Today it's unheard of for a musician to back two artists on the same show. After the tour was over, we again went to the *Hayride*'s Horace Logan and Frank Page and told them that they should sign Elvis to a contract. We knew he had the voice and the talent to be a member. No other artist had the stage presence he did. He was driving all the girls crazy. Even the men liked and respected him. So we knew great things were about to happen.

In 1955, the *Hayride* sponsored us with Elvis, Jim Reeves, and Slim Whitman at the Jimmie Rodgers Celebration in Meridian, Mississippi. They designed and built a beautiful float for us to ride on in the big parade. I guess you could say that Jim Reeves was the star of the event. Elvis was just getting started, and a lot of the folks didn't really know who he was. Many of the artists there seemed very jealous of him.

Some of the deejays wouldn't even play his record. One of them made an ugly remark to Elvis that I just couldn't take. I gave him a piece of my mind right there in front of God and everybody. His reply was, "You can bet your sweet ass I'll never play another Browns record again." I don't think the SOB ever did, but who cares? We didn't need narrow-minded people like him in the business anyway.

We met Elvis's parents, Gladys and Vernon, at the Ellis Auditorium in Memphis in March 1955, where we were booked with several other country artists. They reminded us so much of our own parents that we insisted they all come to one of our shows so they could meet our folks. They did in Texarkana, Arkansas. Elvis was getting so popular by then that the auditoriums and clubs where Tom was booking us couldn't hold all the people. So he booked us at the ball field in Texarkana. Our stage was a flatbed truck. My God, it was awful! There were no dressing rooms and certainly no bathrooms close by. I always had a small bladder. We had to change into our costumes in the back seat of the car and hope that nobody would see our unmentionables. One of the artists on that show was Chet Atkins. Little did we dream that someday he would become our producer at RCA Records.

Later on, Tom put together a tour with us, Elvis, the Wilburn Brothers, Ferlin Husky, Faron Young, Martha Carson, and the Carlisles. I think we had more fun on those tours than we did during the rest of our career. We were one big, happy, crazy family. Ferlin Husky was everybody's favorite, especially when he did his Simon Crum comedy routine.

We were all having dinner one night after our show and getting ready for a long haul to the next big gig when Ferlin asked our waitress, "What kind of soup do you have?"

She said, "Well, we have tomato, mushroom, chicken, and pea soup."

Ferlin ordered chicken soup. As the waitress walked off, Ferlin stood up and hollered as loud as he could, "Hold that chicken and make it pea."

Everyone died laughing. I thought Elvis was going to crack a rib he laughed so hard. I felt like crawling under the table. Ferlin was always the hit of the deejay conventions; he kept everyone in stitches. Sometimes in that old Andrew Jackson Hotel in Nashville the good times got a little wild—downright X-rated. When pickers cut loose after months on the road, they're worse than cowboys after a roundup. Lord, there were always snuff queens and diesel sniffers hanging around to party with the guys. One convention night Curly Harris, Faron Young's fiddle player, ran right through the crowded lobby naked as a jaybird, singing and kicking up his heels. He ran right up to the third floor and jumped out the window, aiming for the pool. He surely would have been killed if he hadn't been so drunk.

Then there was the time that two of the greatest steel guitar players in the business, Jimmy Day and Buddy Emmons, learned a lesson in aerodynamics. It seems they were having a party of their own on the third floor of the Hermitage Hotel, which was just across and down the street about a block from the Andrew Jackson. They were drinking and popping what Jimmy C. Newman called "Don't Get Scared Pills." Buddy decided he wanted to get back to all the action at the Andrew Jackson and decided the best way to do it was to fly, unaided by any vehicle, of course. In making this attempt, he fell out of the window and broke his leg. When Ralph Emery asked Jimmy why he didn't stop him, Jimmy replied, "Hell, I thought the SOB could make it!"

• • •

From the moment Tom Perryman took over as our manager, he set out to free us from the recording contract Fabor Robinson held over our heads. Finally, he was able to strike a deal with the old devil. But we had to pay a dear price. Fabor would give us a release, providing that we let him have all the royalties from our past record sales. This meant we'd continue to get nothing from our big hits, "Looking Back To See" and "Here Today and Gone Tomorrow." On top of that, Fabor wanted ten thousand dollars in cash. Hendrix Rowell, our attorney, said we could wait a year until the contract expired or we could go ahead and pay our way out then. What we should have done was to hire a real entertainment lawyer, because I doubt if Hendrix or any other attorney in Arkansas knew enough in those days about dealing with recording companies. But J. E. was so disgusted that he didn't want to wait a whole year to be free. He and Hendrix went to the bank in Pine Bluff and arranged for a ten thousand dollar loan. When we weren't doing shows, J. E. worked double shifts in the logging woods with Daddy to make enough money to pay off the loan. It wasn't easy.

Jim Reeves was in the same bind with Fabor and had struck a similar deal. We had no alternative if we ever wanted to record again. Fabor didn't have us over a barrel—he had us in it. So we signed away our recording rights, sent him a check for ten thousand dollars and vowed never to look back. This should never have happened to kids just starting out. There are more laws—and lawyers—to protect singers nowadays. But this doesn't mean performers don't still get stiffed. Whenever there's talent and money to be had, there's always a Fabor Robinson.

The only contract J. E. and I ever signed with Fabor was a recording contract for "Looking Back To See." When Bonnie cut "Here Today and Gone Tomorrow" with us no new contract was signed or even offered. If one had been presented to us, our parents would have had to sign it since Bonnie was then only seventeen. (Looking back now, I realize that J. E. was also under age when we signed.)

Fabor never suggested we sign a songwriter's contract. We didn't even know about such things at the time. It wasn't until several months later that Tom Perryman found out we had never signed with Broadcast Music, Inc. (BMI), which collects money for songwriters and publishers when their songs are played on radio, television, or other public places. He insisted that the next time we were in Nashville we go to BMI and sign up. But by this time, we had already missed out on getting paid for all the airplay "Looking Back To See" had earned. It had been recorded by Guy Lombardo, Rusty Draper, Justin Tubb, Goldie Hill, and several other artists, but we were never paid until we joined BMI. Years later, Fabor sold his publishing company, Dandelion Music, to Jamie Publishing. That's when we learned that a signed contract did indeed exist for our songs. But we knew we didn't sign it.

• • •

We went on the road again, while Tom worked at lining us up with a new record company. We struck out for the wide-open spaces, deep in the heart of Texas. It was free and easy, bumpy and cramped and smoky, and it was wonderful. Tom had booked us all over Texas, Louisiana, and Mississippi with Elvis, Scotty, and Bill. I think Elvis would have starved himself if we hadn't bought him so many bacon and tomato sandwiches. In those days, he didn't have a cent and didn't seem to care. Many times we paid his cleaning bill and bought his food—bacon and tomato sandwiches for breakfast, dinner, and supper.

That's about all he would ever eat. His cleaning bills were enormous because those pink pants and black shirt had to be cleaned after every show. Elvis got one hundred dollars for each show. Of that he paid Scotty and Bill twenty-five dollars each. The Browns earned $125 per show, which we split three ways. Since we liked to eat high on the hog, we never seemed to have any money left over, either. But we all had more fun than you would believe.

When my folks' twenty-fifth wedding anniversary was approaching, several of the country singers who'd made Momma's kitchen their second home decided to throw her and Daddy a big party. Tom Perryman took charge and rented a lavish dining hall down in Gladewater, Texas, for the celebration. Among those attending were Elvis, Scotty, Bill, D. J. Fontana (who was now playing drums in Elvis's band), Red West (Elvis's new bodyguard), Floyd Cramer, Tom Tall, Jimmy Day, and, of course, the entire Brown and Perryman families. It was a big thrill for my folks because they loved all those guys and thought of them as family. Afterward, we all went into Shreveport for the *Hayride*.

Elvis's mom and dad went down to the *Hayride* occasionally when Elvis was singing there. Often they'd go through Pine Bluff and make the trip south with my folks. They'd always sit together during the show and afterward we'd all go out to dinner together at the Al-Ida Restaurant and Motel owned by our good friend Junior Cloud. One night when Elvis walked off stage after taking about five or six encores, Gladys got him by the arm and led him over to the side of the stage away from everyone and said, "Elvis, don't you have any drawers?" He said, "No ma'am, the only pair I own was dirty and Maxine wouldn't wash 'em."

I guess that's the only thing he could think of to say at the moment. I thought I would die laughing. But I had to keep it to myself because there was no way I could ever let Gladys know that her little boy didn't like to wear "drawers," especially on stage. Hell, he knew what he was doing! Gladys would always remind me to please take good care of her son while we were out on the road. I guess she though I could watch over him because I was the oldest member of the group. But Lord have mercy, who was gonna watch over me while I was watching over him?

Elvis began to spend a lot of time at our house in Pine Bluff after our shows rather than make the drive on to Memphis. Scotty and Bill, who were both married, would go on home. Elvis hung around our house and the Trio Club. Since our house was small, Norma would give Elvis her bed and sleep on the couch. Funny thing, though, Norma's bed was in the same bedroom with Momma and Daddy. But Elvis loved sleeping in the same room with them He said he had grown up that way and liked the security of a mom and dad nearby. Momma told us that Elvis was a troubled sleeper and had 'the nervous leg." The proof of that was the way he ripped up Momma's sheets with his toes. He'd start a small hole and keep wiggling his foot in it in his sleep. By morning, he'd have that sheet almost in shreds. But Momma didn't seem to mind. She'd tell him she needed some new sheets anyway because everything she had was "hole-y."

Elvis couldn't sleep much at night no matter where he was. He never slept over three or four hours at a time at our house or in the motels where we stayed. Gladys always told us that he couldn't sleep at home either. I think the best sleep he ever got was in the back seat of the car while we were traveling from show to show. But even then he didn't sleep much. He was always pulling pranks on us as we drove along. Most of the time, he rode in our car with Bonnie, and I rode with Bill Black and Scotty Moore.

• • •

Working that close together and being in each other's company on the road made it inevitable that sparks would fly between Elvis and Bonnie. She was truly a striking young woman with a very fair complexion, raven black hair, and gypsy eyes. Her figure was even more stunning. I don't want to exaggerate, but I can safely say that Dolly Parton had nothing on Bonnie. I remember the first night she sang with us on the *Hayride.* We introduced her as "our little sister Bonnie," and when she walked out on that stage, dressed in her tight-fitting outfit, we thought the guys in the audience were going to tear the place down.

Strangely enough, there wasn't any flirting between Elvis and Bonnie—at first. Elvis had many, many admirers, and he did pay some attention to several of those little queens. But toward the women in the *Hayride* cast, he was well mannered and gentlemanly. He and Bonnie got started over a practical joke he pulled.

We were all out in west Texas, killing time before a show by lounging around a motel pool. Bonnie had her hair up in curlers. Elvis came running along, saw her, laughed, and pushed her into the pool. He dived in after her, and they had an awful fight. He apologized, and after that they were together all the time. I think it was the first time Bonnie had fallen in love. It wasn't just puppy love or a crush either, because Elvis was all moony-eyed over her, too. That was obvious. Bonnie stayed out late after our show and when she came in, I knew she had been with Elvis.

One night she came in, woke me up and told me that Elvis had asked her to marry him. Given the circumstances, I thought she should have looked a lot happier than she did. I asked her if she wasn't excited and pleased. "Yes, I am," she said. But this wasn't the Bonnie I knew. If she had been thrilled over the idea of getting married, she would have been cutting up and hollering to beat Dixie. She didn't say much more about it, only that they were in love and wanted to get married but would probably have to put it off for a while.

I think Bonnie had another worry too, although she never brought it up. They were both very young and neither had tried out their wings very much yet. Maybe my little sister was afraid of what I always feared when it came to love—that it would be here today and gone tomorrow. Bonnie told us later how Elvis had come into a restaurant where she has having dinner, all loved up with this other girl. He didn't know Bonnie was there, and this was only a few days after he had asked her to marry him.

It wasn't very long until the talk of marriage between Bonnie and Elvis stopped altogether. Bonnie was all for partying and having fun, but she had a level head too. I think she realized even then that life with Elvis, or with any other music star, would have more valleys than peaks. So it was Bonnie herself who broke it off with Elvis. I think it hurt him too. He moped around some on the last part of our Texas tour. Then he took up with J. E., and they began carousing together.

Those of us on the tour witnessed their antics and speculated that J. E. and Elvis must be betting on how many girls they could score with in a single night. I'd never seen anything like it in my whole life. Those girls would absolutely stand in line outside their motel rooms, waiting to be next. I know because some of us eavesdropped and counted them. Tom Perryman came by, saw what was going on, shook his head, and said, "By God, those boys are gonna wear those things out if they don't slow down."

• — •

There were never any hard feelings between Bonnie and Elvis after they stopped seeing each other. They were truly good friends. It sounds strange, but that's the way it has to work on the road, not just back then but nowadays, too. Elvis still spent nights at our house rather than driving on to Memphis. Momma put on a feast one night for Elvis, his band, and the Carter Family. We were all playing a show together, and they came to our little house at 34 Cypress Drive. My, that was a time! Elvis was in charge of the evening's entertainment. He played the piano and got all of us singing—the Brown Trio, Mother Maybelle Carter and her daughters. I was always amazed as the years went on at how well Mother Maybelle had taught her kids to play and entertain and still be the most polite young Christian girls you'd ever meet. Most people don't realize that June Carter was an outstanding comedienne before she gained fame as a singer and the wife of Johnny Cash.

That night Elvis was at his very best. He was sweet and gracious and utterly charming, showing that winning side of his nature. Then, a few months later, he showed the other side. Late one night, we got a phone call from him. His car had broken down in the little town of Brinkley, halfway between Memphis and Little Rock. He wanted us to come and pick him up. Bonnie got out of bed, and she and Daddy each took one of our cars and drove all the way to Brinkley to see if they could get Elvis's car running. But his car had had it. It was a good thing Bonnie and Daddy had driven separately. You would have to know my Daddy to see how generous and willing he was to help out a friend. He told Elvis, Scotty, and Bill, "I'll let you boys borrow my brand new car."

Daddy had just bought a brand new Pontiac, and he let Elvis take it to his show date while Elvis's own car was being repaired. Well, it didn't work out that way. Those boys kept Daddy's new Pontiac for six weeks; Elvis never even called during all that time to let Daddy know when he'd bring the car home. When they did finally bring it back, it had twelve thousand miles on it, plus some dents, scraped fenders, and worn-out tires. The fellow who brought it back (Elvis was careful not to bring it back himself) never so much as gave Daddy a "thank you and kiss my foot." I have never seen my daddy so mad. It was a pretty tacky way for a king to act.

"You can't trust a hillbilly singer," Daddy said. This was one time we had to agree.

Elvis bought himself a new pink Cadillac right after this happened. The picture of Elvis and his first Cad was in all the papers. I felt sure he would make amends to Daddy for what he had done. But he never did.

• • •

Elvis's star was shooting high, but ours wasn't doing badly either. Our record was still riding high, and though we weren't ever to receive royalties, we became increasingly popular and made more and more appearances all over the country. Jimmie Davis, the legendary singer and writer of "You Are My Sunshine," had gotten himself elected governor of Louisiana. We first met him when we were singing on the *Louisiana Hayride*. When he ran for reelection, he invited us down to dinner at the governor's mansion and asked us to be the entertainment on his campaign trail. The idea sounded like a lot of fun. While we were discussing it at dinner, we were served pheasant under glass. Talk about your uptown fancy. I had never eaten anything served so elegantly, and I had to watch the governor and Mrs. Davis before I caught on. It tasted OK, a little like wild duck without the wild. Just being there, as an honored guest, was special enough for us. Talk about the "other side!" I was plumb in the middle of it.

We hit the campaign trail old-fashioned style, stumping from one little town to the next, singing our songs and stirring up some crowds. When Jimmie won the election, he credited us with helping him get it. I'm not sure if we helped, but it was a unique experience, part of a passing scene of America. Later, we'd do a little bit of campaign singing for Gov. Frank Clement of Tennessee and, of course, in our home state for the great governor Winthrop Rockefeller.

In the meantime, we had gotten our release from Fabor Records. Tom Perryman got us booked on the *Big D Jamboree*, a highly successful show in Dallas. One more time we, or at least J. E., would get caught in a trap—with Elvis Presley right in the middle of it all. The Browns and Elvis were the featured acts on the *Jamboree* that night.

We all stayed at the same motel, which was not too far from the auditorium. I remember a rather slinky, black-haired girl who kept hanging all over Elvis and J. E. She followed us to and from the auditorium and to the restaurant where we ate, but Elvis and J. E. didn't have anything to do with her. She wasn't as pretty as the others they had waiting. Still, she followed us back from the *Big D* that night, and Bonnie and I watched her for a long time as she went from one room to the next, wanting one of them to let her in. Finally, we saw Elvis open his door and let her inside.

J. E. packed up his things, because he knew we were waiting for him outside for the trip back to Pine Bluff. "That old girl just won't take no for an answer," J. E. told us "I don't think Elvis will have anything to do with her, but the other boys in the band might."

About two months later, we were once again booked on the *Big D Jamboree*. Just before we were to go on stage, we got word that there was a death threat out on J. E. Someone, we were told, was in the audience with a gun and was going to kill J. E. for "seducing his daughter." This was the damnedest thing we'd ever heard of. Why would J. E. ever rape or seduce any girl when they were throwing themselves at him all the time? Before we went on stage, we got the additional information that the threat had been made by the father of the same black-haired girl who had been hanging around Elvis and J. E. the last time we were there. If anything, the irate father should have been after Elvis. But Elvis hadn't made this trip. So I guess the guy was settling for whatever he could shoot at. Poor J. E. was trembling in his boots as we went on.

Bonnie stood on one side of J. E. and I stood on the other, trying to shield him the whole time. Without a doubt, this was the shortest show we had ever done—and probably the dullest. We were too scared to open our mouths to sing. Ed McLemore, the *Big D*'s manager, told us we'd better get the hell out of Dallas. He said we didn't have to stay for the second half of the show, that he was afraid this thing would turn into a brawl or a killing. He said he thought J. E. had been set up by somebody. But he went ahead and paid us for our appearance, and we left without saying goodbye to anyone.

On our way from Dallas to Tom Perryman's house in Gladewater we were scared to death every time we went through a town. We kept a constant lookout for police cars, praying that we'd get through this sick joke someone was playing on us. It was just daybreak when we reached Gladewater. We were feeling a little better and thinking that maybe it was all just a hoax. But as we entered the city limits, here came some flashing lights behind us. I was driving, and J. E. was lying down in the back seat. We told him to stay put and pretend he was asleep as I slowed down and pulled the car over. We hoped it was nothing, but we knew instinctively that it was something. Two policemen came around the car and started asking us all kinds of questions.

"You are the Browns, aren't you?" asked one cop. "Is Jim Edward Brown in this car? We're going to have to arrest him."

"On what charges?" I asked.

"He'll find out."

Thank God the policemen knew Tom Perryman. They let us go on to his house while they followed. When we told Tom and Billie what was happening, they almost went crazy. They knew poor little ol' J. E. was innocent. He might love the girls, but he wouldn't harm a fly. The cops had a warrant and insisted on putting J. E. in their squad car and transporting him all the way back to Dallas. J. E. started crying and asked, "Sis, what in the world am I going to do?"

I was so scared I couldn't think straight. Billie Perryman was the one with the level head. She had Bonnie stay there with her and their kids, and Tom and I followed the police car all the way back to Dallas. When we got into the city, we still didn't know what was going to happen. Surely, we thought, they'd ask some questions, see that it was all a hoax and let J. E. go. But they took him in, fingerprinted him, and booked him on "seducing" and "paternity" charges. The girl was accusing J. E. of fathering her yet-unborn child. They locked J. E. into a cell and wouldn't allow us to see him. We'd have to get a lawyer and a bail bondsman, they told us. Thank God Tom was with us. I couldn't have handled it all by myself. Tom arranged for a bondsman, but we had to find a lawyer. I hated calling my folks worse than anything, but I had no choice. Daddy didn't go off the deep end at all. He said he'd have our lawyer, Hendrix Rowell, come to Dallas as soon as possible

When the bondsman showed up, he asked me how much money I had. We had seven hundred dollars on us, so he said, "Well, that's what it's gonna take to get him out."

In the meantime, Hendrix was on the phone getting the bond and the trial date set. Late that Sunday afternoon, they released J. E.

from that stinking hole of a jail. We could have gotten down and kissed the ground. Instead, we went back to Gladewater, picked up Bonnie, and got our butts out of Texas. It had been a horrible nightmare. Later, we all went back down to Dallas to get ready for the trial. Momma and Daddy came along, and our lawyer took care of everything. But it never came to trial. By the time we started into the court, we found out that the irate father had dropped all the charges. Everybody in and around the court said that they knew J. E. was innocent, and a couple of the officers went so far as to say they suspected it was all a set up, that somebody had to put that old man and his daughter up to it.

With the help of Tom Perryman, we did some investigating on our own. There is a grapevine in the country music business that will usually lead you to the bottom of ugly business. We discovered that a certain deejay on a local Dallas radio station had worked with another man (a Fabor Records distributor) to cook up the scheme. It all came down to our refusal to record anymore under their label. Later, Tom also learned that the father had done some snooping and learned that our Daddy had some money and that the Presley family didn't (although they certainly would later). The old man knew he could get a large sum by blackmailing J. E. Daddy agreed to give him ten thousand dollars if he would drop all the charges. He tried to get more, but our lawyer and Daddy told him to take the money or they would see him in court. Knowing he would never win, he took the money and dropped the charges.

Fabor tried to blackmail Jim Reeves in the same way, but Mary, Jim's wife, was too smart for him. Mary knew Fabor was a mean person and capable of just about anything. But this time his plot backfired. Jim was physically incapable of fathering a child. Obviously, Fabor didn't know this when he hired a snuff queen to call Mary and write letters to the effect that she was having an affair with Jim and expecting "their" baby.

Jim loved children more than anything, and at one time he and Mary were thinking about adopting. Once during our Pacific Northwest tour, he spotted a little boy peering through the rails of a wooden fence. He stopped the car and shot a whole roll of Super-8 movie film of that precious little boy. Jim carried the memory of that little face with him for the rest of his life.

Another Legend is Born

While we were getting our new act together, my folks' new Trio Club was going great guns. The only trouble was that, as always, Momma was working herself to death. Thank goodness she had Dido Rowley from the Hayride staying with her and helping her run the club, because now we were on the road most of the time.

Momma booked some good local acts into the Trio. One time when we were home, she told us of a new singer she wanted us to listen to. She'd given this singer his first real chance, and the crowds took to him so fast that he was making quite a name for himself.

"You remember I told you that Elvis Presley would be a big star," Momma said. "Well this new young boy might just make it bigger than ol' hound dog Elvis."

That was a big "might" since Elvis was already on his way to superstardom. Still, we always trusted Momma's judgment above all others. And so we made a point to stay over and listen to this new guy. His name was Harold Jenkins. He was from Helena, Arkansas, and his singing style was what they called "rockabilly" back in those days. We listened to him do one song—and we loved him. After that first night, we became Harold Jenkins's biggest fans. We often went on stage and sang a bunch of songs with him and his band and had the time of our lives.

Harold quickly became a headliner at our club on weekends. How he loved country music! Like other singers just starting out, he was trying to get a recording contract. We spent many an hour sitting around and talking with him about the pitfalls of show business. We told him that no matter what else, he must sign with an honest record label, one that had a good reputation for treating its artists fairly.

Harold was also a good songwriter. We tried out some of his

earlier tunes and were among the first singers to record them. One night, after he finished singing at the Trio, he and I got together and wrote a song called "Just in Time." It became a good harmony tune for the Browns.

Again, Momma turned out to be right in her assessment of talent. Young Harold Jenkins would go on to record more number one country hits than any other artist in the business. Back in those early days, he changed his name to one that he thought might attract more attention. The world now knows him as Conway Twitty.

• • •

After we'd been performing for some time on the *Louisiana Hayride*, we heard of a new country music show that had sprung up in Springfield, Missouri—the *Ozark Jubilee*. Besides being a stage show, it was also carried on TV and getting widespread attention. Airing every Saturday night, it was hosted by the great Red Foley. The *Jubilee* had the distinction of being the very first network country music show—even beating out the *Grand Ole Opry*—and I think the show's immense success had a lot to do with Foley's warm personality and character. He was more than simply a nice guy with genuine charm; he had what the industry now calls "credibility" but which we used to call "honesty." TV talk pioneer Dave Garroway had that same kind of warmth. From big-name artists to green newcomers, everybody loved Red and wanted to be on his show. Some of the regulars on the *Jubilee* were Brenda Lee, Porter Wagoner, Bobby Lord, Webb Pierce, Billy Walker, Marvin Rainwater, Wanda Jackson, Norma Jean, Willie Nelson, and Sonny James.

Tom Perryman called us one night and said he'd been in touch with Si Siman and Lou Black, the men who booked most of the talent on the *Jubilee*. Tom was very excited because he'd just booked us a spot. "You'll not just be singing on a big show," he said, "You'll be seen on national TV by people all over the country." As we drove up to Springfield that first time, we were even more excited than we had been that first time we went to Nashville to sing on the Ernest Tubb show. I guess we were a little bit camera shy that first time, but Red Foley had a way of settling you down and making you believe in yourself. All I know is that he gave us a wonderful intro and we sang our hearts out.

Red gave us all a big hug after the show and told us we were special. He said he wanted us back on the *Jubilee* the very next week. We left Springfield to do some other shows that week, and while we were on the road we got a call from Si Siman. "You Browns were the hit of the show last week," Si said. "You should see the fan mail that's waiting for you. It's stacking up all over the place."

Si confirmed what Red had told us—that we had a place on the *Jubilee* just about anytime we could arrange it. The TV exposure had put us in the national focus. We were a little dizzy-headed over it all. We'd already had two hits, but because of Fabor's greed and larceny, we hadn't reaped many benefits The *Ozark Jubilee* proved to be our real breakthrough.

Breakthroughs don't always come without drawbacks, and we were confronted by a new problem. We were still regulars on the *Louisiana Hayride*, but now having the opportunity to appear just as regularly on the *Jubilee*, we knew we'd have to give up one or the other. Red made us a firm offer to join the *Jubilee*, and we just couldn't refuse. We told Horace Logan of the *Hayride* what we'd decided to do. He got mad at us. He had given us our first break and considered us ungrateful. Of course, we weren't. Many performers in those days were suspicious of TV. They said it was a flash in the pan and would let us all down. But most of us knew better.

Many years later the *Hayride* had a special program on national TV that showcased every artist who had ever been regulars on the show—everyone, that is, except the Browns. Tom Perryman told us that some of the wheels ramrodding the special were mad because we wouldn't let them have our movie film of Elvis to use on the show and that was why we were left out. I don't think Horace ever forgave us for quitting the *Hayride*, but like Jim Reeves, Elvis, and many others, we had done as much as we could on the *Hayride*. We simply couldn't afford to turn down this big opportunity, not after the many bumpy roads we'd already traveled.

So we appeared on the *Ozark Jubilee* again and got to be a part of the Red Foley family. It was fun, exciting, and revitalizing. While Red was clearly the big star of the *Jubilee* you wouldn't know it from the way he always pushed others into the limelight, both stars and newcomers. I remember being on stage and joining the ensemble when Red sang his classic "Peace in the Valley." I was especially moved when he sang that wonderful hymn, "Precious Memories." I think just about everybody has felt—at some time in their lives—that "stillness of the midnight" in their souls that the hymn refers to. Red had a beautiful way of singing straight to our hearts and spirits.

The public never suspected that poor Red was often inebriated when he sang those beautiful hymns. Before every TV show, Siman and Black would have to sober him up with a pot of black coffee. It was a well-kept secret among all the entertainers because we all loved him so much.

· · ·

Tom Perryman was always trying to work angles for us. He let Siman know that we were looking for a new label to record for. "Here Today and Gone Tomorrow" had finally dropped off the charts and we had received absolutely no royalties from it. We knew we had to have a legitimate record company or else we'd fade like the proverbial rose of summer. When we went back to sing on the *Jubilee* again, Si came to us and said, almost matter-of-factly, "I hear you kids are looking for a label. Maybe I can help. Which label do you prefer?"

"Any good one that'll take us," J. E. said. Bonnie and I agreed eagerly. We had spent years trying to break into recording and had been taken advantage of like the three little pigs. Now here was this big-time agent hinting at how easy it could be. Just pick a major label, he seemed to be saying, and we'll line it up.

Si looked at me with a twinkle in his eye, as if to say that he knew all about the hard times we'd been through. "What label do you like, Maxine?" he asked.

"Well, what about RCA?" I said right out. "That seems to be a pretty fair outfit." I thought I was joking. RCA was Big League, but our good friend Jim Reeves was on RCA, so why not?

"RCA, huh?" Si went on. "OK. We'll see what we can do."

It was just that simple. Si said he'd contact Steve Sholes, who headed RCA's country music division. Jim Reeves had already talked to RCA about us and said he'd told Sholes that he should sign us up. A few days later, we got a call from Sholes. Not only was he interested in having us record for RCA, he said he had put a contract in the mail to us that very day. The RCA contract, big, fat, and solid as a brick outhouse, was waiting for us when we got home to Pine Bluff.

We were in ecstasy. RCA! The label of the great ones. And the Browns were going to record for it. Roll over Beethoven and tell Tchaikovsky the news! We recorded our first song for RCA in March of 1956 in the studios of radio station KWTO in Springfield. The song was "I Take the Chance." It was very special to me because Ira Louvin wrote it for us. Actually, he wrote it for me—at least that's what he always said. I'll admit that there were always some sparks flying between Ira and me. But he was married, and we both knew nothing could come of our feelings. Still, he wrote the song and sent it to me and included a note that said, "Maxine, this is the way I'll always feel toward you."

It was a beautiful song. Sad songs always go better than happy ones. Sadness is the thing we all have in common, no matter what style we sing about it in. The words of "I Take the Chance" give a lot of insight into the sensitivity that made Ira Louvin a great songwriter: "I take the chance/to lose my soul, my life, my pride/I take the chance/to be with you."

The musicians who backed us on the recording session were great, especially Harold Morrison and Jimmy Gately, who played twin fiddles on the arrangement. They made a beautiful song even more beautiful. I think everybody present that day knew "I Take the Chance" was going to be very special for a long time to come. The song hit the charts within a few days of its release and climbed almost overnight to the number two spot nationally in *Billboard*. It stayed on the charts for twenty-four weeks—for nearly half of 1956.

J. E., Bonnie, and I were in full swing. During the coming months, we would be nominated for and win all sorts of awards. And I'll never forget that first royalty check we got for the record—the first one we'd ever received for our music. It was for three thousand dollars. We floated on air for days. We were more than thrilled—we had finally proved ourselves as recording artists. Having a number one record is wonderful, but having a record company that will actually pay you for it is even better.

But our happiness was short-lived. In the blink of an eye but through no fault of our own, the Browns were forced to break up. J. E. got drafted. My little brother received his "greetings" from Uncle Sam the same week "I Take the Chance" peaked on the charts. Here we were, being flooded with offers, and J. E. had to report for his Army physical and get his boot camp assignment. The whole Brown family was upset. We couldn't stand the thought of J. E. having to go off to the danged old Army. Our trio was just about to make it big. If J. E. had to drop out, we'd be forgotten quicker than a junior high love affair.

J. E. was sent way out to Fort Carson, Colorado, for his training. Then he was told he would be stationed in Germany. Daddy got in touch with our congressman, Wilbur Mills, and told him what was going on. He explained that J. E. needed to be close to home so he could help out whenever possible. Remember, Daddy had only one leg and J. E. was his only son. Congressman Mills managed to get our brother transferred to the Pine Bluff Arsenal, which was only about ten miles from our house. But that didn't happen until after all the ordeals Bonnie and I went through trying to keep the Brown Trio alive.

Our little sister Norma was only twelve years old at the time, but Bonnie and I started rehearsing her as a replacement. She learned to take the lead and did a good job in substituting for J. E. on some of our songs. So we were able to fulfill some of the dates we already had booked. Norma couldn't take off from school, though, and we had one trial after another keeping the Browns afloat.

We did take Norma with us to play a date down in New Orleans. We were appearing on the *Showboat* with some very big stars. One of them was Dan Blocker, who played Hoss Cartwright on the popular *Bonanza* series. He was acting as master of ceremonies, and when he introduced us, he reached down for Norma's hand to swing her on stage. Well, her feet slipped out from under her, and she went sailing off the stage on her rear. She wasn't hurt, just embarrassed to death. We were all terribly nervous in front of that huge crowd. But the folks seemed to like our efforts and gave us a tremendous round of applause when we finished. Really, it was much more than we deserved. I've always thought they felt sorry for us over what happened to Norma. Maybe we should have put that in the act every night.

After the concert a bunch of us were invited out to eat at Diamond Jim Moran's famous restaurant in the French Quarter. Diamond Jim himself came over to our table and told us how much he had enjoyed the show. He ordered us a whole lot of complimentary wine and special dishes, including those snails they call "escargot." Diamond Jim's was world famous for its snails, so he stood right behind me and waited for my reaction to his specialty. Bonnie kept eating them right down and telling Diamond Jim how good they were. There was no way, though, that I was going to eat one of those slimy things. I put one in my mouth. Ugh! I held it for the longest time, but I couldn't wait for Diamond Jim to turn around. I had to spit it out in my napkin before I choked to death. Diamond Jim just laughed and laughed. He thought we were about the funniest kids in show business. We had grown up on the poorest land in the poorest part of the poorest state, but we never once had to eat worms.

Lord 'a mercy, New Orleans was some glittering place. I gawked at everything down Bourbon Street. Why, you could walk along among the drunkest people in the world and look into doorways and see naked girls. But the music was wonderful—Dixieland and blues and a lot of other styles mixed in. It was a whole other world, wilder and nuttier than even California.

Hank Locklin had also played the *Showboat* and was out with us that night. We were all walking along Bourbon Street when this bum came up to us begging for money. Hank said, "Look, buddy, I'm working this side of the street tonight. You're supposed to be on the other side." Well, that old hobo, who'd been acting like he was crippled, straightened up all of a sudden and said, "Thanks, old buddy. I didn't think you were gonna show tonight so I was working your side for you. Here's a couple of bucks."

• • •

Before J. E. got transferred back to the Arsenal, he got a few furloughs home, and we'd meet in Springfield to do the *Ozark Jubilee*. When he couldn't make it, we'd do our show with other singers— Bobby Lord or Webb Pierce and occasionally Red Foley himself. They were wonderful and giving folks on the *Jubilee*. A few times, Bonnie and I tried to go it alone. I thumped on the guitar and we tried singing our songs. But it wasn't the same as with J. E., and we didn't go over at all. We always remembered the place we did the poorest: Rising Sun, Maryland. Many years later we could laugh about it, but it was painful then, bombing in Rising Sun.

The booking agency at the *Jubilee* got the wild idea that we should get a replacement for J. E. At least we could take advantage of our hit and do a lot of big-money dates. Billy Walker had filled in for J. E. on the *Jubilee* a couple of times and his voice blended in with ours well enough. We really didn't like the idea of using a substitute, but we had to go along. Billy traveled with us on a tour up through Washington, D.C. We did all right on the tour and we got to see such old friends as Patsy Cline and Jimmy Dean.

Billy was terrified of Bonnie's driving. She took the inside of some of those curves at ninety miles an hour just to scare him—or to keep him in his place. When we finally clued each other in as to what was going on, we decided to do something about it. We drove on to the D.C. airport, gave him the money he had coming and told him to catch a plane home or else call Lou Black and see if he could work the remaining dates alone. Bonnie and I knew we might get sued because we canceled those dates, but we didn't really care. We were not used to working with anyone except our brother. Luckily, Jimmy Dean lived close by. So we went to his house to get our wits about us. Jimmy and his wife were very understanding and gracious to us about the ordeal. We called the agency in Springfield and canceled the rest of the tour, and we told them why. Here we were, stranded again, two Arkansas girls facing a long drive home by ourselves.

An old deejay friend that everybody called Smiling Jim was at Jimmy Dean's house that night. He said he could fix us up so we wouldn't get sleepy on the long drive to Pine Bluff. He had a pocket full of all kinds of colored pills and assured us they were harmless but would do the trick. We took some. Since I always got sleepy on the road, I took two pills instead of one as Smiling Jim had prescribed. After that, I could have driven all the way home and back with a side trip to Florida thrown in. Even after I got home, I climbed the walls for three days and nights. I never closed an eye. I don't know what kind of pills they were, for I had never taken any before. And believe me, I never took another one. As Tom T. Hall says, "Taking pills and drinking whiskey . . . can be mighty risky."

On our way home that night, we kept seeing this big old Cadillac in front of us with Tennessee license plates. We knew it must be some-one from the *Opry*, maybe someone we knew. Being way out in the middle of nowhere can be frightening to a couple of country girls. So we kept following that Cad. We would pass, then they would pass and we'd wave. Sure enough, they recognized us and after a while we both stopped. It was Ira and Charlie Louvin and their band. What a wonderful stroke of luck. From there on to Nashville, we traveled in a caravan. We would stop in at all-right cafes and talk our heads off. Ira told me he was working on another song for us, this one called "The Last Thing I Want." And he said this chance meeting was a certain sign the song was meant to be a good one. It took Ira a few months to finish writing it and we later recorded the song for RCA. The words always remind me of that scared, lonely time on the road.

Some of the sweetest songs ever written never get heard by that many people. I think "The Last Thing I Want" would have been a hit. But the other side was the one that went on to become a smash. It was called "I Heard The Bluebirds Sing." It jumped on the charts in September 1957 and soon outsold our earlier hits.

That first Nashville recording session in the RCA Victor Studios in July of 1956 is indelibly imprinted on my brain. Standing there in the footprints of all those living, breathing country music legends was the stuff of pipe dreams. (It's hard to imagine now that the studio was only a two-track facility.) The first song we recorded was another Ira Louvin composition, "Just as Long as You Love Me." And it was the one RCA released as a single. The other side was "Don't Tell Me Your Troubles."

We began rehearsing our songs there in the studio and getting acquainted with all the musicians, but one particular gentleman stood out from the rest. He had a nice, down-home smile that seemed to put everyone at ease. He strolled over to us and said, "Hi, kids, my name is Chet Atkins. I want to welcome you to the RCA Victor family. Jim Reeves has told me all about you—so I've been looking forward to this for a long time. I'm going to be producing your session and also pick guitar."

Oh my Lord, the great Chet Atkins playing guitar for us! From that moment on, Chet would play the biggest, most important role in our career and lives.

. . .

After our ordeal on the road with Billy Walker, Bonnie and I decided that we would not book any more shows until J. E. got out of the Army. So we worked in the Trio Club and helped Momma at home. We did get the chance to go back out to California once—not to see old devil Fabor, but to christen a battleship. The ship was the U.S.S. Jefferson County, named for the county where Pine Bluff is. It was a big honor for us. J. E. was granted a furlough so he could be there for the ceremony, and it turned out to be the most impressive event we had ever taken part in. While we were on the coast, we did a lot of shows, including the *Town Hall Party* in Bakersfield. That area of California was a hotbed for country music. We met many of the West Coast artists on that trip and made some lasting friendships, among them Freddie Hart, Buck Owens, and Tex Ritter.

We called home several times while we were out there to let our folks know how things were going, and we learned they were also having the time of their lives. Gambling was legal in Hot Springs, and Momma was not only winning at the races but had learned how to roll the dice too. It was a good feeling to know they were able to take a break from hard work every so often to enjoy themselves. Gambling wasn't legal in Little Rock, but it was there if you knew where to look. On occasion Momma and Daddy would go to the Westwood Club for dinner. Then they'd slip back behind the "green door" to shoot dice. Momma was having such a long stretch of good luck that I think the owner, Barney Levine, hated to see them coming.

• • •

Finally, J. E. got his transfer to the Pine Bluff Arsenal. This enabled him to be home a lot, but his time was restricted by his service duties. So we couldn't play any big booking engagements. We sat back and waited, hoping that we'd stay in the public's mind long enough to get the Browns going again. Another country singer was about to go into the service around the same time J. E. did. But his induction got worldwide attention. That singer, of course, was our own Elvis Presley. Late one day in December 1956, we were in the Trio Club getting ready for the night's show when that cute boy from Memphis walked in and yelled to Momma, "What's the matter? Have you forgotten your adopted son?"

Momma whooped and hollered and gave Elvis a big bear hug. It had been over a year since we'd seen him, and we were thrilled to have him come by for a visit. (We'd all had time by now to forget about the way he'd treated Daddy's new Pontiac. You learn to get over hurt feelings in this crazy music business.) J. E. happened to be home that night and we all got in a booth over in the corner to have a quiet supper and talk over old times. Elvis was on his way to Shreveport for his final appearance on the *Hayride*. He had a contract with the *Hayride* and Horace Logan was holding his feet to the fire.

Elvis arrived at the Trio Club about 8:30, driving a new white Cadillac. He was accompanied by Hal Kanter—the screenwriter and director of *Loving You,* Elvis's second motion picture—and his bodyguards, Gene, Junior, and Bitsy Mott. The crowd kept piling in, and pretty soon we couldn't get a word in with Elvis. He gave away his sport shirt, a white silk scarf and all the pencils from his pocket to some of the fans who recognized him. As the crowd grew, he became restless and left with his entourage around midnight. Someone must have called the newspaper, because the next day they had a picture of the three of us and Elvis on the front page.

We all knew why he had come by. He wanted to see my Momma and sit around her kitchen like old times, maybe store up some home feelings before he took off to change his life forever. That night I caught Elvis and Bonnie looking at each other a lot, not saying a word but kind of smiling and looking sad at the same time. I think they still had it pretty bad for each other, but they knew it could never be. The Elvis Presley who left our club that night was not the same as the one the world grew to adore.

Elvis had invited us to come by and see his new house in Memphis. So on one of our return trips from a recording session in Nashville, we drove out to Graceland to see his fancy digs. His folks were the same great people, and Elvis was prouder of that mansion than old King Solomon was of all his riches. Elvis ushered us into the ice cream parlor he had installed in the house and took great delight in fixing each one of us monstrous ice cream sodas.

The grand mansion and grounds were, as any Elvis fan knows, as fantastic as the Arabian Nights. We sat out on his veranda and talked a long, long time with him and his mom and dad. He seemed content there. We were proud of what he had accomplished, and he knew it. But he seemed a little uneasy about having all the finery and riches. He kept asking us what we thought. Finally Bonnie told him, "This is all just great, and you deserve it if anybody does because you earned it." I think she sensed that he was feeling guilty deep down because he and his folks had been so poor all their lives. I really think it was a battle that Elvis fought inside for years to come. Maybe that's what drove him so much and accounted for all his excesses. When you can have it all, you find out it doesn't mean that much, because you can never quite get over the times when you knew you didn't have anything. While we were there at Graceland, Elvis's dad, Vernon, took me over to the far side of the swimming pool and told me Elvis was in love with Bonnie. He was planning to ask her to marry him.

• • •

In the early part of 1957, we once again stopped by Graceland to visit with the Presleys. Elvis told us how much he loved the words to our single "Money." He said he wanted to record it but that RCA and Elvis's manager, Col. Tom Parker, wouldn't let him. I said, "Elvis, that song isn't your type. It's a fast waltz and doesn't even sound like you."

"I would change the beat," he said. "Here, let me show you."

He tapped out the beat on the hood of our car and sang all the words. It was so beautiful. I can remember thinking, my God, if only we had done it to that beat, we might have had a hit. I think this showed just how talented he really was. I've often wondered why those words meant so much to him so early on in his career before having too much money became one of his problems.

I Finally Meet My Childhood Idol

After we started making it on a grander scale, Nashville became our second home, just as it's been for countless other singers and pickers. Most of us have a favorite among the stars who have settled in Nashville, and my "all-time best" was Eddy Arnold. To me, he symbolizes all that is good and great about "Music City." Despite our successes, I was still such a starstruck kid the first time I ever met my idol in 1957. We had been with RCA—which was also Mr. Arnold's label—nearly two years before I finally got to meet him. RCA was hosting a going-away party for us just before our first tour overseas, and my idol was one of the many invited guests. Since the Browns and Mr. Arnold were labelmates, everyone at the party assumed that we'd already met. When no one bothered to introduce us, I went up to him and just stood there, fidgeting like a schoolgirl. Oh how I wanted to just throw my arms around him and say, "I've loved you all my life!" In fact, that's what I nearly did. I couldn't think of a thing to say. *So I asked him for his autograph.* That was the first and only time I've ever done that to another artist.

There he stood, the tall, strong, handsome man I'd listened to for years and dreamed about. And he just laughed at me for asking. "I'll give you an autograph you'll never forget, Maxine," he said. He hugged and kissed me like I'd never been hugged and kissed before. My thoughts went back to those early days on our poor dirt farm in South Arkansas when I'd sit up late at night listening to the *Grand Ole Opry* and waiting to hear Eddy Arnold sing. I felt like that kid again—and I know I acted like it.

In all the years that followed, I never once had cause to lose my admiration and high esteem for this man. Some others I thought were great when I viewed them from a distance turned out petty in person.

But not Eddy. We have remained through the years the greatest of friends. Ironically, though, we never worked a show date together. Years after our trio broke up, Eddy was appearing at the Arkansas State Fair, and rather than use the limousine provided him, he told the fair folks he wanted me to be his personal escort throughout his stay. It was indeed my honor.

No one else has ever come close to showing the true class that carried Eddy Arnold to international stardom. He used to bill himself as "the Tennessee Plowboy." But whether he was wearing an old pair of work jeans or a tux and tails, Eddy was always the same perfect gentleman. They say that Hank Williams never wrote a single bad line, and if that's true, then Eddy Arnold never sang a single bad note. I heard a quotation once and have always remembered it because it seemed to fit one man in particular: "Many stars have blazed brilliantly for a moment, then flickered out, while a few have taken the spark given them and nurtured it into an enduring flame." That's my idol, Eddy Arnold.

• • •

For years, the most familiar voice in all of Nashville belonged to Ralph Emery, the ultimate deejay and a fine goodwill ambassador for country music. Ralph used to host an all-night program on famous WSM, the radio station from which the *Grand Ole Opry* originated. When we went to Nashville to record, Ralph was most kind to us and often had us on his show. There's no telling how many lost souls Ralph Emery helped stay on the road just with his kind voice going out over the radio waves. I know he helped us tremendously, not only by promoting our songs but also by offering useful criticism. We would always take our new recording session tapes over to Ralph for his opinions. He had an uncanny knack for spotting foul-ups and trouble spots.

One night while we were on his show, we got a phone call all the way from Pine Bluff. The caller wasn't just a fan wanting to say hello. It was somebody who wanted to tell us that a fire had struck the Trio Club. Of course we ran out of the studio, jumped into the car and took off for home. We couldn't believe the old Brown family curse had struck again. Sure enough, when we got home, we saw the blackened walls and the smoke still rising. True to the family spirit of not giving up, we all pitched right in and started cleaning up the mess. The building itself hadn't been destroyed, though it might have been better if it had. Everything—all the fixtures and furniture—was smoked. It took us months to clean up the few things that could still be salvaged.

The fire happened in March 1956, but we couldn't get the Trio opened again until almost summer. My dad was depressed because the insurance company wouldn't pay but a fraction of the damages. "To hell with insurance," he always said after that. "I'm not ever going to carry any again. You're just making a bet against yourself and hoping you'll lose."

Soon afterward our spirits received a lift. We had another record out called, "It Takes a Long, Long Train with a Red Caboose To Carry My Blues Away." The song was doing well on the charts, and RCA asked us if we'd like to join a big tour they were putting together for the March of Dimes. It would give us the opportunity to perform in every big city on the East Coast. We jumped at the chance. The Army granted J. E. a furlough so he could take part in the tour.

Many top-notch artists were appearing on the tour, including Jaye P. Morgan, Julius LaRosa, Jack E. Leonard, Dorothy Olsen, Ann Gilbert, Janis Martin, David Houston, and Mickey and Sylvia (whose big hit, "Love Is Strange," had just been released). RCA paid for everything, including our plane fares and expenses. We rode a train along the tour route for two weeks and got the red carpet treatment all the way—a far cry from Fabor Robinson's sleazy tour we'd suffered through. At each stop, we'd get out on the rear platform and entertain all the folks who crowded around the train stations. It was cold weather up East, and I had what I thought was a pretty nice cloth coat. But I saw that Jaye P. Morgan and the other women all had full-length fur coats, all mink, so I was ashamed to go out on the platform in my old cloth one. I went without it and almost froze my butt off. Putting up a front sometimes can be downright uncomfortable.

In Buffalo, New York, Bonnie got off the train to buy us a pizza. The train was supposed to stop there longer than it actually did. All of a sudden, the train pulled out. I ran to the window and sure enough there Bonnie stood on the platform, waving a pizza at the train. Knowing she didn't have an extra cent in her pocket, I became almost hysterical. I ran through all the cars trying to get somebody to listen to me, but I couldn't find a porter or the conductor anywhere. Finally, I saw J. E. and David Houston sitting in the club car; I ran to them, crying and tearing my hair, and told them what had happened to poor little Bonnie.

J. E. went and talked to Brad McCuen, an RCA executive on the train, and Brad said he'd take care of it. He radioed back to the train station, told them to find Bonnie and give her a ticket to join us on down the line. I was still worried sick. How in the world would Bonnie ever get by? She didn't have any money and she might starve to death. I sat up all that night worrying and crying. Sweet ol' Jack E. Leonard sat by me for hours trying to give comfort. Jack E. was one of the best comedians in the world, but even he couldn't make me smile all night.

This agony went on for another day and night. Finally, way up in Detroit, Bonnie caught up with us. When I saw her, I just jumped for joy. I ran and threw my arms around her; I was never so glad to see anyone in my whole life. "My poor little sister, my poor little sister," I kept saying. "Are you all right? I know it was a horrifying experience . . . my little sister lost . . . with no money."

"Huh uh," she said in that typical sassy voice. "They treated me like a movie star!"

"Well, I wish somebody had told me," I smarted.

"Now, Maxine, don't be mad. You're acting like you wanted me to suffer or something."

I felt like a complete idiot. All that worrying and crying on poor old Jack E. Leonard's shoulder all night, while she was somewhere back down the line living it up and having a high old time!

We worked harder on that tour than any we'd taken part in before. When it was finished, the RCA folks came to us and said, "Of course you're getting paid for the tour, but everybody is contributing their earnings to the March of Dimes and we're sure you'd like to do so, too."

Er, yeah, why sure. We'd made a little money off our records, but nothing like these big-time stars, and it was taking all we earned for expenses. But we had to go along with it. The thing is, RCA had paid our airfare to New York—but only one way—and we actually didn't have the money for the trip back home. After we'd contributed our tour earnings, we had to borrow money from RCA for the plane tickets. All I could think about on the plane home, with my old checkered coat on my lap, was the dazzling image Jaye P. Morgan made in her luxurious mink.

My Momma was psychic, I do believe. For Christmas that year, my folks gave me a long, gray coat with a real mink collar. I know I had never mentioned the classy ladies in their minks, but my mother must have sensed it anyway. My new mink-collared coat came from the most exclusive store in Little Rock, and I thought it was the prettiest thing I'd ever seen. Why, I'd be proud to wear it alongside Jaye P. Morgan anytime.

Some months later, we were working with David Houston, and he told us that he had flatly refused RCA's request that he donate his tour money to the March of Dimes. He told them he needed it too much. I don't think anyone needed the money as much as we did. Why in the world were we so gullible? But it wasn't long after this that RCA dropped David from the label. Were the two related? In this business, who knows?

• • •

So we'd gotten ourselves a big recording contract with RCA, we'd christened a ship in California, and we'd rubbed elbows with the toast of New York. But we were still waiting for J. E. to get out of the Army. Meanwhile, I was waiting tables at the Trio Club. I had seen this handsome young man come into the Trio every so often, but always with some ugly doll hanging all over him. Still, I was a little stuck on him and made it a point to wait on his table. I was so brazen as to do little things to try to make him notice me. But he never did. Finally, I gave up. I didn't even go near him. Then one night he came in alone, picked me right out and asked me for a date.

"I'm sorry, but I don't go out with strangers," I said.

"I'm not a stranger, Maxine Brown. You've seen me in here a dozen times." "I don't even know your name," I tried to argue.

"Yes, you do. I'm Tommy Russell. I'm a lawyer and I think you're cute as a bug. Come on, go out with me."

"I can't. I have to work."

"Not every night."

"Yes, I do. I work here in the Trio and I work in my Dad's liquor store next door."

"That's all right. We'll have a liquor store date then."

And that was our first date. Cute, lovable, and worthless, Tommy Russell would steal my heart in a damn liquor store! We began to keep steady company. Tommy would stay with me at the liquor store until closing, and sometimes he'd go in back and take a nap. One time my Daddy caught him asleep back there, and I caught some real hell over it. There was no way I could explain that we were getting serious and the liquor store was just about our only dating place. Later we dated on weekends, mostly on Sundays when we were both off. It was a crazy arrangement, but it was leading to deeper and deeper feelings. I just couldn't get him out of my mind.

Pretty soon he asked me to marry him and I blurted out, "Yes!" I guess I would have walked through fire for him. He was one slick, inspiring young lawyer, and everybody said he had the potential to be big and important someday. I began to daydream about being a lawyer's wife, maybe even someday Governor Russell or Senator Russell's wife. I'd never had any security on my own. Surely I'd have it now because Tommy was obviously a winner.

J. E. and I had always been very close, and I swore I'd never marry a man who didn't live up to my brother's standards. But there I was, twenty-five years old, and everyone kidding me about becoming an old maid. I guess I convinced myself that Tommy had the same high qualities as J. E. did. Besides, he was so doggone *good looking.* I was as blinded by love as any schoolgirl.

We set the wedding date, and I notified J. E. that his Sis was getting hitched. Well, he couldn't believe it. Neither could my folks; they said we hadn't known each other long enough and had too many obstacles in our path. How was I going to keep up with my singing and stay married?

"It'll be too hard on you, Maxine," my Momma said. "You might as well get ready for some heartaches." Of course, I didn't pay any attention to her.

I didn't pay attention to anyone, not even our friend Elvis. I had invited Elvis and his parents to my wedding, but I knew they would be unable to attend because he was getting ready for his tour with *Grand Ole Opry* star Hank Snow. Elvis was never one to write or call anyone. But somehow I knew he would call, because, after all, we were the best of friends. And he was sort of like a family member. Instead of calling to wish me well, he called and begged me not to get married.

He said, "I'd like to meet the dude first. Besides, I don't think you know him well enough." He went on to say, "You know you're gonna break a lot of hearts, especially Bill's."

We talked quite a while about Bonnie, Jim Ed's Army life, and what our opinion was of Colonel Parker, but we talked very little about my impending wedding. I remember telling him that if I didn't hurry up and get married I was going to wind up an old maid for sure. Well, he swore from that time on that that was the only reason I was getting married. And this is what he told Bill Black.

I knew that Bill was in love with me. So did everyone else. He always said if I'd just say the word, he would get a divorce. I truly cared for Bill, but there was no way I would ever be the one to break up his marriage. (Just a few years later—in 1965—Bill died from a brain tumor.) Pictures and stories about my wedding appeared in all the county music magazines. *Country Song Roundup* even put a picture of me in my wedding gown on its front cover. I had a big church wedding and everything was beautiful. I don't know how many times the words of my Momma and Elvis have come back to haunt me: "You'd better take time to know him."

Tommy could always sweep me off my feet. But he could not get me in bed. He wanted us to have sex before we were married. In fact, he'd been after that since our first date. But on this one thing I stood firm. Those old country values I grew up with were still with me. I was still a virgin. That must have set some sort of world record for girl singers on the road with all those horny pickers. Anyway, Tommy kept after me, but I wouldn't do it until we got married. Thinking back, I believe I was a big challenge to Tommy's macho image. Maybe that's why he wanted to marry me in the first place.

I stayed married to Tommy Russell for seven years, seven years of pure hell. Eddy Arnold once recorded a song called "Seven Years with the Wrong Woman (Is More Than a Man Can Stand)." Well, just turn that around for me. Tommy could never leave other women alone and was becoming a bad, bad drinker to boot. He drank when I first met him, but I never realized how much. Women continued to call him about every day of our marriage. He had a pet name for each one, a man's name. "Hi, Jack," or "How're you doing, Willie?" He thought I'd never catch on to his little game, but it didn't take long to figure out anything about Tommy. Sometimes I would overhear him bragging to his law cronies that "lonely women make the best lovers." He was one to know. Many a time he didn't charge a woman for getting her a divorce; he just took it out in trade. I'm not sure he ever considered his wife a lonely woman, but it was something that happened to me right in front of his blind eyes. And he never changed his ways, not even after we had our beautiful children. He seemed driven to drink more and chase more as the years passed. He never knew what he had until it was too late. It all sounds familiar, doesn't it, country music lovers?

The famous Trio Club, showplace of the South. *From the collection of Maxine Brown.*

This is a picture of the second Trio Club, which later burned. This is where Elvis, Scotty, Bill, and other artists would come when they came through town. They loved Momma's cooking, and if she didn't cook them something at home, she'd have them come to the Trio restaurant and supper club, where she would always feed them. *From the collection of Maxine Brown.*

Tom and Billie Perryman threw this party at the Mimosa Tea
Room at City Lake in Gladewater, Texas, in honor of my par-
ents' twenty-fifth anniversary in 1955. Included in this picture
are all the guys we had been working with and loved dearly.
Clockwise from left are Floyd and Birdie Brown, Norma, Jim
Ed, Scotty Moore, Bill Black, D. J. Fontana, Floyd Cramer, Red
West, Tom Tall, Jimmy Day, Elvis Presley, the Perryman family,
Maxine, and Bonnie. *From the collection of Tom and Billie
Perryman, Tyler, Texas.*

Maxine took this picture when The Browns were backstage
with Elvis at the *Louisiana Hayride* in 1955. He was just coming
out of the bathroom. *From the collection of Maxine Brown.*

Elvis Presley and the Browns at the Trio Club in Pine Bluff, Arkansas, December 15, 1956. The Trio Club was Elvis's favorite hangout in the early days; he loved Momma's cooking. He came by for a visit with us on his way to the *Louisiana Hayride*, where he was making his final appearance before heading to Hollywood to make his first movie. This picture appeared on the front page of the *Pine Bluff Commercial*. Elvis looks so sad . . . I wonder why? *Courtesy of the* Pine Bluff Commercial*; photographer Bruce Clegg*

This snapshot was taken at the Jimmie Rodgers Celebration in Meridian, Mississippi, in 1956. *From the collection of Maxine Brown.*

The three Browns at the *Ozark Jubilee,* wearing costumes made by Nudie's of California. *From the collection of Maxine Brown.*

J. E. and Maxine performing a duet on a televised broadcast of the *Ozark Jubilee. From the collection of Maxine Brown.*

Bonnie, Eddy Arnold, Maxine, and Jim Ed. *From the collection of Maxine Brown.*

Maxine and Bonnie singing on the *Ozark Jubilee* with Webb Pierce while J. E. was in the army, in 1957. *From the collection of Maxine Brown.*

Del Wood, Jim Reeves, Dick O'Shaughnessy, Herb Shucher, Eddy Arnold, and Bonnie Brown. This was at a press party hosted by RCA prior to our first European tour in 1957 (I think I was in the bathroom). *Courtesy of RCA.*

This was taken at the Andrew Jackson Hotel, outside the hospitality suite of Tree Publishing Co. during one of the DJ conventions promoting Tree. Roy Horton, Jim Ed (in white coat), the Tree Publishing Co. secretary, Hawkshaw Hawkins, Bonnie, and Johnny Cash. I was, no doubt, off somewhere looking for the tree! *Courtesy of Les Leverette, Nashville, Tennessee.*

Our first trip to Germany, sponsored by the European Armed Forces in 1957. Back Row: Billy Harlon, Tommy Hill, Hank Locklin, Louie Dunn, Jim Reeves, Mary Reeves, our escort officer, Janice Martin, Maxine Brown, Del Wood. Front Row: Bobby Garrett, Dick O'Shaughnessy, Leo Jackson, Bonnie Brown, Jim Ed Brown, and Tommy Russell. *From the collection of Maxine Brown.*

Above: Maxine, Bonnie, and J. E. on stage in Germany in 1957. *From the collection of Maxine Brown.*

Right: Norma, our baby sister. Norma was a great sub for Bonnie and me when we were sick or pregnant, and also for J. E. when he was in the army. *From the collection of Maxine Brown.*

Europe

In 1957, the Brown Trio made its first trip to Europe. J. E., Bonnie, and I were working regularly all over the country and happened to be on the East Coast when it was time to go. We'd been on tour for about two weeks and were scheduled to join other groups in New Jersey for a grand European tour. Boy, were we ever excited! The tour had been arranged by our good friend, Jim Reeves, and his manager, Herb Schucher, in conjunction with the United States Air Force. We flew out of McGuire Air Base in New Jersey, and from the moment we took off until we landed back on good old U.S. *terra firma,* that trip was the most unorganized, chaotic, and strangely enjoyable tour we'd ever been on.

Nothing seemed to go right. I remember Jim Reeves bitching about it the whole trip and constantly blaming poor old Herb. Luggage got misplaced, hotel reservations didn't get made, and the bus was never on time. No one seemed to mind except Jim, and I think he was making a fuss now and then just because he thought he had to. Anyway, it was the first time in Europe for most of us and we loved it. I got to see a part of the world I know I would never had gotten to see had we not been in show business. Jolly Old England was, in those days, truly jolly. We watched the changing of the guard at Buckingham Palace, woke up each morning to the tolling of Big Ben, toured Scotland Yard, and frolicked around Trafalgar Square. I think the most interesting part of London was seeing the devastation that remained from the war. A lot of big buildings had been bombed out and still weren't rebuilt. It gave you an eerie feeling and made you happy you were an American.

On the tour—besides the Browns and Jim and Mary Reeves—were Hank Locklin, the Blue Boys (Jim's band), Del Wood, Dick

O'Shaughnessy (a great comedian who was just making a name for himself in Hollywood), and a cute little girl singer named Janis Martin that RCA was trying to turn into a female Elvis Presley. (She was good all right, but being a female Elvis made about as much sense as trying to be a male Minnie Pearl.)

My husband Tommy came along on the tour, too. We had just recently married and decided we'd use the tour as a kind of honeymoon. It was also his first trip abroad, and he was like a kid. It was all sweet and wonderful. We didn't know it then, but it was to be the happiest time of our marriage. Tommy spent most of his spare time at the House of Parliament watching the lawyers and judges in their long wigs and observing the way they conducted court. I went with him a few times and found it an interesting part of history.

We had heard of the notorious part of London called Piccadilly Circus, so we all went to have a look at it. It was wilder and crazier than the Strip in Hollywood. Prostitution was legal in London, and Piccadilly Circus was crawling with hookers. Those flashy girls came right up to the men, even when their wives were with them. They'd say in that fast, clipped accent, "What's your pleasure, lad? Two bob for doing it standing up, three bob for a taxi, or would you like it in my flat?" Boy, this was quite a shock, especially to us country girls. I thought that old devil Fabor Robinson would be right at home there.

Mary and I went back to the hotel to rest up, and while we were in our room, Tommy and Jim decided to play a prank on us. They sneaked out and locked us in! Whatever possessed them to do that, I don't know, but Mary was mad as a hornet. She thought they'd done it so they could go and mess around with those Piccadilly floozies. We tried again and again to get that door open but couldn't. There was no telephone in the room, so we couldn't even call down to the front desk for help.

Mary was terribly jealous of Jim, and maybe she had a good reason to be. She was determined to get out and try to find Jim. Now I'm a big coward, but I let Mary talk me into climbing out on the window ledge with her to try to make it down the fire escape. There we were, several stories up, climbing down like a couple of nanny goats! We had just reached the ground when here came Jim and Tommy, laughing their heads off at us. They'd been at one of those pubs and had had their share of strong English ale. They staggered on into the hotel and ducked into the "lift." When we got back to our room, we now found ourselves locked out! At first, it was kind of funny. It took forever to get them awake to let us back in. They never asked us how we got out. I guess they were afraid we'd have a few Piccadilly questions to ask them.

•   •   •

After England, our tour moved on to Germany. It was there that we had the time of our lives. Our music was very popular, not only with the American soldiers stationed there, but also with the German people. We loved singing for them both. I guess we cut up some, too, perhaps more than we should have. Once, Dick O'Shaughnessy almost got us all arrested. He had a trick he played that involved putting a pair of scissors on a telephone cord in a way that made it impossible to remove them. The incident that caused us trouble happened in our hotel lobby in Munich as we were waiting for the bus to take us to an Air Force base. Sure enough, Dick did his scissors trick on the phone at the front desk. The little German clerk tried to pull the scissors off just as we were leaving. We heard him jumping up and down and jabbering at the top of his lungs. We all thought it was funny.

But it wasn't so funny when we got back to the hotel that night after our show. The local police were waiting for us. They announced that all of us were under arrest. Pretty soon the whole hotel was a madhouse. Dick finally came in, saw what was going on and offered to take the blame, thinking that an apology would get us off the hook. Wrong. The police arrested Dick and escorted him out. They warned the rest of us not to leave the premises until a magistrate could hear the case. It took a couple of sharp Air Force lawyers to get Dick out of jail. We still couldn't understand why there was such a fuss. After all, it was just the kind of stupid practical joke we'd seen almost every night on the road. Finally Dick came back and told us everything was all right and we were free to leave. They did kick all of us out of the hotel that night, but not before Dick sneaked another pair of scissors onto a telephone cord in an empty room.

Still, Germany was our favorite part of the tour. I guess that was because everybody was acting so crazy and wild. We got a kick out of pert little Janis Martin. Evidently her folks had forbidden her to see this one certain boy who was stationed in Germany that she was crazy about. But they managed to meet at our hotel in Nuremberg and get a room by themselves. They disappeared into it and didn't seem to come out for the rest of the time we were there. We learned later that Janis and her soldier had been secretly married back in the States and that this was their honeymoon. I remember going down the hall every morning and passing the other performers coming out of their rooms.

"Are they still in there?" somebody would ask.

"Yep."

"Lordy, are they ever gonna come up for air?"

Our hotel had a pond right in the center of the courtyard. Nothing but beautiful white ducks occupied the pond, and they were the prized possessions of the entire hotel staff. Everywhere there were signs posted: "Please Do Not Feed the Ducks." One morning one of the pampered quackers was found dead. It had choked on a condom. The hotel was in an uproar.

Jim Reeves thought he knew where the condom had come from. So he went to have a talk with Janis's new hubby. It turned out that he had flushed so many of the devices that their commode was stopped up, leaving him no other route of disposal but the window. Jim told the passionate young litterer to get outside and pick up any of his remaining souvenirs or else his goose would be cooked—not to mention ours. We knew if they found out it was a member of our troupe who caused the little duck's demise, we'd all be arrested. It was hard for us to keep a straight face in front of the hotel staff after that. But we had to. We had a lot of fun kidding Janis, but she was very good-natured about it and kept that sweet little smile on her face.

While we were in Germany, Del Wood almost went bald. We all found the incident very funny, and I guess it served Del right. She had always dyed her hair red. But while we were in Germany, she ran out of dye. She looked all over but couldn't find the brand she used. So she finally settled on a substitute. I remember she came in one day with this big packet of dye, saying she'd bought enough to dye her hair— "all of it." It wasn't two hours later that she started going crazy. She broke out in a terrible rash and finally had to find a doctor. Her hair started falling out and she cried and carried on in pain for a long time.

"My God, girl," I told her. "You're going to lose all the hair on your head."

"That's not the only place I'm losing it," she moaned.

Del's rash cleared up fairly quickly, and her hair started growing back. But she had this funny, spraddled walk for quite a few comical days.

• • •

While we were in Germany, Jim Reeves and I stole some of Hitler's personal beer steins. We couldn't resist. In our off hours, we went to a beer hall where Hitler and his cronies had first started the Nazi party—at least this was the story some of the old-timers there told us. Anyway, the beer was wonderful and the German band that played in the hall was especially good. We started going to the place every night. Some of the locals found out we were singers and musicians, and pretty soon Jim Reeves, the Browns, and some of the others were up front singing and playing and having a great old time with the crowd.

Behind our table was this huge glass shelf filled with fancy mugs and steins, all under lock and key. Our waitress, who could speak a little English, was funny and friendly and managed to get us loaded on strong brew every night. We bought her a drink every time she served us a round, and pretty soon we all became as close and friendly as first cousins.

"See those mugs up there?" our waitress said. "They once belonged to Adolf Hitler."

"Hon," Jim Reeves said to her, "I'll give you a whole American sawbuck if you'll get me one of those mugs."

"No, I could not. Lots of people try to get those mugs." She explained they were more valuable than anyone could imagine.

"Aw, come on. There must be a hundred. Nobody's gonna miss one little mug," Jim begged, as he kept getting her drunk.

The little waitress refused; she was afraid she'd get caught and lose her job. Besides, we could get arrested, again.

Jim went up to sing for the crowd, while those of us who had already done our turn sat back, feeling no pain. Then it was time for Hank Locklin to take the stage. At that time, Bobby Helms had a fast-rising single in America called "Fraulein" (which Hank would record for his 1958 album, *Foreign Love*). Seeing the obvious relevance of the song, Hank promptly broke into "Fraulein." The crowd went crazy. I'd never heard such loud applause and singing-along our entire time in Germany.

Here was our chance for the mugs. Since we had our guitar cases beside our tables, Mary Reeves got the idea that we could smuggle the mugs out in them while all the wildness over "Fraulein" was going on. Our little waitress was about three sheets in the wind by then, and with the bribe Jim was offering dangling in her face, she agreed to open the case and get us down some of the Fuhrer's collection. She got one down, Mary stuck it in the guitar case, and then here came another one.

The crowd was still going wild over Hank, so we kept stuffing those Hitler mugs into our cases. We got out of there that night with a whole load of them. We had to have been pretty drunk ourselves to pull a stunt like this. I wonder what would have happened to us had we been caught at customs with ol' Adolf's mugs? They would probably have put us under the jail instead of in it.

•　•　•

From Germany, we moved on to other parts of Europe. Each time we took off, we traveled in an Air Force transport plane. Actually they were the planes used to parachute soldiers during the war. And, would you believe it, each time we got on one of those big planes, we all had to wear parachutes. Back in those days, women didn't routinely wear slacks or pantsuits, so it was quite an awkward deal to strap one of those chutes between your legs. All the guys enjoyed seeing us strapping those contraptions on. They fit sort of like a fat G-string. I never felt so stupid or embarrassed in my life.

The Air Force had assigned a young, good-looking sergeant from public relations to travel with us through Germany. He kept everything running smooth and in order. I don't know what poor old Herb would have done without him. During our six-week stint in Germany, he fell madly in love with Bonnie. She was very laid back, soft spoken, and beautiful. Our Air Force sergeant said he had found the "perfect lady of my dreams." They agreed to keep in touch with each other and that, as soon as he could get back to the States, they would take up where they had left off.

Finally the tour came to an end. We went back to London, with Bonnie's admirer in tow, to await another Air Force plane back to the good old U.S.A. We had a few hours to kill, so we all stayed in the airport lounge laughing, talking, and telling jokes. Out of the clear blue sky, Bonnie stood up and said she had a champagne and beer joke she wanted to tell. In her soft, sexy voice she said: "When I drink champagne, I picture myself on a lonely island. As I walk along the shore in the hot, soft, white sand, a cool wind caresses my nude body. I look out into the sea and see an Adonis rise up out of the clear blue water. He comes closer and closer to me. He grabs my hot nude body. I grab his hot nude body, and we fall into the hot, soft, white sand. But when I drink beer, I fart!" Everyone died laughing at Bonnie's joke—everyone, that is, except our Air Force sergeant. His face turned red, and he never cracked a smile. With that one joke, she had completely destroyed his dream that she was a perfect lady. He never told her goodbye, and she never heard from him again.

When we got back home, we found out that Jim Reeves had a big hit record on the charts. It was called "Four Walls," and I guess it goes down in country music history as one of the very top songs of all time. While we had been gone, "Four Walls" had been released and had already climbed to number one. Jim didn't even know it was out. Also while we were away, our booking agent, Hubert Long, had accepted awards from both *Billboard* and its competing trade magazine, *Cashbox,* naming the Browns as best vocal group of the year. It made for a delightful homecoming.

Before we left New York, on our flight back home, we were booked for three appearances on Dave Garroway's popular *Today* show. While we were on that show, we received a message from Dee Kilpatrick, the manager of the *Grand Ole Opry,* which read, "Congratulations on your European tour. The *Opry* would like the Browns to make a guest appearance the first Saturday night you have available." The *Grand Ole Opry*! They wanted these poor country kids from Arkansas to sing on the *Grand Ole Opry*! We had always dreamed about it but somehow never believed it would happen. Yet here was the invitation.

We were so nervous when we first walked onto the *Grand Ole Opry* stage at Nashville's historic Ryman Auditorium that we were probably shaking like kites in a high wind. The song we were doing, "I'm In Heaven," surely fit our mood. The only problem was that I was so nervous I couldn't utter a sound. I opened my mouth to sing, but nothing came out. I was so overwhelmed and embarrassed that I started choking. I had to run off stage, trembling all over. Then someone put his arm around me and said, "You can do it." It was my good old friend, *Opry* staff musician Lightnin' Chance. He got me all calmed down and breathing normally again. He led me back on stage, and the crowd started applauding. We started the song again, and I guess we did pretty well this time, because we got an encore. As we left the stage, there stood Lightnin,' my old friend and supporter, saying, "Attaboy, girl."

That night, Dee Kilpatrick extended the Browns an invitation to join the *Grand Ole Opry* as permanent members and performers. It was truly the highest honor that singers like us could ever hope to receive. I don't know if we deserved it yet or not, but I felt my life had reached its highest peak.

The Browns' Younger Sister and Momma's Stroke

14

We didn't join the *Grand Ole Opry* following our European tour after all. The reason was that we just couldn't afford it. Joining the *Opry* back then would have required us to be in Nashville nearly every weekend. And it would have cost us dearly to put up the kind of front expected of *Opry* members. Then there was the fact that I had recently married and my husband's roots, both personally and professionally, were in Little Rock. Finally, my folks needed our help with the Trio Club and Daddy's lumber business.

So after our European tour and our first appearance on the *Opry*, everything was a big letdown. We went a long time without working any personal appearances, and although we kept recording at RCA, we couldn't come up with another big hit. We recorded a very pretty song called "Alpha and Omega" that we thought was a surefire winner. It was written by Bill Anderson, who's an international celebrity now. In those days, Bill was a deejay down in Georgia, but he was already writing some pretty songs. However, "Alpha and Omega" never caught on. It didn't even make the *Billboard* charts. But it's always been one of my favorites. Listening to it again today, I still can't understand why it wasn't a number one. That's always the way it is in show business. Jim Reeves thought "Four Walls" would never even get released. Elvis used to say that "Hound Dog" was the silliest song he'd ever sung and thought it might sell ten or twelve records right around his folks' neighborhood.

By now the *Ozark Jubilee* had folded up, so we didn't have that as a base or the old *Louisiana Hayride* either. J. E. had finally gotten out of the Army, but the Brown Trio was sort of at a standstill. We didn't even have a booking agent any longer. Tom Perryman was still managing us, but he was limited as to where he could book us—mostly down around his East Texas territory. We still journeyed down to play the Longhorn Ballroom in Dallas and the Reo Palm Isle in Tyler, Texas. But that was about it.

J. E. went back to work for Daddy at the sawmill, and Bonnie helped Momma run the Trio Club. I was a married woman committed to making a good home for Tommy in Little Rock, although I did go and help out at the club as often as I could. To tell the truth, I could never quite adjust to living away from my family. Tommy was gone all the time, and I was lonely and miserable. Tommy bought me a puppy, Prissy, to keep me company. Day in and day out, it was just Prissy and me and a big, old empty house. I guess, too, that show business was in my blood. I never thought I'd admit it, but I missed being on the road.

While we were doing recording sessions in Nashville we had met Hubert Long, one of the biggest booking agents in the industry. Hubert had made Faron Young a big star, and he had several other big-name singers in his agency, including Ferlin Husky and others from the old *Louisiana Hayride* and the *Opry*. We contacted Hubert to see if he could line us up some really good dates, not those killer one-nighters that sapped all your energy but didn't allow you to break even. Hubert was a very nice guy. He said he'd be happy to get us on the right track again. "Shoot, The Browns are a number one act," he said. "I can't understand why you're not making it bigger than you are."

The reason we weren't making any money was because we were three people. A top act gets paid the same amount whether it's one person, three or five. After taking our expenses off the top and then splitting the remainder three ways, we found ourselves going further and further in the hole. We would have to have more money to break even.

Sure enough, Hubert came across with a great booking for us, an extended tour with Faron Young, Ferlin Husky, and some others. The tour was to take place in two months. We got all excited. We were guaranteed more money than we'd hoped for, and the tour accommodations would be first-class. My spirits lifted immediately. I decided I would spend the next two months getting my wardrobe and my body in good shape.

Lo and behold, I came up pregnant. Oh, Lord, I thought, I want to have a baby, I want to have a big family just like my folks had—

but not right now, not when we've got a chance to finally make it. But it was no use. The idea of the tour was out of the question. I couldn't perform as a pregnant, singing cowgirl. That idea was bad as the morning sickness I'd started having. I guess my Momma sensed that I was down and depressed, for she came to see me one day. None of us kids could ever fool Momma. She knew the instant she laid eyes on me that I was pregnant. She also knew about the big tour and guessed right away what I was thinking.

"Well, you're going on that tour anyway," she said. "It's less than two months away, so you won't be showing that much. I'll get busy and make you some special costumes to hide yourself under."

Dear good, strong Momma. And poor Momma, too. No matter how much work she had to do at home and in the club, she never failed to help her kids. She pitched in and made me these wonderful costumes. It meant sitting up half the night to do it, but she got them all done on time.

I wasn't showing much at all on the day we were to leave for the tour. I drove down to our house in Pine Bluff to join J. E. and Bonnie. From the moment I turned into the drive, I knew something was wrong. J. E. was just standing in the living room; Bonnie was in the dining room with her back turned, and I could tell she was upset and about to cry. Momma stood there in the kitchen trying to smile. Something had happened to her in the night, and she was trying to hide it until we were gone. But she couldn't hide her problem this time. During the night, she had had a stroke. She couldn't speak clearly, and her right side was paralyzed. I took one look at her and it broke my heart. "You all go on," she tried to say, her voice raspy and broken.

We took Momma to the hospital and called Hubert Long to tell him we couldn't make it for the tour after all. Being such a great and understanding guy, Hubert told us to stay and take care of our mother. Then, if she got better, he said, we could join the tour somewhere along the way. Momma was worse off than even she knew. It took months for her to recover, and we never did catch up with that tour. But taking care of Momma was our first priority; the Brown Trio would have to wait.

• • •

Not too long after we missed the tour, Chet Atkins called us with some good news. RCA wanted us to do an album, and Chet himself was going to produce it. We had been down and depressed one minute, and suddenly we were back up again. With Momma on the road to recovery, we busied ourselves planning our first album.

When we got to Nashville, we saw that RCA's Brad McCuen was laying out a big to-do over our album. We dressed in our stage clothes and went out to the famous Belle Meade mansion to shoot the picture for the album cover. J. E. had forgotten to bring along his guitar, but luckily Hawkshaw Hawkins was at the mansion having some publicity photos made, too. So J. E. borrowed Hawkshaw's guitar. It turned out to be a good move for Hawkshaw. When our album came out, there was J. E., holding a guitar with Hawk's name emblazoned plain as day across the front. This oddity has made the album a collector's item.

One of the songs we recorded for the album was "I Heard the Bluebirds Sing." When the album was released, deejays started playing "Bluebirds" so much that RCA put it out as a single. Within a few weeks, it rose to number four on the *Billboard* charts—our best showing since "I Take the Chance." With another hit on our hands, we were suddenly in demand again.

Hubert Long called us every day to say that he could book us anywhere we wanted to go. But I was faced with a big dilemma. I knew I was going to have a baby and understood that a woman of my age, twenty-six, ought to settle down and raise a family. I was very happy about having a baby, but I so wanted to stay in show business.

This time fate stepped in. I was three months' pregnant and having all sorts of physical problems. I could tell something was wrong, and my doctor thought so, too. Finally I got to hurting so bad that my doctor put me in the hospital. After further examinations, the doctors at the hospital agreed that I was in the process of losing my baby. They wheeled me into the operating room and prepared to perform an operation. I remember praying as hard as I could. I knew my baby was dead, but I kept praying and praying for it to live anyway. Then a miracle happened: the doctor had made an incision and was about to take the baby when it started breathing again. My little baby was going to live!

They sewed me back up and a few days later I went home with my baby still inside me. I had to take special care of myself and remain in bed for most of the rest of my term. But on May 18, 1958, I had the most beautiful, healthy baby boy in the world. I named him Tommy Jr.

While I was convalescing, my little sister Norma took my place in the Brown Trio. She was still a teenager, but she was very talented. She could sing harmony with Bonnie or do the lead. She had just recently won the title Miss Oakland Park and had a dozen boyfriends at any given time. Because she was still in school, she didn't get to practice much with us to work herself into the act. That was probably a mistake on our part. By not taking the time and trouble to work Norma in, we deprived her of the chance to sing on any of the Browns' hit records.

Norma was still substituting for me a few months later when the troupe from the *Louisiana Hayride* came to Little Rock to play a show. There was no way I was going to miss that. I got up out of bed and did the show with J. E. and Bonnie—and wound up back in the hospital. Afterward, I wished long and hard that I had let Norma sing in my place.

Norma did go with us to Nashville for one recording session in 1957. She sang on a song called "Man In the Moon" and another one that I wrote, "True Love Goes Far Beyond." She did a wonderful job with us and got a lot of attention and publicity. She was pretty and full of spunk and added a lot to our stage presence. Everybody thought she would be a full member of the Browns from then on, but for several reasons it didn't work out.

I think Norma was resentful that we didn't fully take her in, and I really can't blame her. It's strange to think of now, but Norma might have been the one who could have held us all together in the troubling years ahead. We have always regretted not taking the time to teach her four-part harmony and at least bring her into our recording sessions. Chet tried to show her the part she would sing, but she couldn't "hear" it. He wanted us to work with her to cultivate her voice and teach her that fourth part. But hell's bells, I never could hear that fourth part myself.

• • •

Big things were starting to happen to the Browns. We could feel it in the air, and we vowed that nothing would stop it this time. All the deejays were playing our records, and we were getting big write-ups in all the trade journals. Our records always got a "spotlight" or a "bullseye" (except, ironically, for "The Three Bells," which would prove to be our biggest hit). We were in *Cashbox* and *Billboard* almost every week. There were lots of feature stories and interviews. We were hot!

Still, there were nagging problems. We had lots of rehearsing and traveling to do, which confronted me with the never-ending chore of hiring baby sitters and live-in housekeepers for little Tommy Jr. It was a constant worry, not just for me but for all the other women singers who were attempting to balance a career with family life. I don't think there ever was a girl singer who was successful at both. If you're going to be in show business, you haven't got a chance of being a normal person, much less a normal mother or wife.

Even now, it's hard for me to fully appreciate just how big the Browns became in the late '50s. In 1956 and 1957, we won virtually every award the country music industry had to give. We did big TV network shows such as *Country Music USA* and *Big D,* both on CBS; the *Louisiana Hayride* when it was televised on NBC; the *Ozark Jubilee* and the *Grand Ole Opry.* Looking through my scrapbook, I see stories, photos and certificates that proclaim us and our records "Number One Vocal Group," "Number One Up and Coming Group," "Number One Most Played Record," and "Number One Favorite Record of the Year." Bonnie and I were even nominated by the deejays as their "Favorite Girl Singers." *Cashbox* named us its "Best Vocal Group" for 1957. That same year, *Billboard* and the Juke Box Operators voted us "Number One Vocal Group." In 1958, the Music Operators of America presented us its "Number One Vocal Group" award at its annual convention in Chicago.

Since J. E. had served in the Army, we were called upon to do a lot of Army recruiting shows for TV. Almost anytime you turned on the TV in those days, you could see the Browns singing our special Army theme song called "Would You Care."

We were attending the 1958 Disc Jockey Convention in Nashville when we received some more devastating news. Jim and Mary Reeves had invited us over to their house after the festivities, and we called home to tell our folks we'd be staying over an extra night because our recording sessions were running longer than expected. When I heard Daddy on the phone, I could almost tell from his voice what he was going to say. I had been through so much trouble by then I could sense it coming.

"Well, the damn ol' Trio Club turned down again," Daddy said, his voice just totally whipped. Just three years before, fire had nearly destroyed it. This time the destruction was complete. I remembered Daddy saying after that fire that he wasn't going to fool with paying insurance again because it never paid off. I couldn't sleep all night for worrying about this new ruin that had come to the Brown family.

We had to get through the recording session the next morning, and somehow we did. It was bitterly funny how the song we were recording—one that I had written—fit our mood. It was about the sun shining beyond the darkness.

It was a sad bunch of Browns that came back home to Pine Bluff that next day. We rode along in the car for miles without saying a word, and then Bonnie started in humming an upbeat song. Pretty soon J. E. joined in, and what else could I do? I had to put some harmony to it. It was the Browns' way of not giving up on ourselves or the hope that someday those clouds of darkness would fade and our sun would shine once more. "Beyond the Shadows" never became a big hit. Oh, it got considerable radio play and climbed to number eleven on the charts. But then it faded away, like so many other pretty songs and dreams had done.

John D. Loudermilk, one of the truly great country songwriters, had written a song we recorded for the other side of "Beyond the Shadows." Ironically, it was called "This Time I Would Know." Maybe we should have known from all these lyrical hints that things would never be easy for us.

●　■　●

Although we had never really been away, we sensed that the Browns were making a comeback. Because we had not worked together regularly through the years J. E. was in the Army, we never got a string of number one hits going. Even so, we were certainly big in Britain. The UK Country-Western Express Popularity Poll voted us "Best Vocal Group of 1958." I think the reason we were popular there was because of the tour with Jim Reeves.

We got fan mail from England all the time. One such letter was from a group of boys who were trying to make it in the music business. They wore their hair like the character of Prince Valiant in the then-popular comic strip. Five or six years later, these same guys were in this country on tour and Dick Clark was interviewing them on

American Bandstand. When he asked them who their favorite American singers were, one of the acts they cited was the Browns! I was in my house in Little Rock and just happened to have the TV on that day. I nearly died when I heard John and Paul of the Beatles mention our name.

• • •

Despite our evident popularity, we felt our career was slowing to a standstill. Back in those days, you were only as good as your last number one. And we couldn't get even a Top Ten record, no matter what we tried. We were making a lot of personal appearances but no money at all after expenses.

"You've had a bunch of big hit records and you're still broke," our always-skeptical Daddy kept telling us. Maybe he was right, or maybe we heard him say it so often that we began to believe it. So we just decided to quit. Give it up entirely. No more singing, no more pounding the road, no more vain hope.

Helping me make up my mind to quit was the fact that I was pregnant with my second child. Tommy and I were hardly getting along now. Even though I was home most of the time, he always found excuses to be gone. It didn't matter. I was a mother of one, expecting a second, and I had an obligation to make a home. That was the way I was brought up, and that's what I believed, even when I was on tour and singing in front of big crowds. Still, I couldn't help feeling resentful. Giving up my life on the road was doing nothing to keep my marriage from failing. Tommy was gone at all hours, and sometimes he stayed out for two or three days at a time. Our life together was in complete turmoil. Maybe the best thing I could do was raise my babies and forget everything else.

J. E., Bonnie, and I got together and talked it all out. The hardest thing we've ever done was call our friend and producer, Chet Atkins, and tell him our decision. All those years he had stood by us and given us encouragement. Now we were letting him down. We truly loved him, and making that call was about as painful as calling someone to tell them a good friend has died.

"I understand, kids," Chet said on the phone. "I don't blame you at all." But he reminded us that we still had a few months to go on our contract with RCA. "So why don't the three of you come on back to Nashville and do one last session?" he said. "We'll call it the

Browns' farewell. Pick out any song you've always wanted to record, and I promise we'll do it."

At first, we didn't even want to do it, but the more we thought about one last recording session, the more it began to stir us up. Why not do one last record and put our hearts and souls into it? So we called Chet back and told him we were coming.

I was six months' pregnant at that time, but it sure didn't bother my singing voice. The three of us got together and rehearsed incessantly. We brought our voices back up to performance level and found that we enjoyed singing together more than ever. We turned our attention to finding that special song that would serve as our farewell to show biz and all that.

Back home, Bonnie had been hearing a particular song on a local radio station. She contacted the deejay who was playing it and ended up getting a copy of it. It was a French song called "Les Trois Cloches," which translated to "The Three Bells." It told the touching story of a little boy's tragic life. Bonnie kept talking about that song so much that we decided to try it out and see how it sounded. I wasn't too sold on the song. But, of course, I had never picked a hit in my life. My all-time favorite Browns' song was "Ground Hog." Ever heard it?

We worked on "The Three Bells" all through the long drive over to Nashville. But we still had one problem with it. How could we cut it down to under three minutes? The deejays, we had often been told, would never play a record that was more than three minutes long. We kept singing it and timing it and finally got the verses and choruses to come out at exactly three minutes.

The recording session was something special. Chet brought in Anita Kerr to help with the arrangement. A musical genius, Anita had been instrumental in creating many hit songs before she went on to establish the Anita Kerr Singers, a truly first-class act. After our first run through on "The Three Bells," Chet was so excited that I thought he was going to pop a vein for sure.

"This is it!" Chet kept saying. "This is the big one. You've got the biggest hit ever!"

By the time we finished the session, Chet had calmed down a little. But he made this bold statement: "I've just recorded you a million-seller. There's no way you'll be quitting the business."

The next week Chet was on the phone making an appointment

with all the RCA executives in New York. He took the master tape of our session and had his boss, Steve Sholes, set up a tape player for the meeting. According to what he told us later, Chet said to the executives, "I've produced a lot of hits from Studio B, but you have never promoted any of my artists. This time, I want you to listen to what could be the biggest record RCA ever had." Then he played them "The Three Bells." He went on to say, "If you don't get behind the Browns and this record, then you'll have to hire a replacement for me as A&R in your Nashville office."

You would have to have known Chet, who was normally low-key, to realize how out of character this was for him, especially when it came to standing up against the giants at RCA. But from that day forward, he was the biggest giant of them all.

Sometimes artists know when they've come across with a great recording. Sometimes though, you may just be pipe dreaming. As some wise man once said, "You make a hit the same way you make a failure." Who's to know? There are so-called experts in New York and Nashville and L.A., professional golden ears who get paid megabucks for deciding what is and isn't a hit. The truth is that on this matter, there is no such thing as an expert.

Still, there are times when a singer or producer has an uncanny feeling that something great is about to happen. Chet Atkins had that feeling when we were recording "The Three Bells." And it rubbed off on us. Chet had a good track record when it came to choosing and producing songs, and his confidence in this one was exactly the encouragement we needed. I think that on this session, the Browns sang better than we ever had before.

We recorded "The Three Bells" on June 3, 1959, and RCA released it on July 3. Not only did the song soar to number one on both the country and pop chart, it even made it to number ten on *Billboard's* rhythm and blues chart. And it became a million-seller many times over. It wasn't a "fast-burning" hit either. "The Three Bells" stayed at number one for ten weeks on the country chart and for four weeks on the pop chart. Whatever a "classic" is, "The Three Bells" fits the definition. It has become one of the most-played records of the post-war era. And for three kids who had decided to quit show business, the song turned a sad ending into a bright new beginning.

PART FOUR
Sweet Sounds

"The Three Bells" (Little Jimmy Brown)

Driving back home from Nashville, we felt as low as the old wayfaring stranger. We just knew we had reached the end of our singing career. We didn't sing while we drove, as we usually did. We didn't laugh and tell jokes. We didn't talk. And we were almost indifferent when the first reviews of "The Three Bells" came out. If we had any hope, those first awful reviews cinched it. *Cashbox* gave the song a meager B-plus; *Billboard* listed its sales potential as only three-star; *Music Reporter* even picked the other side of the record, "Heaven Fell Last Night" (a nice song written by John D Loudermilk) as the potential hit. These were absolutely the worst reviews we'd ever gotten on any song we'd recorded. A fitting end to a bitter career, I thought. "Might as well go out with a whimper instead of a bang."

It was late July, 1959, and I was seven months' pregnant. The only thing I had to look forward to was taking care of my babies and trying to live with a man who didn't care for me or his children. I was determined not to feel sorry for myself. I made myself so busy with cleaning house and taking care of little Tommy Jr. that I didn't have time for self-pity. But at night, I couldn't keep the sweet sound of singing out of my mind, out of my dreams.

About two weeks later, all hell broke loose. Momma called from Pine Bluff to say that RCA had been calling almost every hour wanting to talk to us. J. E. was back working with Daddy at the sawmill. Momma said, "Maxine, I think you better call RCA to find out what they want."

I sure couldn't guess what it was all about. Maybe RCA wanted to sue us for quitting. Instead of calling them myself, I drove down to Pine Bluff to wait for J. E. to come in. But before either of us could call back, the phone rang again. It was the RCA office in New York. They said "The Three Bells" was setting all kinds of records and was a smash hit!

"Your song is selling thirty to forty thousand copies a day!" the RCA executive said. "We've never seen anything like it!" He added that the label had all its record-pressing plants working day and night and had even hired other pressing plants to keep up with the demand.

I looked at J. E. He looked at me. Was this some joke? At that moment, they could have told us anything and we would have been skeptical. Sure, sure, sure. We've got a smash-hit; Fabor Robinson is a saint; Elvis doesn't like girls; and we're going deep-sea fishing tomorrow in the Sahara desert.

Good Lord Almighty, though, it was true. The next day, Chet Atkins called and told us to rush back to Nashville because we needed to cut an album fast to follow up on the rocketing success of our "last" single.

• • •

I was only a few weeks away from my delivery date when we journeyed back to Nashville to make the new album. I wasn't sure I could sing all the notes; I thought I might have the baby right in the middle of the recording session. Since Norma was out of school for the summer, we took her along with us. RCA titled the album *Sweet Sounds By the Browns*. It was probably put together quicker than any other album on record. With only the shortest of notices, we had to record eleven more songs. But with Chet's guidance and Anita Kerr's help, we managed to do it.

"The Three Bells," of course, was the album's lead song. Then we blended in some new titles and some old favorites to complete the package. We put a rendition of "Unchained Melody"—which had been a pop hit for four different acts in 1955—on the album. I had trouble reaching one of the high notes on the song. I was so big that I had trouble breathing even. So we decided to let Norma step in and sing that one note I couldn't reach. It was a funny kind of situation. I'd sing with J. E. and Bonnie until we hit the phrase "are you still mine " and Norma would step up, hit the note, and step back. It worked out great after a few run-throughs (although we had to hold ourselves to keep from laughing right in the middle of that deadly serious song).

All of a sudden, the Browns were in big demand. In late August, RCA arranged for us to appear with Dick Clark on *American Bandstand*. I was so close to having my baby that I couldn't make the trip. Norma took my place, and they lip-synched "The Three Bells." Just about every singer on TV was doing lip-synchs of their records then, so it went over perfectly. While J. E., Bonnie, and Norma were in New York, they had pictures made for the cover of *Cashbox*. Chet Atkins flew up from Nashville and they had this big group picture with Chet, Steve Sholes, and George Marek, the vice president at the label. I missed out on it all. But I got a beautiful little baby boy that made up for it.

After the New York trip, RCA sent J. E. on a promotional trip all around the East and down through the South. When he got back, the Browns were booked for autograph appearances in just about every big city in the country. J. E., Bonnie, and Norma went on a whirlwind autograph tour. They appeared at dozens of record hops and called to tell me they were getting mobbed everywhere they went. The executives at RCA calculated that if the records kept selling at its present steady pace, it would soon top ten million copies.

I remember the first time I heard the song played on the radio. I was changing Tommy Jr.'s diaper. When it started playing, I ran into the living room to listen, leaving Tommy Jr. on the changing table. It's a wonder he didn't roll off. Before the song was finished, I rushed to the phone and called my husband Tommy at the governor's office. Tommy was in big then with the Arkansas politicos. He was Gov. Orval Faubus's administrative assistant and right-hand man. Everybody in the world knew Faubus in those days.

"Tommy," I said, "I've just heard our record on the radio and it really sounded great."

"I know, hon," he said. "Everybody's heard it. It's all the talk out here at the Capitol. Everybody's calling me Mr. Brown."

* * *

Because the subtitle of "The Three Bells" was "The Story of Little Jimmy Brown," some people thought the song was in some way about our family. It wasn't. But on September 4, 1959, my own "little Jimmy" was born. On that same day, our song was perched at number one in all the music trade publications. Several of the magazines did cover or feature stories on the Browns. We had become, they said, a unique singing group. We were the first group ever to cross over from country to the pop charts and have a number one single on both at the same time.

RCA was planning more and bigger things for us. It was time for me to get down to serious business and get my figure back. I was so anxious I couldn't wait another minute. Jimmy was only two days old when the nurses came into my hospital room and found me down on the floor beside the bed doing exercises. It scared them half to death, and they ran out of the room yelling, "Stat! Stat!" as loud as they could. They must have thought I was having convulsions and had fallen out of bed. But I was determined to get back into performance shape.

My doctor made me wait two weeks before I went back on the road. By that time, I had a better figure than I did before I got pregnant. One thing happened while I was in the hospital that moved me deeply. I received flowers and messages from fans and friends all over the world. RCA sent me two dozen orchids. Little Jimmy was one popular baby.

Now that we had hit the big time, we needed a manager badly. We had always followed closely in Jim Reeves's professional footsteps since he was our closest friend and ally. He told us we should talk to his manager, Herb Schucher, who we knew from our European tour. Herb was willing to take us on. He hired a fellow named Bobby Brenner to book us on some of the bigger shows and to renegotiate a new contract for us with RCA.

Plunging into all this wheeler-dealer business turned out to be a mistake on our part. We were big-time, all right, but that meant we had to pay bigger commissions to more people than we could twang a guitar at. By the end of our run, we discovered we had paid out more money to managers and agents than we kept for ourselves. Still innocent kids, we learned that when you're a hot act, you're a minnow waiting for a hungry carp or catfish to swallow you.

When we were in New York, Brenner routinely took us out to eat at places like Trader Vic's and Sardi's. He was very good at getting us tickets to Broadway shows and picked up the tab on just about anything we did in the Big Apple. We were very grateful to him, too.

But, then again, he should have done all those things for us. He was making a mint off us—more than we were.

Our personal appearance tour lasted a month. I had left Tommy Jr. and little Jimmy with a housekeeper, and I was dying to see them. I found out that Tommy Sr. was never at home to look after the babies, so my folks had to keep in close touch with the housekeeper. I remember getting anxious when I called home and Momma would be a little closed-mouth about the arrangement. Finally, she told me she didn't think the woman keeping the children was treating them right. And that's what I discovered for myself when I came back home that first time.

When I got home, I found little Jimmy asleep. He looked frail, and his skin had a yellow tint. Momma had told me on the phone that when she went to the house little Jimmy seemed to be asleep too much. I wasted no time in scooping up the baby and rushing him to the doctor's office. I found out that the old bitch of a housekeeper I had hired was feeding my baby paregoric—a liquid made from opium—to keep him quiet. I almost went into hysterics. To think that I had risked my children's lives with a mean, lazy witch like that. I also found out that she had left the children by themselves sometimes at night while she slipped out to meet her boyfriend.

Had the children's father been any kind of responsible person, I wouldn't have had this problem. But instead of staying home to keep an eye on the housekeeper and our kids, he ran around even more. As far as I could tell, he never stayed home a single night. Besides that, he took most of the money I was there making to finance his harebrained schemes.

I was a big star, but I felt like the worst mother in the world.

• • •

I finally found another housekeeper and sitter, and I didn't even ask Tommy to stay home now and then. I managed to keep our show dates, hopping from one coast to the other and then back to Little Rock every extra week I got off. Being on the road now was far more hectic than exciting, and I couldn't find any enjoyment in it because I was thinking constantly about my children. If I had to do it over again, I would bundle them up and take them with me. Where they couldn't go, I wouldn't go.

I'll never forget the time we were working on the West Coast for six weeks. Our next engagement was somewhere on the East Coast, and we only had a week to get there. J. E. and Bonnie took me to the nearest airport so I could fly home and spend two extra days with my family. They had to drive back east through Little Rock, anyway, and arranged to pick me up there. I hated to leave all that driving to just the two of them, but I had to see my babies.

When I got home and walked in the door, I realized I'd been gone too long. I hugged Tommy Jr. and said, "Look, Tommy. Here's Mommy." He walked outside, looked up at the sky as if staring at an airplane and said, "No, there's my mommy." That broke my heart. When J. E. and Bonnie came through to pick me up for another extended tour I so badly wanted to say, "You two go on by yourselves. I'm never gonna go off and leave my babies again." But I did go.

All in all, 1959 was a spectacular year for the Browns. When the National Academy of Recording Arts and Sciences—that's the Grammy people—came out with their top five recordings of the year, the list was a mighty impressive one. It consisted of: "High Hopes" by Frank Sinatra, "The Three Bells" by the Browns, "A Fool Such As I" by Elvis Presley, "Like Young" by Andre Previn, and "Mack the Knife" by Bobby Darin. If you are known by the company you keep, then we were doing all right. That same year, we were nominated for a Grammy for Best Performance By a Vocal Group. Our competition was the Ames Brothers, the Kingston Trio, and the Mormon Tabernacle Choir, which won the award.

One of the big thrills we had that year was knocking Elvis Presley and his song, "A Big Hunk O' Love," out of the number one spot on the pop charts. A lot of honors were falling in our lap, too. In 1959, we won an award for Best Country Vocal Group. We even came in second to the Fleetwoods—whose big hit that year was "Come Softly to Me"—as the Most Promising Pop Group. We also won the Certificate of Achievement Award from *Music Vendor* for having "the longest consistent run by a vocal group on the official *Hit Parade* charts, 1959." (Sad to say, this award was destroyed some years later in a fire in J. E.'s Nashville office. Fire seems to have followed us all our lives.)

By September 1959, "The Three Bells" was number one country, number one pop, number ten rhythm and blues, number one on the Honor Roll of Hits and the number one bestseller in sheet music. So many dates were pouring into Herb's office that he had trouble picking out the best ones for us. I'm sure he could have booked us every day of the year if we had let him.

"The Three Bells" topped the million mark in sales at almost exactly the same time our original contract with RCA expired. You can imagine the frenzy those RCA execs were in trying to get us to sign a new one. They were afraid we would go to another record company, and I suppose if we had had some dog-eat-dog blood in us we would have sold ourselves to the highest bidder. But there was never a doubt in our minds about re-signing to RCA. We'd been a part of that family for a long time and dearly loved Chet Atkins—far too much to think of leaving him.

We instructed Herb to negotiate the new contract. For some reason that we weren't aware of, Herb allowed MCA, then a powerful booking agency, and Bobby Brenner to intervene. This made RCA furious. They thought J. E., Bonnie, and I had something to do with it. I guess they thought we were trying to put the squeeze on them. I was having coffee with Steve Sholes, RCA's manager of pop singles and albums, during one of the conventions, and he brought the matter up. He implied that we were trying to get too much and wouldn't get away with it. He said it would be easy enough for RCA to put us on the shelf if it wanted to. I discovered that he was referring to the fact that MCA had made the label rewrite the contract and give us a better deal than we had in the one we had recently signed.

I couldn't really grasp what Steve was talking about, but I knew he was angry at us. I broke into tears right there in the coffee shop of the Andrew Jackson Hotel. I tried to tell him that we had had no say in the matter at all. But I couldn't make him believe we were that innocent. This episode symbolized what usually happened to recording artists back in those days. There we were with a huge hit, making RCA bushels of money and in the end they tried to put a guilt trip on us. If you don't think a big record label can rule your very life, putting you on the shelf or taking you down like a can of beans, then take my word for it. They can, they will, they do.

Just as soon as we finished up one concert tour, we were booked for another. Herb called and had us go back to New York for some big TV shows. RCA also wanted us there for some new publicity pictures and stage costumes. The first thing we did when we hit New York was go to Sydells for fittings. I'll never forget those first dresses Bonnie and I bought. We were having them made especially for our appearance on Arthur Murray's popular TV dance show. They were beige, with rhinestones all over, and, my God, I think they weighed twenty-five pounds apiece. When they told us the price for each dress—six hundred dollars—I almost fainted. I tried my damnedest to get something cheaper, but we had already decided. Never in my life had I paid that much for something to wear. I kept thinking of those tacky brown stockings I had to wear as a kid.

To cap it off, we had to get fitted for another outfit to wear on the *Ed Sullivan Show*—and these cost five hundred dollars each! They made us another dress for the jukebox-operators convention in Chicago where we were also scheduled to perform. These dresses were purple with a slit up the middle and long flowing ruffles. I can't remember how much they cost, but it was a bundle. I don't know what J. E. bought for himself, but by the time Bonnie and I got our shoes and jewelry, we walked out of there looking like two rich bitches. And that wasn't all. RCA told us that we'd have to have our hair and makeup done for our publicity photos.

Eddie Sine's was the fanciest makeup establishment in New York. The place was full of well-to-do women and men, some in show biz, some just New York swells. Bonnie and I had a complete overhaul. It took several hours for Eddie and his assistants to change our whole look. We were quite pleased with it—even though it certainly wasn't the real us. We got ready to leave, and I went up to pay the bill. It was $853! I just stood there in a daze, counting out every last dollar I had in my purse. Bonnie didn't know how much it had cost and as we started to leave, she said, "Maxine, you didn't tip them. Let's go back and give them a good tip. We look so beautiful."

"Oh, let's not," I said meekly.

"Yes, we really should. They deserve it."

I finally got close enough to whisper to her that this beautiful makeup business had cost us $853 and that I didn't have a red cent left. "$853! $853!" she gasped. Now it was her turn to faint, and I think she almost did. We had never had anyone do our hair and faces before. This was a real first for two country gals. Talk about putting on that almighty front. If we ever got out of the Big Apple, we knew we'd be broke flat as a fritter.

. . .

The *Arthur Murray Show* was one of the very first TV shows in color. Everything about it was beautiful and first class. Murray, of course, was then a world-famous dance instructor, but his wife, Kathryn, really ran the show. She had a hand in everything. It was her lilting personality that made the show so popular. She treated us like royalty and had someone there to cater to our every need. She even had fresh flowers delivered to our dressing room. Arthur and Kathryn must have known this was our first big show because they really worked at putting us at ease. On the show we sang our hit, "The Three Bells," and afterward Kathryn presented us with our first gold record.

Back home, Momma and Daddy had swapped in their old black and white TV for a big color console, just so they could watch us in color. Since the show was taped, we got back home in time to throw a big party and watch ourselves on network TV. On the *Arthur Murray Show* we did our new single, "Scarlet Ribbons," as an encore. It was hot off the press and presented us a golden opportunity to preview it. Surprisingly, this folk-type song went over better on the show than even "The Three Bells." Kathryn raved and raved about it afterward and later sent bouquets to our hotel room with a note that said, "I'll present a second gold record to you for 'Scarlet Ribbons.' Wait and see."

. . .

We were the number one vocal group in England in 1959. Herb was hustling like mad for us. He booked us for a one-time shot on the BBC's popular variety show, *Boy Meets Girl* We flew out of New York one morning and were scheduled for rehearsals in England that night. Word must have gotten around there we were coming because a bunch of kids met us at the airport and at our hotel. In the crowd were those cute Liverpool boys again. We recognized the Beatles right away, and they grabbed our luggage and went up to our rooms with us. They said they had been working on some of the songs from our *Sweet Sounds By the Browns* album and sang a little bit for us. It was surprising the close harmony they got.

Our appearance on British television was very exciting. A lot of people talk about how reserved or stuffy the English are, but we never found that to be the case. The crowds at the show were wild and wonderful. And we always felt right at home. While we were in Europe, we didn't get to see Elvis, who was then stationed in Germany. But we called and talked to him one night. I think we stayed on the phone for way over an hour. Elvis was so excited to hear that we were on tour fairly close by that he said he would try to get a weekend pass to come visit with us. But we never could make the right connections. Elvis's father, Vernon, talked to us a long time, too, and I think he was really homesick. He told us that Elvis couldn't wait to get back to the States and back down to Pine Bluff for some of Momma's cooking.

Elvis and Bonnie talked a long time on the phone. I guess that even after all this time had passed, the old spark was still there between them. She was very quiet afterward, and I could see a tear in her eye—and a smile too. Theirs was true young love, and that's the hardest kind to get over. Bonnie told me that night that Elvis had asked her to wait for him until he got out of the Army.

• • •

When we went back to New York, we got ready for another round of TV appearances. We went on the *Jerry Lewis Telethon* and back to Dick Clark's *American Bandstand* for another guest spot. "The Three Bells" had been on Dick's top ten list for three solid months. Later, we made several other appearances on Dick's shows and became close friends with him.

One year Dick came to Nashville for the Country Music Association Convention. It was his first time to attend the convention and be celebrated on our turf. We had the pleasure of introducing Dick to all the VIPs in the RCA hospitality suite and to several of our artist friends he admired and wanted to meet. By this time, we knew almost all the executives of the various record companies. So it was a really big honor for us to say, "I'd like you to meet our friend, Dick Clark."

Finally, we got to return home for a long spell. It was October, and our new Trio Club was rebuilt and ready for a grand reopening. This time it was truly the showpiece of the South. But it wasn't the only one. My folks had built a beautiful new home right behind the club. It was so big and elaborate that Momma had to hire a full-time maid to help her keep the place clean. Daddy swore that this time he had built the club so well that nothing in it could burn. A lot of big stars came for the opening and returned for guest appearances on many occasions afterward. Momma was still cooking that great food of hers. By now, she had come to be known as the "best cook in the country" by all our fellow performers.

Because of our popularity, the Browns had run up huge expenses. But there was considerably more income too. Our first big royalty check for "The Three Bells" was for $68,000. Wow! Now that sum may not seem like much for a recording act today, but to us it was a fortune rivaling King Solomon's treasure. When I showed the check to my husband Tommy, his eyes bugged out. I finally had something to show for all the hardships and strain I'd gone through for so long.

"I want to invest this money for us," Tommy said. "I have my eye on some property."

"No, sir," I said. "I'm putting part of this money into the Trio Club."

We had a terrible argument that night and he stormed out.

I gathered my babies around me and had a good cry. It should have been the happiest moment of my life, a moment I'd been dreaming about almost since I was as little as these babies. But all I got out of it was an empty feeling of being lost and alone.

• • •

Since we were working big time TV shows now and our manager had us booked for so many nightclub dates, Bonnie and I felt we needed complete new wardrobes. We needed a lot more formal wear than the three outfits we had purchased at Sydells. Momma happened to see a newspaper ad for a "trunk showing" of original costumes made to clients' specifications. Bonnie and I had always dressed alike on stage, but finding matching dresses had become a real problem. We didn't have as much time to shop as we used to. So we went to see what all this trunk showing was all about. The man holding the showing was named Yancy. His wife was a seamstress and costume designer for strip-teasers all over the country. They owned their own costume business in Fort Smith called Helaine of Arkansas. (Helaine would later make stage clothes for singer Anita Bryant.)

After we met and talked with Yancy, he called his wife, told her of our dilemma and made an appointment for us to go see her later that week. She took all our measurements and immediately started designing some of the most beautiful dresses we had ever seen. And they were certainly less expensive than the ones we had recently bought. Each dress had long zippers, which made it easy for us to get in and out of. This was probably a strip-teaser's trademark. We loved it. Each dress had the slip or crinoline (if needed) sewed onto the waist and a built-in bra. She always made sure mine was padded. I needed that! Now Bonnie and I no longer had to search for matching outfits. All we had to do was call Helaine. She was one of the best things that could have happened to us—and at just the right time.

"Scarlet Ribbons" and "The Old Lamplighter"

Every artist who has ever had a number one record knows the anxiety and frustration of finding just the right song for a follow-up. We spent the two days before our next recording session with Chet Atkins, our producer, listening to tapes of new and old songs, trying to find a hit to follow "The Three Bells." At the end of the second day, we still hadn't decided on anything. So we all went to Printer's Alley, the Nashville entertainment mecca, for dinner and a show by Archie Campbell. We planned to go back to Chet's office afterward and take up where we'd left off.

Archie was known for his humor and always kept the crowds laughing. We never knew he had a serious side. So that night when he sang the heartbreaking ballad "Scarlet Ribbons," you could have heard a pin drop. He had the crowd mesmerized. We knew by the look on Chet's face that he was thinking the same thing we were. "That's it!" we all blurted out. "That's our follow-up!" The next day—September 24, 1959—Archie came to the RCA studio and taught us the melody and all the words.

"Scarlet Ribbons" was released in November 1959, and all the trade magazines picked it to be a hit. And it was. The great singing duo of Doyle and Teddy, the Wilburn Brothers, came up to us in the lobby of the Andrew Jackson Hotel in Nashville during Country Music Convention that year and asked us what our latest recording was. When we told them "Scarlet Ribbons," they asked, "Why in the world would you record a song that's been done a hundred times and never has been a hit?"

"That's why we did it," I said. "It's a beautiful song, and we're going to be the first to ever sell a million on it."

"I'll bet you fifty bucks it doesn't," Doyle said.

"You're on," said J. E.

Sure enough, "Scarlet Ribbons" turned out to be one of the biggest hits of 1959 and 1960. It sold well over a million records and stayed on *Billboard's* pop chart for fourteen weeks. When we saw Doyle and Teddy a few months later, they were fit to be tied. They said they wished they'd recorded the dadgum song themselves, but I don't think J. E. ever collected on that bet.

In 1958, the Disc Jockey Convention began to transform itself into the Country Music Association. The next year, the Browns were chosen to entertain the new organization at its convention. We were booked with Leon McAuliffe, Homer and Jethro, and many others. For our part of the program, we previewed "Scarlet Ribbons," and everyone in the room was completely silent. There we were in front of not just any old audience but the greats of the whole country music industry. When we finished the song, the applause rolled out, and it didn't seem like it was ever going to stop. We got a standing ovation. There are very few moments like that one, when you know you've gone beyond just your own voice and your own talent. The feeling is indescribable. It comes only once or twice in an artist's whole career and is so magical that your mind and body and soul all seem to be on perfect pitch.

We first heard our recording of "Scarlet Ribbons" on the radio while we were driving to a show on old Highway 101 in California. J. E. was asleep in the back seat, Bonnie was driving and I was talking a mile a minute to keep Bonnie awake. We were listening to some pop music station and our song came on. All at once Bonnie said, "Hey, that's us!" and pulled the car over to the side of the road. We sat there in silence listening to the song. When it was over, we got out of the car without saying a word and walked over to a cliff overlooking the big, wide Pacific. And we both started crying. The song was truly beautiful and I was so homesick to see my babies that hearing that song released all the emotions inside me. It was the first time that one of our songs got to me in a personal, hurting way.

But I couldn't go home that night. I was on the road, and I had to smile for the next crowded auditorium, the next smoky hall. Still, hearing our song for the first time was like getting a warm hug from my kids.

When I did get back home, I found out that my new house-keeper was mistreating my children. Momma had run her off and was taking care of the kids herself. When I found out what that old crab housekeeper had done to my kids, I almost died. She had made little Tommy sit for hours on his potty-chair, just because she didn't want to change him. And she had given him a bunch of filthy "funny books" to look at. Momma and Daddy had come in and found the house in a mess. So they just booted her out and stayed in the house for several days waiting for my husband Tommy to come home. When he didn't appear, they bundled up the kids and took them to their house in Pine Bluff.

I cried for a whole day. I was caught in the middle of an awful predicament. I couldn't go off and leave those babies again, but I couldn't let J. E. and Bonnie down either, especially now that we had reached the top. I began to have splitting headaches and I was in a daze most of the time. But my dear mother came to my rescue again. She got me aside one day before J. E., Bonnie, and I were to start out on another tour. She knew I was deeply troubled and that I was thinking seriously about quitting the trio for good.

"Maxine, you're not going to quit," Momma said. "Ever since you've been about as little as these younguns of yours, you've dreamed of this time, and I'm not going to let that dream die. I've already talked to Aunt Maggie, and she's agreed to come and take care of your kids while you're gone. So don't you worry any more."

Aunt Maggie was my Daddy's great aunt. She had raised a pas-sel of kids and was a godsend to me. I guess I knew all along that this was no way to raise kids and that maybe I'd pay for it someday. Life on the road does something to you. It won't ever let you be a nor-mal person. Like so many others before me, I was trying to do the impossible. Show me a singer or a picker who's had kids and I'll show you more heartaches than you'll find in all of Hank Williams's songs.

• • •

Our manager, Herb Schucher, got it into his head that the Browns should work up a full nightclub act, complete with witty talk and even choreography. Because we were getting a lot of offers, Herb and our agent, Bobby Brenner set us up with the Hollywood talent agent Harry King. Mr. King was an old-time stage performer who worked with lots of movie stars to teach them stage presence and dance. His son was Bobby Van, a great dancer in the movies and a big hit in those days teamed with Mickey Rooney.

Mr. King came to Arkansas to meet us and see us perform. He was one of the nicest men we'd ever met, kind and very patient. Later we flew out to L.A. for a month to take dance lessons from him in one of the Hollywood studios. How he ever taught us three wild mustangs to dance I'll never know, but we did manage to work up a passable routine. I had always had two left feet, especially in high heels, and I ended up having to have a plantar wart between my toes removed. But I suffered through all the practice and lessons because it was costing us a bundle—about ten thousand dollars—for that month in Hollywood. And this didn't even include the cost of arrangements. We took a song called "An Old Pair of Shoes" from our *Sweet Sounds* album and worked up a soft-shoe dance routine. In the end, we managed to perform it on stage without getting hit in the face with rotten tomatoes.

Mr. King gave us his undivided attention while we were in Hollywood. I suppose we were a great challenge for him. He was obviously determined to turn these three clumsy cows into dancers. He also invented a new routine just for us that he called Cool Square Dance. It caught on for a while back then, although not through our tripping the not-so-light fantastic. Mr. King also wrote a really fine song for our show's finale called "Glory Train." It always went over well with our audiences. Then he worked us up a neat stage arrangement to "They Call the Wind Maria," a popular "folk" tune from the Broadway hit *Paint Your Wagon*. It was the best stage number we ever performed. Later, Chet Atkins let us put it on one of our albums. We had several hits during our career, but Ralph Emery, probably the best-known deejay in country music, always told us that "They Call the Wind Maria" was the best song we ever recorded.

Mr. King treated us like family during our stay. He had us out to his house and took us to Chinatown for the most delicious food we'd ever eaten. He also showed us all the sights of Hollywood. I still cherish that time, and I can't keep from comparing that trip with that terrible one we had taken years before to Fabor Robinson's studio in Los Angeles. While we were in California learning our nightclub routine, we got booked on a number of television shows, including the popular country music series *Town Hall Party*. We saw some of our old friends there, including Buck Owens, Freddie Hart, and Tex Ritter. We also met a lot of new artists whom we came to love, among them Harlan Howard and his wife Jan, Tommy Collins, and the great Merle Haggard.

One day we had a visitor at the studio where we were rehearsing. This very nice gentleman, dressed in jeans and a cowboy hat, came up to us while we were clunking around and applauded and cheered. But this was no ordinary Hollywood cowboy. It was our childhood idol, Gene Autry. Gosh, I had worshipped him for so many years that I couldn't find my voice to say hello. Gene told us he was a fan of ours and had all our records. He invited us out to his Hollywood ranch for the day, and we had the grandest time in the world. Gene recommended that J. E. take a screen test for the movies.

"I think Jim Ed could be a big movie star," Gene said. "He's got the looks and the voice. All he needs is a few acting lessons, something I never had, but that didn't stop me from fooling a whole lot of people."

Gene insisted that J. E. take a screen test and even helped set one up. My little brother was a handsome guy, for sure, a lot more of a hunk than those Troy Donahue types who were then the rage. But J. E. never took the test seriously because he was doing exactly what he'd always dreamed of doing. So he brushed aside a studio offer to set him up with acting lessons so they could cast him in a movie. I don't think he's ever regretted passing up that chance. Just working up a fakey stage act was enough of Hollywood for him.

"Shoot," Gene Autry told him before we left, "if Elvis Presley can get by with his acting, I know you can."

"One kicker from the *Louisiana Hayride* is enough," J. E. told him.

• • •

The first chance we got to show off our new nightclub act was back home in Arkansas, of all places. We had been booked as the headliner act for the big Press Association convention in the resort city of Hot Springs. We were very excited to try everything out, especially the arrangements of our songs for a full orchestra. The arrangements had been done in Hollywood by noted arranger Norman Haas—to the tune of eight thousand dollars. We got to Hot Springs early to rehearse with the stage orchestra that was playing for all the acts. You'd have thought we were auditioning for the old *Barnyard Frolic* all over again. They told us the other acts were rehearsing and that we would be last. By that time, a large crowd was already gathering. We didn't get to go over a single song with the orchestra. We gave the orchestra lead sheets of our new arrangements, thinking surely they could read through them without any problem. It was a total fiasco. That local orchestra couldn't make heads or tails of a really professional arrangement. They messed us up so bad that it made us look like total amateurs. The crowd was polite, but we rushed off stage in embarrassment at the end. The next day the state newspapers crucified us. They said we couldn't carry a tune or follow the beat. To make matters worse, my husband Tommy had told Bonnie a joke to tell on stage. The joke was a personal, inside joke on Tommy's boss, Gov. Orval Faubus, who was in the audience. Well, the joke went over like a bullfrog loaded with buckshot. When ol' Orval Eugene came on stage later to present us with an Arkansas Traveler Certificate, he let us know he didn't appreciate that joke. He said, "I'm presenting you with this certificate, but I hope from now on that you'll stick to singing and leave the bad jokes alone." He was really ugly to us. But then, in his own way, he was ugly to a lot of people and had pulled a really bad joke on the whole state.

After that calamity, we wanted to redeem ourselves in the eyes of our state. Every chance we got, we went into the Trio Club to work on our new act to get it down pat. I still couldn't dance very well because of my bad feet, and to this day my damn "dogs" keep me from doing a lot of things I'd like to do. It's pretty awful to buy a nice outfit and have to wear brogans with it.

It seems we were constantly being called upon to do some sort of benefit show in Pine Bluff and Little Rock. But some of the local deejays were acting downright hostile toward us, a few of them refusing even to play the Browns' hit records. A little known singer—Dick Flood—had come out with a cover of "The Three Bells," and the Little Rock and Pine Bluff deejays played that version instead of ours. Then there was the fact that we had made such a name for ourselves on our European tour that when we returned to New York and Nashville, the press and a lot of fans showed up to greet us. But when we arrived in Little Rock, not a single person was there to welcome us.

Arkansas is a peculiar state in this respect. I've heard other native artists and writers make the same complaint. It never seems to change. After puzzling over this trait for years, I think I know why Arkansas puts the knock on its own so much. It's always been a poor state and maybe too self-conscious. Therefore, it cherishes a humble image—and woe unto its children if they get above their raising.

• • •

Chet Atkins came up with a wonderful song for us so we could string another hit to "The Three Bells" and "Scarlet Ribbons." He suggested we record "The Old Lamplighter," a dreamy, nostalgic tribute to the men who used to ignite the street lamps one by one in the days before electricity. It was a pop hit from 1946, written by Charles Tobias and Nat Simon, and recorded by Perry Como, among many others. It had always been one of Chet's favorite songs, and he was anxious to hear the harmony we could get on it. We recorded "The Old Lamplighter" on December 3, 1959, and it was released in February 1960. *Billboard* gave it a "spotlight," *Cashbox* awarded it a "bullseye" and every one of the other trades picked it to be a smash hit. For fifteen straight weeks it stayed on the hot one hundred charts and went on to sell a million copies. Ironically, the song only reached the number twenty position on *Billboard*'s country singles chart, though it reached number five on *Cashbox*'s charts. And there was a reason for it: politics. The flip side was a song called "Teen-Ex." The publisher, Acuff Rose, and the writers, Felice and Boudleaux Bryant, used their muscle to push their own song, and they pushed so hard that "The Old Lamplighter" suffered a great deal. We wound up with a split record. ("Teen-Ex" reached number forty-seven on the *Billboard* pop charts.) That sort of thing happened all the time in the music publishing business. It was the proverbial cutting off the nose to spite the face. Eventually, the record companies began putting the same song on both sides of the record. They did away with A and B sides in order to avoid having split records.

Our three hits in a row landed us on the *Ed Sullivan Show* on May 8, 1960. It was something of a landmark for country music, or so they said. Our old *Louisiana Hayride* buddy, Elvis, had already made his famous high-camera-angle appearance; but by then he was already being billed as the King of Rock and Roll. We were country in the best sense of the word, critics said, and were paving the way for a lot of other pickers to appear on network TV. We were back in the Big Apple again, and everyone was treating us like superstars. I was really afraid to meet Ed Sullivan because people had told us he was such an old grump. We sure got fooled. When we went into the studio to meet him, he was as kind and considerate as any host we'd ever met. We fell in love with him immediately. Pop singer Gordon MacRae and his actress wife Sheila were on the show that night, and they stayed around for our rehearsal. Afterward, they were very complimentary. Ed told us they all enjoyed listening to our harmony and our southern drawl. Ed knew we were nervous about being on his show, but he was so warm and friendly toward us that we felt as though we'd known him for years. He was certainly no old grump.

The network had these little morality snoops we called "blips," who did nothing but evil-eye you. They were the ones who tried to get Elvis to quit using his pelvis. At our first dress rehearsal, Bonnie and I had to go back to the alteration lady and have a piece of material pinned onto the front of our dresses. (We wore our blue chiffon dresses from Sydells. They had to call and have some of the same material sent over to the studio.) We were showing a little neck, not cleavage, and that would never do. We couldn't believe it, but that's how it was back then. You had to wear high-neck dresses, and you couldn't do any movements at all, not even a little rumble to the beat.

We were going to sing our current hit, "The Old Lamplighter," on the Sullivan show, and a funny thing happened to us when we started to rehearse with the orchestra. Martin Bloch was for years the prime music conductor and arranger for the show. Well, we had our arranger in Hollywood wire all the arrangements for "Lamplighter" to New York so that we'd have them for the show. But it turned out the violin arrangements were missing. Mr. Bloch told us not to worry, that he'd write the music for violins himself. He had us come in one morning so he could hear us sing. He sat there and listened very quietly as we sang through the song. Then he got up, looked all around and just shook his head. Was there something wrong?

"You kids can really sing," he said. "That harmony you get is something special. But I can't write your parts. The kind of harmony you get can't be written."

We were stunned! We had no idea what he was talking about. "Don't worry," he said. "You kids are unique, you know. Your harmony is so pure that we can't match it. But I'll work it out and it'll be great."

We found out something about ourselves from talking to Mr. Bloch. He said the kind of harmony we'd always sung naturally was called "tempering harmony" and couldn't be matched with musical instruments. A few other singers have had that kind of harmony, notably Larry Gatlin and the Gatlin Brothers, Tompall and the Glaser Brothers, and Bobby and Sonny, the Osborne Brothers. Anyway, Mr. Bloch showed that he was a real genius. He wrote sustaining chords for the orchestra's seventeen violins. When we performed "The Old Lamplighter" on the *Ed Sullivan Show*, it all came out beautifully.

We got outstanding reviews all over New York, and suddenly we weren't just "hillbilly singers." We were "sweet styled vocalists," "balladeers," and "folk song artists."

Another show we always enjoyed working in New York was *Shake The Maracas* with the great orchestra leader Vincent Lopez. It was staged at the Taft Grill and broadcast over ABC radio. The Browns had a standing invitation to be on his show every time we were in town. We loved it because he was so much fun to be around.

Immediately after the Sullivan show, we were booked solid. We worked sold-out concerts, big state fairs, and pop music tours with such acts as Ricky Nelson, Fabian, the Casuals, and the Fleetwoods. The Browns were really riding high. Nothing was going to get in our way this time.

One afternoon when we were doing a concert with Ricky Nelson and the Casuals in Orlando, I walked into Bonnie's hotel room and overheard her talking to her new beau back in Arkansas. I was happy that she was pretty stuck on this new guy. He was not only a good-looking young man, he was also a class act. His name was Gene Ring, though everybody called him "Brownie," and he was in medical school and on his way to becoming a fine doctor.

"I think we should tell them," I heard Bonnie say.

Whatever it was they were talking about, Bonnie wouldn't tell me until we got back home to Pine Bluff. I think I already knew, though, because Bonnie and Brownie were really sweet on each other. When we got back home, Brownie was there waiting for Bonnie, and they took off together for the whole day.

The next day, we were all having a big family get-together.

Brownie was there and nervous as a bobcat stuck in a culvert. After we finished Momma's great Sunday dinner, Brownie asked everyone to sit down because he had something to tell us. We could tell he was nervous. He had one cigarette burning in the ashtray, another going his mouth, and he was fumbling to light a third. Bless his heart. He was so fidgety and little-boyish that we all fell in love with him right away. All of us started laughing, and Bonnie had to yell out over the noise, "We're married!" They had eloped to Hernando, Mississippi, and I think every member of the family had already figured it out.

"Well, dadgum it," Brownie said. "You can't put anything over on this crowd!"

The whole Brown clan was as happy over their marriage as we could be. It didn't dawn on us then that a change was coming about, starting that very day. We were no longer those "cute little Brown kids that sing like songbirds." We were all grown up and starting families of our own. We had ventured out into a harder world and made our marks against some tough odds, but we all understood that the bonds that held the family together were the only source of strength we could always come back to.

It wasn't long after that our friend Elvis was discharged from the Army. Actually, it was just a few weeks after Bonnie eloped. Shortly after Elvis's discharge, Col. Tom Parker and Tom Diskin invited the Browns to a party and press reception in Memphis. It was an honor to be a part of this prestigious affair. The guests were all the VIPs from RCA, the press and some of the star's close friends. When Elvis saw Bonnie, he called her to one side and asked, "Did you wait for me?"

When Bonnie replied, "No. I'm married now and expecting a baby," he left the party and never returned. Some sad events transpired after this, but I never discussed them with Bonnie too much. She was married to a man she loved and all of us respected. I'm sure Bonnie has a lot of secret, special memories locked away in her heart forever.

We were invited back for a repeat performance on the Sullivan show but had to cancel because Bonnie was pregnant. Then we had to cancel our booking on the *Perry Como Show*. It seemed that every time we came in off the road, one of us would wind up pregnant. Remember, this was before the pill. I think poor J. E. had gotten to the point he hated to see us come home. He knew what would happen.

Over the next five years, we would go on to achieve some even higher marks in our careers. But we would also face a lot of hard choices and some bitterness before we were through. During this time, Brownie became a pillar of strength for the whole family. I don't think we could have held together without him. Through all the years that lay ahead, Bonnie would be the only one of us to keep her marriage and family happy and together. If there's one hero of this story, it is without a doubt the wonderful, patient, giving Brownie.

• • •

In 1960, the Browns were the hottest act in the country. Thanks to three bestselling records, everyone knew who we were. Our records were being played on virtually every pop, rock, and country station in America. We dearly loved most of the disc jockeys, and they loved us. But during this era, there were some newer and younger deejays who refused to play records by any country artists that had crossed over into the pop charts. It wasn't just the Browns they targeted. It was also Skeeter Davis, Faron Young, and Jim Reeves. During the Country Music Convention that year, one of the newer deejays seemed to take sheer delight in telling us he wouldn't program a crossover record on his show, and he named several of us artists he refused to play. I had to tell him what I really thought. I said, "Look, you so-and-so, none of us give a big rat's ass whether you play us or not." Well, that's all it took. He went around telling anyone who would listen that Maxine Brown was a shit ass. It didn't matter to me, though. I could never stand narrow-minded people like him.

That year, Bonnie and I thought it would be a good idea to bring along our husbands, Brownie and Tommy, since they had never been to the convention before. They couldn't believe some of the things that went on in that great old Andrew Jackson Hotel. They thought the best way to keep us from attending any more of those wild functions was to keep us pregnant and bare-footed.

It was not long after the 1960 convention that we got the news that Johnny Horton had been killed in an automobile accident. Johnny always believed in some peculiar things, among them reincarnation. He even predicted his own death—when, where, and how it would happen. The country music world had lost another great artist, and we had lost a dear friend. I couldn't sleep all that night; I kept hearing Johnny's voice singing "North to Alaska" and "The Battle of New

Orleans." The next day we learned more about the tragic accident. Johnny had been driving and was killed instantly. His guitar player, Tommy Tomlinson, and his manager, Tillman Franks, were seriously injured.

Pickers and singers are more superstitious, I swear, than ball players or racetrack plungers. Everyone we met on the road had some sort of good luck charm, and I began to believe in that stuff a little bit myself. We had gotten to know Johnny Horton and his band really well. Tommy Tomlinson used to share his lucky rock with me. He carried it everywhere he went, on stage or on the road. It was just an ordinary old gray rock with a dent in it about the size of my thumb. He had handled it and rubbed it so much that it was slick as glass. He always made me rub it before I went on stage, telling me that I was guaranteed good luck for the rest of my life. We worked with Tommy later on other shows, and he always had his lucky rock with him. He said he was holding it during the crash. The accident that took Johnny's life was one of those freakish, unavoidable things. We simply had to accept that his time had come.

But Tommy's lucky rock—somehow I could never bring myself to touch it again. I always believed that some of Johnny's superstition had rubbed off on Tommy. I never really believed in any of those things. But later on in the Browns' career, I came to believe that three was a lucky number for us. Of course we were a trio and we had a huge hit with "The Three Bells." We had three million-sellers in a row, and many of our hits were either recorded or released on the third day of the month. We joined the *Grand Ole Opry* on July 3, 1963, and I had three children. It seemed that almost every important thing we did was associated with the number three in one way or another.

PART FIVE

The Beginning of the End

Johnny Cash and Paying the Price for Crossover Records

Our schedule had become so hectic by now and our big shows were so far apart that we began to travel by chartered airplane. Some of our experiences were like scenes out of the movie *It's A Mad, Mad, Mad, Mad World*. On one occasion we chartered a plane to take us way up to Ottawa, Canada. Our regular pilot wasn't available, so we had to settle for this guy who looked like a yokel. We hadn't even gotten out of Arkansas when the plane began to bump and dip and make scary noises. Pretty soon, the Gomer at the controls yelled out, "This thang's overloaded! We'll have to throw out the heavy stuff or we're gonna go down."

Throw out the heavy stuff? Our suitcases were full of thousands of dollars worth of costumes that we'd bought at Sydells in New York! No damn way! I'd go into the side of the mountain before I'd lose that stuff.

"You're kidding, aren't you?" Bonnie asked the pilot.

"No, ma'am. We're losing altitude every minute. I'm gonna have to find us a level field to see if I can land this thang."

Pretty soon we were all nearly hysterical and the guy at the controls was shaking like a hound in a frozen ditch. Finally, Bonnie and I crawled all the way up front and J. E. piled all our luggage up against us, and we made an emergency landing on a little strip at Walnut Ridge, Arkansas. We had to go through all our things and leave most of our luggage behind. I guess being on the road gives you courage or makes you crazy, because we climbed back in that plane, and flew on up to Canada like we had good sense.

Ottawa was one of our very best stops. They treated us like royalty at the Gatineau Club where we were playing. Between shows, I learned how to play poker with the guys in the band. Bonnie and I were big hits. The Canadians must have thought we were sexy Latin American types because we had both used a new lotion on the market that applied a quick tan. When we went on stage, the guys in the audience went crazy, shouting and whistling like they were watching a strip show. But later that night when we took a bath, the damn tanning lotion started streaking. We scrubbed and scrubbed, but there was no way we could get the rest of the stuff off. The next night we went on stage looking like a couple of candy stripes. The audience roared with laughter. We had no choice but to explain what had happened. We made a big joke out of it, and the crowd just ate it up. Still, I'm not sure whether they were laughing with us or at us.

A few days later, we settled in for a weeklong engagement at the Shell House Club on Long Island. All the big wheels from RCA were there to see us, as were the top brass of *Cashbox* and *Billboard*. Opening night was a disaster. The club's orchestra couldn't read our arrangements (although the orchestra in Ottawa had no trouble with them). We managed to stumble through the first night's show, but we were embarrassed to death in front of all the bigwigs. For the second night's show, we dismissed the orchestra and did our whole act with just a guitar. All the executives in the audience scowled at this. Steve Sholes, who headed RCA's country division, let us know right away that the label was very upset with us. The only person who was kind to us during that ordeal was Bob Austin of *Cashbox*.

"Lousy bands can mess up the greatest singers," he said. Bob even stayed around for the second show, while all the fickle VIPs were beating it out of there. We got terrible reviews in all the papers. The band finally worked out the arrangements, but by then no one was around to hear and see what we could really do. It was the second time that an orchestra had put us in a bad light. Where was Spike Jones when we really needed him?

We learned a good lesson the hard way: never change from the way you were first accepted. You can never fool the fans by trying to be something you're not. We were country in the truest sense of the word and were at our best when performing with a good country band or just with our guitar.

• • •

On October 7, 1961, my sister Bonnie gave birth to her first child, a beautiful baby girl they named Kelly Lee Of course we had bookings stacked up for most of the next year. And now Bonnie began to experience the same feelings I'd had of having to go off and leave a precious little baby behind. One thing was different, though, and it was a big difference. Bonnie had Brownie, a wonderful husband who cared deeply for her and the baby, while my husband was a full-time playboy.

During the tours when Bonnie was expecting, our sister Norma came once more to our rescue by stepping in to sing with us. She had taken both Bonnie's place and mine when we were having children, and she had even taken J. E.'s place briefly, back when he was in the Army. I guess Norma was the most unselfish one of the Brown children, and I know we took advantage of her. There's an old saying that fits: if you have a free horse, you'll ride it to death.

We were booked in Syracuse, New York, this time at a snazzy place called The Three Rivers Inn. Appearing with us for that week was none other than our fellow Arkansan, Johnny Cash. Now, I must say that the young Johnny Cash, so strongly built in that black outfit and with that sexy, smoky voice, was about the most attractive man I'd ever laid eyes on. The Three Rivers Inn was located out in the countryside, so we all stayed in the motel adjoining the club. Johnny Cash was just down the hall from us. Lordy, there was something extra special about him. Every time he spoke to me, he made my heart do flip-flops. Just once, dear Lord, I kept saying to myself. I knew my husband was probably making out that very moment with one of his dolls, and I'd been faithful all this time.

But Johnny just drove me wild with those long, lanky, limber legs and the way he moved his body. Everything about him stirred feelings in me that no one had ever touched before—not even my husband. So one day I mustered some courage and invited Johnny up to my room. I'm sure we both knew the reason He was one sweet man, and I knew he was having some of the same yearnings I was. We sneaked into my room and started kissing and holding each other. Just as we were about to let ourselves go, we heard a noise in the adjoining bedroom. I looked in, and there lay my sister Norma fast asleep in bed!

After I finished writing this book, I sent Johnny a copy, not only to get his approval of what I'd said about him but to get his overall opinion as an author himself. In his reply, he said, "I have speed-read your book, and I think it's terrific. It's a book I would buy. You brought back some nice memories from the early days, and you documented them very well. I remember so well some of the things we did and said to each other that night in the hotel room in Syracuse. I especially remember the things you said. We had some great times." Time never changed my feelings for Johnny.

We worked with him again in Atlantic City. We were all booked on the boardwalk during the Miss America pageant. This time, Johnny's first wife, Vivian, was there. I remember thinking that it was a good thing; I still melted when I saw him.

Something was very disturbing about that Atlantic City date. I noticed that Johnny didn't look quite the same. I knew he was taking speed, bennies, cadillacs, L.A. turnarounds—that's what they called these pills. Lots of pickers and singers on the road used these pills until the pills began using them back. I was upset and scared about what Johnny was beginning to do to himself. Back in California, when we were learning our nightclub act, we saw Johnny and Vivian and their kids quite often, and I knew Johnny wasn't on the stuff then. I could only wonder why he had started popping. I asked Vivian about it one day, and she told me that Johnny was so nervous over this Atlantic City show that he had to have the pills or else he couldn't go on stage. The great Johnny Cash nervous to go on stage? He was the last one you'd have thought that about. But then I'd recall just how tough this business really is. No one was strong. No one was safe.

• • •

The road makes you crazy. For one thing, there weren't enough restrooms along the highways. I have a bladder the size of a hickory nut and always had to stop about every hundred miles. I learned very quickly to lose my modesty on the road. I used to carry a big, wide-mouth fruit jar on chartered planes. Once when J. E., Bonnie, and I were traveling the wide-open spaces of Colorado, I made J. E. stop so I could get out and pee behind the car. Right in the middle of it, they drove off, leaving me squatting. I screamed and hollered at the top of my lungs, but there they went, waving bye-bye. I could see their taillights disappearing miles and miles away. I stood there, about to panic. They stayed gone for over an hour. (We never learned to play simple or quick little practical jokes.) Where we'd stopped, there was a big sign beside the road that said, "Warning. Dangerous Wildlife. Stay in Your Vehicle." God, I about froze with fear. It started getting darker. At last, here came some headlights. J. E. and Bonnie drove up, both of them laughing like hyenas.

"Wanna lift?" Bonnie asked. "You should see yourself, girl. You look like a scared jack rabbit."

I wouldn't let them have the satisfaction of seeing me so afraid. "It's great out here under the big sky," I said. "Y'all go on. I think I'll just stay here."

I guess they thought they'd break me of having to stop so often, but it didn't work. Just a few more miles down that lonesome highway I made J. E. stop again. No doubt I've left a little part of me in every state of the country.

• • •

The sky is just another crazy road. One good thing about being worked as a pop group was that we got to play weeklong engagements instead of one-night stands. But we still loved doing those one-nighters because they enabled us to see many of our old friends and sing with country bands. One time we were booked on a big package show in Duluth, Minnesota, with Faron Young, Ferlin Husky, the Glaser Brothers, and many others from the *Opry*. It was twenty degrees below zero, and we were in our charted plane again—this time, fortunately, with our reliable pilot. We were flying a mile up, and I was freezing to death. I was huddled up close to the front, and I reached to turn the heater up. At least I thought it was the heater. Suddenly, there was an eerie moment of silence and then the plane started whining like a stuck pig. What I had done was turn off the engine!

The pilot just looked at me and reached to snap the engine back on. It wouldn't start. He tried again. Ice started forming on the windshield and out on the wings of that little plane. Just in a flash we were all terrified, including the pilot.

"Pull us out of this, pull us out of this!" J. E. yelled.

"I can't," the pilot said. "The damn thing won't start!"

Now the plane was swirling around and around. We were still

above the clouds but nose-diving fast. Oh, Lord, we were all going to be killed, and I had caused it!

Finally the pilot got the engine started again, but we weren't out of danger. The ice was by now as thick as stucco on the whole plane. Little by little our expert pilot guided the plane down through the clouds and got as close to the ground as he could without striking the treetops along the way. His aim was to start the ice melting. He radioed an emergency to the Duluth airport and stayed just above the trees until we sighted the landing field. When we touched down, I muttered a prayer of thanksgiving and confessed all my sins. The worst kind of fear in flying is knowing that the plane is overloaded with ice. We surely would have perished had it not been for our wonderful, heroic pilot. After that episode, I took out a lot of life insurance on myself for my children. Sooner or later, this kind of road madness catches up with everyone.

Another thing I remember vividly about that Duluth date was Faron Young wrapping his long coat around my legs to keep me from freezing while we waited on a street corner for what seemed like hours for a taxi to take us back to our hotel after our show.

• • •

Since the Browns had crossed over into three fields of music, we were able to work various types of show dates. We did country, pop, and rock shows in places ranging from hillbilly parks to elegant night-clubs to big concert halls. We worked a lot of rock 'n' roll shows and managed to come up with a fairly decent program. There were two rock songs I think we performed especially well, "Hearts of Stone" and "So Fine."

Some of the best music of all time was the rock and roll of the 1950s and early '60s. Our Momma's favorite songs were "Rag Mop" and "Sixty Minute Man." I can still see her dancing and singing to those two tunes. We worked them into our pop act because Momma insisted, and the crowd loved them. So we started singing them on our country shows as well.

Coca-Cola sponsored the Junior Miss Pageant one year in Mobile, Alabama, and they booked us with a fabulous group, the Fleetwoods. They got very upset with the promoter because we were set to close the show. They had a number one song called "Mister Blue," so we told the promoter it didn't matter to us who closed that evening. Before the show, Bonnie and I were in the dressing room with the two girls from the Fleetwoods, and one of them said, "Oh yeah, we know who you are—you're the group who tries to imitate us."

Well, we had been in the business years before they ever started and we were trying to imitate them? Several years later Chet Atkins wanted us to record "Mister Blue," but we never could get that great sound the Fleetwoods had, so we never recorded it.

One rock 'n' roll artist who made a big impression on us was Bill Haley, famous for the all-time classic, "Rock Around the Clock." At first we were nervous about working with such a big name. Then we learned he was a big county music fan, and that made us feel a little better. Since we didn't have a band traveling with us, he let us use his band, the Comets. Lending out their band was something an artist just didn't do back then, especially if he was the star of the show. We always had a special feeling toward Bill for being so kind to us.

I suppose the rock 'n' roll artist we loved working with most was Ricky Nelson. Tom Diskin booked us on an extended tour in Florida with Ricky and his band. He reminded us so much of our dear friend Elvis Presley. Since he was such a famous movie and TV star, we thought he would probably have a big head. But he didn't. Ricky was young, handsome, and very shy—but full of life. Before the tour was over, we got to know him well. We also learned that he liked to hunt with a bow and arrow. At that time, Bonnie had become a big-time hunter and was being sponsored by the Ben Pearson archery company in our hometown.

During the tour, we noticed Ricky would always phone his dad, Ozzie, after every show to give a full report on how it all went. One night, we all waited for him in his hotel suite until he finished talking to his dad, and then Bonnie surprised him with a complete set of engraved bow and arrows. This was our way of saying thanks for being our friend and for being himself.

• • •

We didn't try to have crossover records. It just happened. Of course, every country artist hoped his records would hit in the pop field because that's where the money was. If a country artist sold fifty thousand copies of a single, he had a big hit. Pop hits sold in the millions.

In those days, some of the county music disc jockeys were also would-be singers. They thought they were as good as or better than the records they were playing. And no doubt some of them were. We dearly loved many of the disc jockeys and they loved us. Even so, some of them refused to play a record if it hit the pop or rock 'n' roll charts. A few of our fellow country artists accused us of deserting country music. That was not true!

One year during the Disc Jockey Convention, Little Jimmy Dickens came up to us in the lobby of the Andrew Jackson Hotel and said, "What are you doing here? You ain't country."

We just stood there, fighting the hurt and tears. I was as mad as an old setting hen and there was no way I was going to let him get away with making a statement like that. I called him a "damn little sawed-off son-of-a-bitch." He, in turn, called me names I had never heard. Tom Perryman saw what was about to happen and pulled me away before things got really ugly, but not before I knocked the little white Stetson hat off Little Jimmy's big head. I've often wondered if Little Jimmy had a change of heart when his "May the Bird of Paradise Fly up Your Nose" became a number fifteen pop hit in 1965. It took years for us to get back on speaking terms, but I'm glad we did. I have a lot of respect for him as a legend of country music. Later on, we had the pleasure of working with him on several shows. Not only is he a great entertainer on stage, he's also great to be around offstage. There's never a dull moment when he's around. He can tell more funny stories than Mel Tillis.

• • •

The Browns appreciated all kinds of music and loved performing other artists' up-tempo songs from time to time since most of our hits were ballads. When J. E. sang Wynonie Harris's 1949 rhythm and blues hit, "I Want My Fanny Brown," at the Trio Club in Pine Bluff, the crowd exploded. I thought his rendition was much better than the original. However, some of our best friends were dyed-in-the-wool country types who refused to accept the new rock 'n' roll.

My old friend Ira Louvin, of the Louvin Brothers, was one of the country artists who resented WSM, the *Grand Ole Opry* station, playing anything but hillbilly or bluegrass music. In those days, WSM carried a live weekly show, the *Friday Night Frolic*. It was held in a studio that held only about four hundred people. Fans packed it every time. On one of the shows, the Everly Brothers got a standing ovation after singing one of their big hits. Ira complained that they were not country and that WSM never should have allowed them to perform on the *Frolic*. He got so upset that night that he threw his mandolin all the way down the hallway and broke it into a thousand pieces.

• • •

I don't think we ever realized when it was happening how big we were or how popular we had become. One thing is sure—we never let our successes go to our heads. If we had been promoted better, we would have made megabucks and probably built ourselves big log mansions in Nashville. Looking back, I wish sometimes we had. But I'm glad in many other ways that we didn't. If you were born and raised on a poor dirt farm in Arkansas, you just don't have it in you to get stuck up. I always paid heed to that old Lester Flatt and Earl Scruggs song, "Don't Get Above Your Raising."

We made a stab at getting back into the good graces of the country deejays in 1960 by recording "Send Me the Pillow You Dream On," which had been a country hit for its writer, Hank Locklin, two years earlier. Dean Martin would have a modest hit with the song in 1965, but Hank told me years later that he made more money from our version than from all the others combined. Chet Atkins, our producer, was convinced that the song could be a hit again because it lent itself so well to our kind of harmony. But we added violins, and the song came out sounding even more pop than our others. It hit the pop charts quicker than it did the country ones, but it didn't go to the top of either. Ultimately, it topped out at number fifty-six pop and number twenty-three country. It was kind of caught in the middle—a little too country for the pop deejays and much too pop for the country deejays. We found ourselves being partially boycotted on both sides. It's no fun being thought of as a half-assed.

Always on the alert for any new opportunity for us, Chet called and asked if we would consider doing a Christmas record. Would we ever! Back in those days—this was in 1964—the opportunity to record a Christmas record was very rare. It was kind of a Catch-22 situation. If you weren't selling, the labels had no incentive for letting you try what was obviously a limited-time niche market. If you had a song on the charts that was selling during the Christmas season, they didn't want you to end up competing with yourself.

Chet had a special song in mind for us, one called "Greenwillow Christmas." While it was pretty enough, it never caught on and charted. Chet let us make our own choice for the flip side, and we picked "Blue Christmas." The song had been a number one country hit for Ernest Tubb in 1949 and had not yet become identified with Elvis. So Anita Kerr went to work and came up with a beautiful arrangement. The moment it was released, "Blue Christmas" took off for us like a streak of lightning. From the reviews in the trades to the glowing early sales reports, we just knew that we had at least a Top Ten record in both the pop and country markets.

Then, all of a sudden, wham! RCA released Elvis's version. Our record immediately crashed and burned. There is an unwritten code in the business that you don't cover a friend's record since that confuses people and dilutes the market. Sure, pop artists covered every single hit the Browns had, but the practice was simply taboo in the country field. For example, Johnny Cash called us from Hollywood about this same time. He had heard that we'd recorded "Little Drummer Boy," which he'd just cut himself. He was very relieved to find out that we hadn't. He said that if we had recorded the song, he'd tell his label, Columbia Records, not to release his version. I'm sure Elvis never knew the Browns had recorded "Blue Christmas" or that it was close to hitting the *Billboard* charts.

Even though we were still riding high in the business, we had entered a frustrating period. I suppose it was brought on by our naive ways. We never thought of singing as a real business, much less as a dog-eat-dog battle. We probably sensed that there'd never be another "Three Bells" or "Scarlet Ribbons" or "Old Lamplighter," but we were giving it the old country try. A lot of country deejays were still saying we were a pop group.

We recorded a sweet little tune in 1961 called "Angel's Dolly," which was a story song that required some effort to grasp. It went over like a pregnant feather. Then Chet came up with another one that he just knew would be a great for us, "You Can't Grow Peaches On a Cherry Tree." The record got picked by all the trades, but for some reason RCA wasn't pushing the Browns. So we wound up getting covered again by a pop group, Just Us, which enjoyed a moderate hit with the song in 1966 under the title "I Can't Grow Peaches On a Cherry Tree."

Around this same time, we recorded "Rhythm of the Rain" and took the tape of it to Ralph Emery to listen to. Always the uncanny judge of the public taste, Ralph said, "You can bet the farm on this one. If ever I have listened to a smash, this one is it." Ralph also warned us not to let RCA bury the song in an album as it did with "They Call the Wind Maria." We tried, but we found out quickly that we no longer had any pull with the label. Promising though it seemed, "Rhythm of the Rain" got buried on the backside of our album, *Our Kind of Country.*

Years earlier, we had been invited to join the *Grand Ole Opry* but hadn't been able to accept. When *Opry* manager Ott Devine extended the invitation again, we jumped at it. The Browns joined the *Opry* on July 3, 1963, fulfilling our lifelong dream. In retrospect, we probably should have moved lock and stock to Nashville in the beginning, but our home ties were so strong that we honestly never saw ourselves as part of that scene. We started recording with a real country sound again. And it was fun being members of the *Opry* and working with Ott. He was a jewel. The first thing he warned Bonnie and me about was our low-neck dresses. There were two no-no's on the *Opry*: cleavage and drums. Things have changed since then, of course. I recently watched a TV broadcast from the Opry, and there were lots of drums and some girls who looked like they were trying out for the Playmate of the Month.

WSM had an early morning radio show called the *Waking Crew.* Even though we had to get up before the chickens to do this show, it was worth it, because they had the best orchestra I'd ever heard. We were the first act from the *Grand Ole Opry* to go in with all its arrangements and sing with this wonderful orchestra. They always said our arrangements were written with such simplicity that no one should ever have any trouble reading them. We were invited back time after time, and I used to think how wonderful it would be if we could take the whole crew on tour with us.

We were working now on the road with such stars as Buck Owens, Jimmy Dean, and Roy Clark. Roy was probably the most talented star we'd ever performed with, and he was just starting his rise to the top. In one big show we were doing, the Browns had top billing. Naturally, we were set to close the show. Roy came on just before we did, and the crowd absolutely loved him. When we got on stage the crowd was still chanting "Roy, Roy, Roy." We did everything we could think of to get the crowd's attention, but it still kept shouting for Roy. Red-faced, we summoned Roy back on stage, and he wowed them for another hour before we finished our part of the show. There are some wise rules to follow in the business: always leave 'em laughing, never let 'em see you sweat, and never ever follow Roy Clark.

• • •

Talent comes at you sometimes out of the dark. My Momma discovered Conway Twitty. Tom Perryman put Elvis on the right track. Jim Reeves helped us get started. One raw winter night way up in a small town in Iowa, we found ourselves stranded after a show. We were the last to go on. By the time we finished, all the others artists had left, and the taxis had stopped running. This skinny kid came up to us and asked if he could drive us to the airport in Waterloo. He was a godsend, and we offered to pay him triple his gas mileage. But he wouldn't take a dime.

"All I want you to do is listen to me sing one song," he said. "If you think I'm any good, will you send my tape to Chet Atkins?"

Sure kid, sure, sure. We were so tired and sleepy that we began to doze off as he started singing. His sound woke us up. His voice was pure and clean as the sun, and the song he sang was truly a hurting, haunting one: "Five hundred miles, five hundred miles/I'm five hundred miles away from home." Driving us along in his old junker car that terrible winter night, the young man nearly had us in tears.

We took his tape and promised that we'd be sure Chet got it. We also promised to put in a good word for him wherever we could. Then a couple of years and a million miles went by. I think we were out somewhere in the far west, dozing to the radio, when we heard this deejay say, "Let's give a listen to Bobby Bare and his latest single, 'Five Hundred Miles Away From Home.'" I think we were as thrilled to hear Bobby singing as we were the first time we heard ourselves on the radio.

Bobby is one of the most underrated artists in the business, sort of the Pete Seeger of country music, you might say. We always felt a special kinship with him because of the time he rescued us. Later we worked with him a lot on the road. And during the terrible ordeals I was to face at the painful end of my own career, Bobby was there to offer kindness and comfort.

Bobby had some other wonderful hits besides "Five Hundred Miles" during his early folk music period, one of which was "Four Strong Winds." Some time after we met him, we were getting ready for a recording session. Chet had given us an acetate recording with two songs on it to listen to. We worked on the first song awhile, then we flipped the acetate over and found "Four Strong Winds." Lord, it was a great song, and we started working it up. When we went in for our session, we started warming up with "Four Strong Winds."

"Wait," Chet said. "Where'd you get that song?"

"It was on the acetate you gave us, Chet," J. E. answered.

"Well, now, Bobby Bare has just cut this song for his next single. You want to go ahead with it?"

No, we didn't. We couldn't. But since we had learned it so well, we went ahead and cut the song for our next album. But we let Bobby have the single. And I'm glad we did, for his version is now a classic. I know a lot of established acts might have been tempted to push their version of a song ahead of that of a newer artist. Did I say "tempted"? Shoot, they'd have jumped on it like a cat on a one-legged mockingbird. But not the Browns.

"Mommy, Please Stay Home with Me"

I came home from a tour one time to discover that my husband Tommy hadn't set foot in the house since I'd been gone. Aunt Maggie was still taking care of my kids. She told me she knew Tommy had a serious girlfriend staked out somewhere. I didn't want to believe it. I still thought he would be happy to see me. But he didn't come home until almost daylight. He gave me a little hug and I could smell the liquor on his breath.

"Hon, I'm so proud of you," he said. "I know y'all are going great guns now, and I was wondering if I could borrow a little money from you. Hon, we're gonna make a killing on that cemetery development I'm working on, but I need to put in the curbs and gutter."

When I was leaving a few days later, he came out to the airport where J. E., Bonnie, and I were waiting to board our charter. I thought he had come to say goodbye. "Maxine, hon," he said, "I need three thousand dollars by tomorrow morning. I need it in the worst way. I know you've got lots of money." I guess I was so embarrassed to see him begging for money that I wrote him a check. He had been hitting me up all along and taking just about all that I made singing. As we were getting on the plane, J. E. said to me, "It's stupid to give him money. You know what he'll spend it on, don't you?" I couldn't answer, for Tommy's behavior that day was nothing new. He was draining me in more ways than one.

I took off in the plane, unaware that Aunt Maggie was trying desperately to get ahold of me. Little Jimmy had pulled over the coffeepot and had scalded himself all over his body. I didn't learn the whole truth until I came home again. It seems that Tommy had gone back to the house after leaving me at the airport and had walked in just after the accident had happened. Aunt Maggie told me later that she begged and pleaded with Tommy to hurry up and rush Jimmy to the hospital. Aunt Maggie couldn't drive a car, and, besides that, she was in a panic. But Tommy, being the self-centered father that he was, had to pretty himself up before going out in public. He let our baby suffer while he took a bath, shaved, and pampered himself. All the while, Jimmy was crying and Aunt Maggie was pleading for him to hurry. It almost killed me when I got home and saw Jimmy. He was so burned all over his body that he couldn't stand to wear a diaper.

This time, I'd had it. I was so furious and guilt-ridden that I could have jumped into a boiling vat myself. After I calmed down, I decided to take the kids and leave Tommy for good. First, though, I had to know the real truth, so I hired a private detective to follow Tommy. It didn't take him half a day to find out that Tommy had his own apartment. It was located above a paint store on Seventh Street, near the State Capitol where he worked. He was living with his own little tramp, and I was the one paying for his love nest.

I made myself go to a lawyer and begin divorce proceedings. When Tommy found out about it, he came crawling to me, begging, and promising to straighten himself up. But it was no use. I could never erase from my mind all the mean things he had done to the kids and me. In all these years, he'd come near me only during his drunken fits or when he wanted money. What passed for lovemaking was about as warm as soured wine.

By divorcing Tommy, I thought I would never have to worry about him again. I knew I would never trust him. For the first time since we were married, I began feeling something akin to peace of mind. And then I got sick and sicker. I felt those stirrings inside my body that could mean only one thing: I was pregnant again. Oh, Lord, oh Lord. I had two babies already, a career that demanded all my time and more, and I was going through a divorce.

Foolish me, I let Tommy convince me not to continue with the divorce. I did take my stand, though. I stopped giving him the money I was making from my singing. This made him furious with me. But after he had cooled off, he started crying and saying he was sorry. He pleaded for us to try again for the sake of the children.

Tommy never knew how to be a father to his two little boys.

Maybe it was because he was an only child and had never been around kids. But he was gone from home all the time. When he was around the kids, he drank constantly. My oldest son, Tommy Jr., was scared to death of his dad.

I didn't go back living with Tommy, but he came around now more than he did when we were supposedly happily married. He didn't let up on me, however. I knew he was still using his apartment and seeing his girlfriend. It wasn't a week after our blowup before he started asking for money again. Soon after she heard about our separation, Tommy's mother began harassing me and threatening to take my babies away from me. "How could you bring the disgrace of divorce on the family?" she moaned. "You'll lose those children. You're not a fit mother."

I thought Tommy's mother would be happy we were getting a divorce since she never considered me good enough to marry her son. And as far as those babies were concerned, she had to be the worst grandmother in the world. She was so caught up with her social life that she never had time for our children.

The next time I had to go to Nashville, I took Tommy Jr. with me. We were recording a religious album called *The Brown Church Hymnal.* One of the songs we cut was "When They Ring Those Golden Bells for You and Me." Little Tommy sat right on the floor beside me the whole time we were in the studio, and he didn't cause a single problem, not one little whimper. Later that night I woke up and saw him sitting on the foot of my bed. He was rocking back and forth and singing, "When They Ring Those Golden Bells for Mommy and Me." I cried my eyes out as I held him close to me. "Momma," I kept saying to myself, "what in the world's going to happen to me and my young 'uns?"

All my nerves shook loose at once, and I just sat there trembling. Old scenes of misery flooded my mind, but I knew I had to go back home and plead with Tommy to quit drinking so we could try and make a home for ourselves and our children. I told Tommy I would quit show business altogether if we could save our marriage. Tommy didn't want me to give up my singing career—he never did—but he did promise to quit drinking. But it wasn't a week until he started again.

I didn't want another baby. The idea of going through another pregnancy, with all the misery between Tommy and me, was too unbearable to think about. Each day I'd wake up and the nightmares in my mind would start once more. One day, while I was almost out of my mind, I climbed up on the roof of my house. I'm not sure what I thought I was doing. All I knew was that my life had become pure hell, and I felt something driving me to escape. I stood up there for a long time, crying and shaking all over. Then something inside me began to form words in my brain. Maybe it was my mother's voice, or maybe it was the spirit of my sweet little brother we had lost so many years ago. At that moment, I knew I had to live and that the little baby growing inside me had to live too. It was God's gift to me, and it would be a special life, as beautiful as any song ever sung. When that little baby was born a few months later, I think I was the proudest mother ever. I named her Alicia. Now a beautiful woman, Alicia has been a source of joy to me all her life.

• • •

Aunt Maggie stayed on to help me with my three babies, and I tried to find ways to remain at home. For long stretches of time, the children and I were almost a family. Then I'd have to go on the road again. There was very little fun left in it. Oh, when we were in Nashville, we loved going out to eat with Chet at Ireland's, a favorite hangout of country music people. When we were back home in the spring, sometimes we'd spend a day at the races in Hot Springs with Momma and Daddy. They loved going to the track, and Momma could always pick the winners. One time after the races, we went to the Vapors Club where pop crooner Frankie Laine was singing. Because we had played shows with him, he called us out of the audience. It became a big to-do, and a lot of hangers on moved in on our party. People did this to us all the time, leaving us with huge checks to pay. But it was part of the business, part of putting on that almighty front. This time it backfired. After the expensive dinner and the floor show were over, Momma, Becky (Jim Ed's future wife) and I sat alone without enough money among us to pay even for one meal, much less the dozen or so that the freeloaders had added on to our tab. It was one of the most embarrassing moments of our lives.

"You girls stay here," Momma said. "I'm going to take what little money that's left in my purse and see if I can't run it up." She meant that she was going into the gambling room at the Vapors to try the dice table. In those days, Hot Springs was a wide-open casino town, almost as big as Vegas. Each nightclub had its own slots and gambling tables. She was spunky enough to try anything to get us out of that awful bind. Becky and I sat there for over an hour, toying with our coffee and stalling. We knew that if something didn't happen soon, we'd have to call Daddy or J. E. to come bail us out.

Bless her heart, Momma came back into the club clutching a whole fistful of greenbacks. She had almost cleaned the dice table out and had won more than enough to pay the bill. She led us out of there, laughing and cussing the ones who'd left us in the pinch. I remember her saying, "Always remember, girls: never trust family or friends. They'll screw you every time." I never fully realized until many years later how true those words really were.

· » ·

We were on our way to fill a date in Atlanta when, just outside Little Rock, we had a car wreck that had devastating aftereffects. Bonnie was driving and some lunatic whizzed too close and forced our car off the road and into a ditch. The impact threw Bonnie's head into the sun visor and knocked her unconscious. J. E. and I managed to get the car back on the road, and we rushed Bonnie to the emergency room in Pine Bluff. She had suffered a pretty serious concussion, but she seemed to revive well enough for us to go on down to Atlanta.

Not long after the accident, Bonnie began having problems with her inner ear. She would be singing and all of a sudden she'd stop, grab her ear and whisper to me that she was upside down. She'd forget the words to the songs and suffer dizzy spells on stage. She underwent treatment for a while, but the doctors could never sense the seriousness of her problems. Finding no relief, she became moody and sullen, which was not at all like Bonnie. Pretty soon, she began taking her problem out on us. She was so irritable we could hardly stand being around her. Instead of improving, she seemed to be getting worse.

I know now that this was the beginning of the end of our trio. I'm sure some of her problems stemmed from the accident, but a bigger problem had surfaced in this emotional time. She had babies of her own now, Kelly and Robin, plus a wonderful husband who was busy with his medical practice. Her problems were the same ones I'd had for years, leaving the kids with a stranger and worrying about them every minute you're gone. Every departure from home was sheer torture and left us both full of guilt. Neither of us could any longer feel a tinge of happiness when we walked out on that stage, and this left J. E. caught in the middle.

It all crystallized for us in October 1963 when we recorded a song called "Mommy, Please Stay Home with Me." It was that great old Eddy Arnold song we'd listened to as kids. Bonnie cried all the way through that session. I cried too, and before it was over, all the musicians were sitting there with tears rolling down their faces. There was so much pain in that recording that we never dreamed it would wind up as such a beautiful cut. It came out in our album called *Grand Ole Opry Favorites,* which was nominated for a Grammy in 1964 as Best Performance by a Vocal Group, along with entries by the Beatles; Peter, Paul, and Mary; The Double Six of Paris; and the Four Freshmen. The Beatles won for "A Hard Day's Night," but in being nominated in this category, the Browns had taken country music into the very heart of pop territory.

It's strange how one recording session comes back so vividly. "Mommy, Please Stay Home with Me" was so maudlin that it was wonderful. I still see all the session people: Chet Atkins making sure everything was just right, Floyd Cramer at his piano, Jerry Reed playing the guitar, Ray Stevens, Jerry Kennedy, my brother J. E., and my sister Bonnie. Our youth and our dreams had all run a race, a mean obstacle course, and we understood then that things would never be quite the same again.

PART SIX
The Last Hard Road

Just a Matter of Time

You hear a song you like so much it seems to become a part of your life and soul, you worship the ones singing it, and you buy all their records and go to all their concerts. When they break up, a little piece of you dies with them. That's why you see people driving along and listening to the radio with tears in their eyes. A golden oldie experience, they call it. We knew it was only a matter of time now until the Browns were going to have to call it quits as a trio. Still, we had a few more hits to make before we were through—and some more bad luck, just to keep things on an even keel.

We had always been popular in England, and after our latest run of hits we were voted the number one group in the United Kingdom. Our manager booked us for another tour abroad. This time we were going back for a series of concert dates with all our musical arrangements in tow. We were the only act on the show besides the London Symphony Orchestra. But we drew huge crowds. Generally, we performed our choreographed routine and then did another fifteen minutes raw—just the three of us and a guitar. The fans seemed to love it. RCA in London treated us like royalty the entire time we were there. They made sure we had everything we wanted or needed, and I'm sure they went out of their way to keep us entertained. I remember them taking us to see our first soccer game. We had never heard of soccer, but it was the top sport in England. I think J. E. and Bonnie enjoyed watching those guys playing kick football, but, for myself, I much preferred indoor sports. Since RCA went to so much trouble getting us special seating for the game, I managed to sit there and pretend I was having the time of my life.

After our final engagement in Liverpool, we found a park bench adjoining the depot where we waited for the train to take us back to

London where we could catch our flight to the good old U.S.A. It was late at night, and we were dog-tired. My mind must have been five thousand miles away, because after we got on the train, I realized I had left all our expensive arrangements on that park bench. I went into hysterics. Thank goodness, J. E. kept a cool head. He had the conductor radio back to the Liverpool station to have someone pick them up and put them on the next train to London. We waited at the London station the rest of the night and damn near missed our plane. But there was no way we'd leave England without our arrangements. Finally, they came, and we were off. (After this experience, we made copies just in case something like this should ever happen again.)

Flying back to the States, we had one of the most horrifying experiences of our lives. Way out over the ocean, the plane started acting up. We began bumping up and down like we were riding a mechanical bull. Things didn't get any better, and pretty soon the stewardess was saying, "Ladies and gentlemen, there's no cause for real alarm. But at this time, we would like to ask you to put on your life jackets." Life jackets? Lord, we were going to crash into the damn ocean!

I looked out my window and saw lights from boats right down there below us. Then an eerie silence set in. All the plane's engines had quit. Everybody was yelling and screaming and trying to get those stupid life jackets on. I looked around and couldn't see Bonnie anywhere. We started hollering for her as loud as we could. Then I heard her voice somewhere below me. She was down under the seat—praying. The captain's voice came over the speaker, telling us all to remain calm. Sure, Jack. I screamed to the high heavens. The captain assured us that if we did have to ditch in the ocean, there were ships close by to pick us up. Somehow, I didn't feel very reassured.

I started praying and confessing all my sins. I asked God to forgive me for sneaking out in my old car back when I was a teenager. I didn't mean it, God, when I drank that much whiskey on the road with all those horny pickers. I even promised to give up my fantasies about Johnny Cash if only God would spare us. Oh Lord, why didn't I ever learn to swim? I'm not sure my prayers got through, but somebody's did, for suddenly the plane's engines started working again. They told us later that the plane came within a hundred yards of going into the water. I never did get that damned life jacket on, and

Bonnie, being too amply endowed, never did ever try to get hers on! I still see those imaginary headlines in my nightmares: "Plane Goes into Drink ... All Aboard Saved Except Brown Sisters ... Life Jackets Found Floating Nearby."

We thought of all the near mishaps we'd had over the years and how every time the Browns had a chance to do something big or make any money, something would always happen to prevent it. Maybe those things were omens. Maybe this mishap with the plane meant that the good Lord was trying to tell us something.

• • •

My marriage finally reached its long and bitter end. Tommy and his family were threatening to go to court to take my children away from me, claiming, of all things, that I was an unfit mother. I loved those kids more than life itself, and in the next few years I would have to fight like hell to keep them. Tommy and I fought each other in court for three years until finally the divorce was granted. Tommy's lawyers had succeeded in beating me down to nothing. I was at the breaking point, so I went ahead and signed the papers. I had spent all I'd ever earned on Tommy's harebrained schemes and investments. When it came time to go to court, he pleaded poverty, and the judge believed him. Tommy agreed to pay me three hundred and fifty dollars a month child support and pay for the kids' education and medical insurance. But he never kept his word. In the end, he contributed very little to his children's welfare. The day after the divorce was final, however, he went out and bought himself a new airplane and a Harley Davidson motorcycle.

I learned the hardest way that the courts are a man's world where women don't usually stand a cotton-picking chance. I had made my bed hard and I've had to lie in it the rest of my life. It's really ironic that I had made it in a business famous for songs about worthless, boozing, whoring men, and here I was, trapped up to my neck in it. You tell me country isn't true!

• • •

J. E. and Becky were married and expecting their first baby. They had decided to move to Nashville. After all these years, J. E. had finally decided to get into show business full time. None of us had ever considered ourselves in the business for good. We'd had so many ups and downs and still felt all those ties to home. With J. E. in Nashville, it wasn't going to be easy to keep the Browns going. Most of the time Bonnie and I stayed in Arkansas and drove over to Nashville to be on the *Opry* with J. E. on Saturday nights. Sometimes we'd have to drive or fly to meet him for the other shows we had booked.

J. E. and Becky bought a home in Iroquois Estates in Brentwood, a classy Nashville suburb. Right after they moved there, Bonnie and I came in to see their beautiful home, do the *Opry* and leave on Sunday for a series of one-nighters in Georgia and Florida. After the *Opry*, I went on back to Brentwood with J. E., while Bonnie stayed behind to go with songwriter Hank Cochran to a party. Hank said, "Don't worry, I'll bring Bonnie home in a couple of hours." J. E. and I got up early Sunday morning to get ready for our trip. But there was no Bonnie! Where in the world was she? Old worrywart me. I became frantic, sure that something dreadful had happened.

It had just gotten daylight when she and Hank drove up the driveway. When she told us what had happened, J. E. and I couldn't stop laughing. She said that she and Hank had to wait until daylight to find the house. She remembered what it looked like, but she couldn't recall exactly where it was located, its street address or J. E.'s phone number. She said they searched around all night. Finally, Hank found a phone booth and woke up everyone he could think of who might know where J. E. and Becky lived or what their new phone number was. Well, I reckon if I had been out to a party with Hank Cochran, I wouldn't remember much either!

With my divorce final, I was a free woman for the first time since I was a young girl. To tell the truth, there hadn't been any romance in my life since I could remember. That sort of thing just didn't enter my mind. Having kids, fighting with a drunken husband, and trying to keep up with the demands of a singing career all kept me from having any sort of personal life. There was one brief episode, though, that got hold of my heart and wouldn't let go. His name was Phil Regan, and he was a player for the Detroit Tigers. I fell head over heels for him. And for a brief time, it was all hearts and roses.

I met Phil in Minneapolis at a nightclub we were working. It was a weeklong engagement, and one night some players for the Minnesota Twins and the Detroit Tigers came to one of our shows. Several of the players came backstage after the show and introduced themselves. Bonnie and I thought they were the best-looking guys, and here they all were in our dressing room. I remember thinking that this Phil Regan was about the handsomest man I'd ever laid eyes on. He was kind of bashful, and I couldn't keep my eyes off him. Lord, it was love at first sight. I guess the feeling was mutual because he called me for a date the next night. During our week in Minneapolis, Phil and I saw each other every spare minute. The Twins team invited us to their game on Sunday, and we even sat in the dugout during the game and had our picture made with some of the players. The picture appeared on the front page of the Minneapolis newspaper the next morning. There I stood, like a wide-eyed kid at the carnival.

A couple of months passed, and things started to cool down between Phil and me. It was the same old story, I thought: here today and gone tomorrow. But this time luck was on my side. We had been a pretty big hit at the club in Minneapolis, so they booked us for a return engagement the same week that the Tigers were back in town. When I got into my hotel room, I had a message from Phil. He wanted to see me again. He was coming to the club where we were performing. We were there a whole week, and it was wonderful, the greatest time of my life. I'd never met a young man like Phil. He was sweet and kind and perhaps the most gentle man I'd ever met.

On our last night there, we planned a big party after our last show, and it was a real blast. We went back to the motel to get packed up for some show dates in Canada. Our good friends, Ray and Marilyn Firnstall, were there with Bonnie, J. E., Phil and me. We were having such fun that we lost all sense of time. I guess we must have had one nightcap too many, for we decided to take a dip in the motel pool, and, hell, I couldn't even swim. I've never been as giddy since—or as hungover. We said our goodbyes and in the harsh light of day started our long drive north.

The love bug had smitten me harder than I would admit. All I wanted to do was stare out the car window and see Phil out there somewhere on the mound, winding up, pitching and smiling as if to say, "Here's another strikeout just for you, Maxine." I know it was corny, but it was beautiful too, especially now that we were apart and not certain if we'd ever get together again I know we listened to the ball game on the car radio because Phil was supposed to pitch that day. But he never came into the game! We listened to the whole game, but there was no mention of Phil. Lord, had I kept him out too late and gotten him in trouble with his manager?

That drive up to Canada was horrible. When we checked into our hotel, I had a note from Phil. The Tigers had sent him back to the farm club for a week, and it just so happened that the farm club was in the same city where we were playing! Talk about your freakish stroke of luck! And what a week we had! Looking back, I guess I was lucky to have a good, juicy love affair, if only for a brief time. Our luck didn't hold, and we found ourselves pushed apart by circumstances from then on. We still managed to see each other every now and then, a few stolen hours between shows and seasons. Phil got traded to the Los Angeles Dodgers as a relief pitcher, and then we just sort of drifted apart. As I said in "Here Today and Gone Tomorrow," "absence never makes the heart grow fonder."

· · ·

Jim Reeves wanted to go back to Germany for a concert tour and asked us to go along. This time it was a well-planned tour with lots of publicity. RCA worked with our agent to make it all run first class. We played most of the Army and Air Force bases over there, plus some personal appearances. It was all very wonderful. This time, no one acted up enough to get us threatened with jail.

The most enthusiastic audiences in the world are servicemen. Jim Reeves was the best entertainer I ever knew, and he certainly knew how to entertain those guys. Since Bonnie and I were the only girls on the show, we naturally wowed them. They never stopped whistling and yelling the entire time we were on stage, except when we sang "The Three Bells." Then they would get as quiet as mice. I don't know how many times we were invited to join them for lunch in their mess hall, and we loved it. We were always craving beans and cornbread, and they never tasted better than they did there.

· · ·

When we got back to the States, we were in big demand. We played a lot of state fairs. One I remember distinctly was in Ohio. The bandstand where we were performing was close to the lion's cage, and when we started singing "The Three Bells," those lions started to roar. We stopped and started over, but sure enough those lions joined right in again. It was like those lions wanted to be a part of our act, and the crowd loved it! We must have started the song six or seven times, and every time we had that same lion chorus. We finally gave up without finishing the song. It's funny that the lions never roared on any of our other numbers. Maybe there was something in the way we harmonized that got to the big cats. So much for the old saying that music soothes the savage beast. Perhaps we should have added them to our act.

Since we didn't travel with our own band, we'd always have to use a local group and rehearse them like hell to get our songs right. One time when we appeared at a state fair, no band showed up to back us. The promoter had goofed. Hank Snow, the Singing Ranger, was booked on the same show with us. Seeing our dilemma, Hank said we could use his band. He didn't have to do that for us, but he knew we were desperate. He was a jewel about the whole thing. Hank also did something else that country artists seldom do for each other. He sent us telegrams of congratulations after "I Heard The Bluebirds Sing" hit big and when "The Three Bells" reached the million mark in sales.

Hank Snow was one of the true gentlemen of our business, but I couldn't say the same for Don Gibson. We had just finished recording a session for our religious album, *The Old Country Church,* and Don had the session immediately afterward. Bonnie and I had fixed ourselves drinks to celebrate finishing our session and decided to stay around the studio to hear some of Don's recording. His session was barely underway before he and Chet Atkins got into an argument. Now Chet was a master at producing great records, and we all knew that Don wasn't doing the right thing. He had come to the session drinking and simply couldn't carry a tune that night.

The argument raged on, and we found ourselves kind of trapped there in a very uncomfortable situation. We saw that Chet was trying to reason with Don so that the session wouldn't be a total loss. He kept trying to get Don to let the band lay down the sound tracks so Don could come back and do his vocals when he was in better shape. But Don wouldn't hear of it. He acted like he'd been insulted. Before we knew it, Don shoved himself right up against Chet and slapped the fire out of him right in front of everybody. Don had his girlfriend with him and she was throwing a few punches herself.

Chet Atkins was then and until his death probably the most respected artist/producer in Nashville. He was also one of the most mild-mannered men in the world. He just stood there, a big gash on his lip and his nose streaming with blood. Bonnie was closer to them than I was. She turned fire red and rushed at Don. Nobody was going to mistreat Chet Atkins, at least not in front of us. Bonnie threw her drink in Don's face! And she told him and his girlfriend to get the hell out of there before she clawed their eyes out. Don had enough sense to leave.

All Chet said to us was, "Well, there's no use wasting three hours of session time. Maxine, you and Bonnie put your drinks down and get some coffee." He told us to get some songs ready and we'd use Don Gibson's wasted time. So we went ahead and recorded some more songs, and we were lucky enough to have the Jordanaires there to back us up. They were Elvis's special back-up group and an absolute dream to work with. They sang on "Taller Than Trees," "Mocking Bird" and "Jezebel" for our album entitled *The Old Country Church*. That project got us nominated for the 1967 Grammy award for Best Sacred Performance alongside Elvis, Dottie West, Red Foley, and George Beverly Shea. But Elvis beat us with *How Great Thou Art*. Still, we were proud to see our old friend win his first Grammy. No one deserved it more.

We always thought it was such an honor to sing with the Jordanaires, and all thanks go to Bonnie for throwing her drink into Don Gibson's face. (I'm sure Don regretted this incident many times. Easygoing Chet went on produce many hits for him.) After the session was over, the Jordanaires called Elvis in Memphis to tell him they had just recorded with the Browns. They told us that Elvis talked about us often and would sometimes say, "Give me some Brown sound" when he was recording a sweet ballad or a gospel song. For years they thought he meant James Brown, the soul singer. Then one night Elvis happened to mention Bonnie, and they suddenly realized he had meant *the* Browns.

Bonnie talked with Elvis a long time that night, and he invited us to come by Graceland on our way home from Nashville that following Sunday. She said Elvis seemed excited about seeing us again and said we had a lot to talk about. No one could have been more excited than we were as we drove up to the big iron gates of Graceland at the exact time Bonnie told him we would be there. But when we arrived, the gatekeeper refused to let us inside. We told him we were expected and pleaded with him to at least call Elvis to let him know we were there. But he wouldn't listen to anything we had to say. In fact, he was downright rude and hateful to us. We left with the heaviest of hearts, wondering what happened. Had we fallen victim to Elvis's Memphis Mafia (as everyone called them), the rude gatekeeper or who? We felt certain that Elvis never knew we were there, and I'm sure he wondered why we didn't come by as we had promised.

There was one other time that Bonnie threw a drink in someone's face. Charley Pride was just breaking into the big time with his first release on RCA. We met him at the disc jockey convention in Nashville. All of us were in the RCA suite at the Andrew Jackson Hotel, having a good time and getting to know Charley. Then one of the deejays started picking on him. No one paid much attention at first to the obnoxious deejay. But then the guy started throwing slurs. "You're a black Negro, ain't you? A black one! Well, you don't have no business in country music. It's not for niggers, you know. Why don't you go on back to Mississippi and pick cotton?' The loudmouth didn't see Bonnie come up to him. She stared him right in the eye and splashed her drink right in his face. She told him off good too, and the jerk didn't waste any time getting out of there. After that, we always made it a point on the road of telling people what a great new voice and talent country music had in Charley Pride.

From time to time, we got the opportunity to help other artists get started. We'd already brought Bobby Bare to Chet Atkins's attention, and quite often Chet would give us tapes to listen to for our opinions. The funniest one we ever heard was comedian Don Bowman singing "Chit Atkins, Make Me a Star." One time we met this sweet gal in the lobby of RCA trying to get up her nerve to go in and talk to Chet. After we listened to the tape she made, we were convinced she had what it took to become one of the biggest stars in country music. Her name was Dottie West, and she turned out to be about my best friend when I later moved to Nashville. Chet always wanted to know what we thought about other artists. He had the genius to know the difference between real talent and a flash in the pan. As our own singing career and personal lives rolled on, we got so busy that we never seemed to have time to search out good material. I believe we grew to depend too much on Chet for this, but he always came through for us. He was finding material for and producing so many other artists that I'm sure he didn't have time to take our careers in hand. But he did anyway and never let on that we were a lot of trouble. His wife, Leona, always treated us like family. Many a time when we were in Nashville, Chet and Leona would have us come out to their home in Belle Meade for a visit and a good home-cooked meal. Chet offered many an artist a shoulder to cry on in those hard old days. I'd throw a thousand drinks in any jerk's face for Chet Atkins anytime.

Speaking of drinks reminds me of the time we were flying out to Arizona for a couple of shows in Phoenix and Scottsdale. I don't know how J. E. put up with Bonnie and me all those years since we were always teasing him about something. Bonnie was critical of his guitar playing, and every year for Christmas she would give him a set of Chet Atkins Easy To Play Guitar Lessons. I, on the other hand, was always fussing at him about spending too much money on his gal friends. If he had one we didn't like we'd tell her, "He's got a house and a wife full of kids."

On this trip to Phoenix, he got us back but good. After we were airborne, Bonnie and I ordered Old Charter and water. Everyone got served except us. We kept asking them to bring our drinks, but they seemed to completely ignore us. Pretty soon, we got downright angry about it and demanded they bring us our drinks. But the hostess said they had run out of alcohol. By this time we were almost to Phoenix. When we got off the plane, J. E. was standing over to the side of the entrance laughing his fool head off. He found pure joy in telling us that he had told the stewardess not to serve us anything to drink because we were alcoholics and he was taking us to California to a drying-out center. He had all of them convinced that what he told them was true and that he had his hands full just trying to keep us sober until he could get us there. I'm sure they believed him, especially after Bonnie and I showed our asses for them refusing us drinks. After this we thought twice about teasing J. E. about anything.

Jim Reeves's Last Flight

So you think it's the big time when you've been in the business almost ten years and had several million-selling hits? That's what we thought all through the next five years of our career. We had made so much money from "The Three Bells," "Scarlet Ribbons," and "The Old Lamplighter" that we had to have our royalties spread out over the next few years for tax purposes. We kept on recording singles and albums, thinking the money from the sales was going into a separate fund from which we would get our royalties twice a year as we were supposed to. It didn't happen.

One day we got a notice from RCA that we were in the red. Red? What the devil were they talking about? RCA had charged against our royalties the costs of recording sessions, production, promotion, and everything else imaginable. I guess every hog between Nashville and Madison Avenue was supping at our trough. All the money from those million-selling songs was gone. We were drained dry, although we thought there was no way that this could be true.

I took it upon myself to try to discover how all our money had disappeared. After all, RCA was a big time, reputable outfit. I went directly to Chet Atkins and told him about our situation. He couldn't believe it. "There's no way in God's creation that you kids should be in the hole," he said. "Why, you should be sitting on half a fortune by now."

Being an RCA executive as well as producer, Chet said he'd check into the matter for us. But he could never get anything out of the people in the New York office. While he seemed as puzzled as we were as to why we were in the red, he must have finally thrown up his hands in despair at trying to communicate with those big city paper-pushers. There didn't seem to be anything we could do, short of getting a battery of accountants and lawyers and going to court. We'd played that sorry old song before. To add insult to it all, one day I got the nastiest letter I've ever received from RCA. The letter told me to stop bugging Chet! The letter was full of criticism of the Browns, me in particular, and in so many words implied that the label was carrying us out of the goodness of its heart. Oh, yeah, carrying *us!* I'm sure RCA made megabucks off our records.

I went to Chet and apologized for bugging him, and he got so mad at RCA for that letter that I thought he was going to blow a fuse. The end result of all this hassle is that we never got a clear accounting from RCA on our financial status. We certainly didn't get a lot of the money we thought was coming to us. We weren't the first singers to get stiffed by a record company, I'm sure, but we were probably the easiest because we were so trusting. It would take almost the rest of our career to get us back into the black with RCA. Today, most performers have powerful lawyers and accountants working for them to lessen the possibility of being cheated, but that wasn't the norm back then.

• • •

RCA built a big, beautiful new studio in Nashville, and we were the very first artists to record there. We were working on a new album when Steve Sholes, the RCA vice president who'd written me the nasty letter, happened to come in. I remember we were recording "Born To Be with You." When I saw Steve, I just froze up. I couldn't sing at all. We must have had at least fifty takes on that one song, and I know we never did get it right.

Not too long afterward, RCA was throwing a big party in Chet's honor in the new recording studio. I didn't get an invitation. What I did get was a little of old-fashioned Arkansas courage, aided by a little Old Charter, and I crashed the party. I had said something to Mary Lynch, Chet's secretary, about being left off the invitation list. Mary was very apologetic and insisted that I come to the party anyway. So I did. I was standing by the door when Chet and Steve walked in. I made a beeline to Steve and got right up in his face and said, "You wrote me a nasty letter, and I want to know why!"

"Why, er ah, Maxine. I don't know what to say. I certainly didn't intend for you to take it that way."

I had just enough Old Charter in me to tell Steve what I really had on my mind, but Chet, gentleman that he was, stepped between us and put his arm around me. "Maxine, I want you to know that I love you and I appreciate you above anybody else in this sometimes sorry business. If Steve thought you were bugging me, he was just wrong."

He was looking right at Steve as he spoke, and at that moment I knew I'd never have a better friend in the world. Let me tell you, though, people in the music business can carry a grudge forever. It was some time later, maybe a year or more, and we were getting ready to record another album. J. E. had come up with a fantastic idea for the album's title and theme, *The Browns Are Blue*. J. E had already tried the idea out on Chet and other RCA VIPs. They thought it was a unique idea, something sort of new in the industry, a "concept" album.

Everything regarding the album came off without a hitch. The album cover was done in solid blue, Bonnie and I wore blue chiffon dresses and J. E. wore a blue suit. Most of the songs in the album had references to the color blue, although that wasn't our overall intention. We just meant to do blue, sad songs, whatever their name.

When the master reached New York, Steve Sholes hit the ceiling. He said he wanted every song on the album to have the word "blue" in the title. But he never mentioned this to us when he was at the recording session. We begged him to hold up the album and let us take "The Whiffenpoof Song," "Lonely Little Robin," and a couple others out and replace them with others that had "blue" in the title. He wouldn't hear of it. He said, "The release date has already been set and I'm not about to change it."

When the album came out in 1960 it was titled *The Browns Sing Their Hits*. Now that was the most asinine thing we'd ever had done to us because there wasn't one damn song on that album that had been a hit for us. But there was nothing we could do about it. Our hands were tied—as usual. Steve was one of the biggest wheels at RCA, and it seemed he was constantly on us from that time on. He'd never forgotten the misunderstanding over our RCA contract when he thought our new agent was trying to jack up our price. When I protested a little bit about our royalty statements, he must have taken it as a personal slap. He once told me that he could make or break any recording artist. But I will say this about him: most of the time he was a big, fat, lovable old huggy bear and I'm glad we got back on good terms before his death a few years later.

Now free of Tommy, I was having the time of my life. In the '60s the only time artists got to really be with one another for any length of time was during the industry conventions in Nashville. Those were wild, wild times. As I've mentioned before, all the record companies had hospitality suites in the hotels to butter up the deejays and other industry heavyweights. The booze flowed like lava down Mount St. Helens, and I've got to admit that I was now in there partying with the best of them. At one convention, I got so juiced on the free booze that I went crazy as a road lizard. I was supposed to meet Jim and Mary Reeves at their hotel room. When I walked in late, I saw Mary waiting for me with our old friends, Tom and Billie Perryman. I saw Jim Reeves lying in bed asleep, probably topped off on booze himself. Jim Reeves was one good-looking hunk of a man, and to tell the truth he'd always had his share of road honeys. With all that Old Charter in me, I just went a little crazy. I proceeded to pull off all my clothes and climb in bed with Jim. There we were, in front of God and everybody, between those lily-white sheets and naked as jaybirds. "I've always wanted to go to bed with Jim Reeves," I sang out drunkenly, "And this is my chance!" I was so bombed I don't remember all the details, but Tom Perryman told me later that I was just a wild woman that night. If Mary Reeves hadn't been such a good friend, I'm sure she would have killed me right then and there.

There's a sober side to such wicked little stories. No matter how much you might be devoted to someone, you can't help yourself when you're on that long, hard Pecker Road. Truly it is not good to be so close to others for a long period of time. Believe me. Jim Reeves was a great friend and maybe the greatest artist country music has ever had. I idolized him from that first time he took us under his wing. I consoled myself later by thinking that I had that one little naughty escapade coming to me. If two people are thrown together too much, it won't be long until there'll be some "he-ing" and "she-ing" going on, and I don't care if you're Mr. Milk or Miss Goody Two Shoes.

As raunchy as my Jim Reeves story is, it doesn't come close to what happened to our good friend Tom Perryman. Tom has some wild tales about his drinking days in Nashville, but the best one is when he and George Jones woke up in the same bed together, naked. Well, Tom wasn't completely naked. He was wearing green cowboy boots and purple socks. To this day, Tom can't figure out where the boots and socks came from, why he had them on or why he was in the same motel room with George Jones. All Tom can remember is that he started drinking at the Boar's Nest, an after-hours hangout, and woke up the next day in a cheap motel room on the outskirts of town with no clothes and no car. And, fortunately for George, no camera. This was a mean, dirty trick some of their drinking buddies played on them. They never were able to figure out who it was.

• • •

It was at a convention that I was first hypnotized. And it nearly turned into a brawl. We had all gathered for a party in Buck Trent's suite in the Andrew Jackson Hotel. (Buck became famous playing banjo in Porter Wagoner's band.) The hypnotist was Leo O'Rourke, who got a lot of bookings in nightclubs. Some of the biggest names in the industry were at the party, and they all gathered around while Leo started his act. Of course, I was the one they chose to be put under hypnosis. I swore to everybody that I couldn't be put under. Leo just grinned, and there I went, just as gullible as Lucille Ball. I don't remember a thing that happened next. All I know was that Leo kept flipping his cigarette lighter, and when he did, I felt someone pinching my butt. Every time some of those pickers or deejays pinched me I'd slap the hell out of them. They said I must have slapped twenty or thirty guys before Leo put his lighter away. I don't remember any of that, but I was truly the butt of all the jokes at that convention. Lord, I prayed that Bonnie or J. E. had apologized for me, but they didn't want to ruin the fun. The next day just about everyone I ran into laughed their fool heads off at me. Well, at least I got the pleasure of knocking the hell out of a few deejays—which is every artist's dream. I just wish I had the satisfaction of knowing which ones.

No one liked to party more than Bonnie and me. One year, both *Billboard* and *Cashbox* nominated the Browns for Best Vocal Group of the year. In the highest of spirits, Bonnie and I latched onto Bill Sachs from *Billboard* and Bob Austin from *Cashbox*. Then the four of us went from one hospitality suite to the next. We partied way into the night.

Finally, we decided we'd go to Ralph Emery's all night show at WSM. We had borrowed J. E.'s new Cadillac and had parked it somewhere while going from one party to another. Now, we couldn't find the dang car. We finally gave up our search and caught a cab out to WSM. This was the worst thing we could have done. Ralph's studio was full of deejays from all over the country, and here we were all giggly and wobbly. For reasons still not entirely clear, we announced to everyone listening to the show that we had lost J. E.'s car.

Conrad Jones, who was WSM's sound engineer, was kind enough to take the four of us back into town to try and find J. E.'s car. When we failed, Conrad drove Bonnie and me out to J. E.'s house. But first, we had him take our two friends back to their hotel rooms, wherever they might be. They couldn't remember that either. After two whole days of searching, J. E. had to get the Nashville police to help him locate his Cadillac. He swore he would never let Bonnie and me borrow it again. We did win the Best Vocal Group prize from both magazines, and Ralph forever kidded Bonnie and me that we had won by "bribing" Sachs and Austin. That's a story we never quite lived down.

• • •

Our lives were changing. Despite having been in the business for years, we never managed to hang onto any money. Maybe I needed to get my act together. Following J. E.'s lead, I made the big decision to move to Nashville. Strangely enough, my Daddy was in favor of the move. He thought it would be a good idea for me to be closer to J. E. We could help each other out and maybe get our singing careers in forward gear.

After I moved to Nashville, Tommy complained that I had taken the children out of state without the court's consent. He came at me with all kinds of threats until I finally agreed to let him have visitation rights in Nashville and keep the children during the summer.

I rented a house in Madison, just north of Nashville. I hated it from the first day. J. E.'s house was a long way from mine. It didn't take long for the old Brown bad luck to rear its head. The second night we were in the house, my little boy Jimmy was pulling on the window blind, trying to get it down. The whole thing fell with a bang right on top of him. Blood gushed from his mouth and nose. My God, I didn't even know where the nearest hospital was!

I got all the kids and my housekeeper, Mrs. Hannah, in the car, and we took off like a shot. I stopped and frantically asked people how to get to the hospital. After dashing here and there, I finally roared up to the emergency room and rushed in with my bleeding little boy. He'd suffered some deep wounds that required several stitches. The sight of him in that hospital almost broke my heart. "So this is the way you greet newcomers, Nashville," I moaned. I'd been in Nashville a thousand times and had always heard it was an unforgiving place. Now I'd experienced it firsthand. Was this an omen?

It was so scary being so far away from my family with my three babies that I never unpacked anything in that house in Madison. Instead, I had a real estate agent find me a house closer to J. E. and Becky. I bought a beautiful home on Caylor Drive in Green Hills, only a mile or so from Music Row. It was still a few miles from my brother, but it was near a big shopping center, schools and doctors' offices.

Not too long after our relocation to Nashville, we did catch a little good luck. We recorded a song in February 1964 called "Then I'll Stop Loving You." Jim Reeves wrote the song, and I remember taking the tape of that session over to his and Mary's house and playing it for them. About the best feeling I ever had in my life was when I saw Jim's reaction to that song. He just about flipped. He played it over and over. "It's going to be a hit, it's going to be a big hit!" he kept saying. And it was. It got great reviews and started jumping up the charts like crazy. Well, I thought, maybe we'd been wrong all those years. Maybe Nashville really was where we needed to be.

I had put my house in Arkansas up for sale, and I kept waiting for the real estate people to call me with some offers. None came. I hadn't been in Nashville but a little while when I got word that Tommy had moved into my house. I had boarded up the place and given no one a key but the real estate office. But Tommy hadn't let that stop him. He removed the boards and took down the For Sale sign, telling the realtor that he was taking the house off the market. He had no legal right to do it, but that never ever stopped him. I contacted my lawyer in Little Rock and went through weeks of red tape (and a lot of lawyer's fees) before I gave up. I agreed to let Tommy stay in the house until it sold. He agreed to make the payments. Sure he did. He lived in that house for over two years and never made one payment. You know, they should have had me sing that song on *Hee Haw,* the one that went, "Gloom, despair, and agony on me." I had that stuff down pat.

• • •

Jim Reeves called me one day in late July of 1964 to say that he and Dean Manuel, his longtime piano player, were flying up to Bull Shoals, Arkansas, to check out some property he was thinking about investing in. He invited me to ride as far as Little Rock with them. I was homesick to see my folks so I quickly accepted the invitation. I'd flown with Jim in his plane before, and so had J. E. and Bonnie. To tell you the truth, though, I was never very confident flying in those little old tree-topper planes. Jim had owned his own single-engine craft for some time, but he hadn't quite mastered flying it, especially in bad weather. His plane didn't have the proper instruments, either, but a little thing like that never stopped Jim Reeves. He liked to fly by the seat of his pants. That was no more threatening to him than driving his car on the highway.

Well, I never got to make that trip with Jim and Dean. At the last minute, my little daughter Alicia got sick. She had developed some infected boils and was running a high fever. I called Jim the night before and told him I couldn't go. He offered to take Alicia and me to our family doctor in Little Rock, but I declined. I could put up with flying by myself, but I didn't want to take any of my babies up in those little planes.

"We've got a show date in Dallas, anyway," I told Jim. "If we get weathered in up there in those Arkansas hills, I'll miss the show."

"Aw, come on, Maxine," he teased. "I won't let you get weathered in. And if we do, we'll have a whole lot of fun being stranded, har, har, har."

So I didn't fly out with Jim and Dean. I took Alicia to the doctor the next morning. By then, she had improved a lot, and her fever had broken. I never gave another thought to the trip Jim Reeves had set out on. J. E. and I drove to Arkansas to pick up Bonnie for our trip to Dallas. I brought my children to stay with my folks. Then we headed out for the Big D.

Somewhere on that long, dreary road between Little Rock and Dallas, we turned on the radio and heard Ralph Emery giving the news that an airplane with two *Grand Ole Opry* entertainers aboard was lost. We drove along in silence for maybe an hour. We had lost so many close friends to wrecks and crashes that we couldn't bear to speak any names out loud. Truthfully, it didn't occur to us that it might be our very best friend, Jim Reeves. I was sure he had flown up to Bull Shoals and had returned that afternoon.

A couple of hours passed, and they still didn't announce on the radio who those two people on the plane were. Then Ralph came on again. He could hardly talk. His voice was breaking. He simply started playing "The Nightwatch," one of Jim Reeves's most moving songs. I broke out in a cold chill. We still couldn't say it, but we knew then that it had been Jim who had been killed in that plane crash. I hadn't felt so dead inside since the day my little brother had been killed.

Then the details of the plane crash came on. Jim and Dean had been killed when their single-engine plane crashed, soon after it disappeared from the radar screen during a thunderstorm. They were on their return trip from Bull Shoals and had almost made it back to the Nashville airport. Another two or three minutes and they would have landed safely, we learned later. J. E. stopped the car, got out and walked off into the woods just off the highway I knew he was there crying his heart out. I was numb all over. All I could do was hold Bonnie in my arms while our tears flowed. I guess we were a little out of our heads, because I remember talking to her as fast as I could.

"Jim's not dead," I said over and over. "I know Jim is not dead. He landed somewhere. They made a mistake. They'll find him alive. I know they will."

• • •

In the wee hours of the morning, we found a phone and called Tom and Billie Perryman to tell them the news. They hadn't heard about the plane crash yet and were in almost total shock. Tom said he was leaving right away for Nashville. The authorities in Tennessee hadn't found the plane yet. Tom said that if there was one chance in a million, he'd go find Jim and get him out alive.

We went on to Dallas to sing on the *Big D Jamboree*. By the time we went on stage, Jim's plane still hadn't been found. We asked the audience to say a silent prayer that somehow Jim might still be alive. It was only with that slim, impossible hope in our hearts that we were able to get through the show. We drove right back to Little Rock, picked up my kids and rushed to Nashville. J. E. promptly joined in the search for Jim's plane.

What a bitter thing it was. They found the wreckage and the bodies in some woods not more than half a mile from J. E.'s house in Brentwood. Sadly, too, Jim had died on Bonnie's birthday, July 31, 1964. We recalled all the times on the road that Jim had sung "Happy Birthday" to Bonnie and had been the life of the party.

J. E. still lives in Brentwood. Every time I go there, I have to pass right by where that sweet man and great singer died. If my daughter hadn't been sick, I would have been on that plane and no doubt would have died with Jim. I wonder if we would have died afraid. Being hardened by the road for so many years, a picker takes fear right along with every song, every chord, every beat. I think Jim probably was afraid in that last dark storm, but I think he was laughing and probably singing. Singing right into the face of that black storm and standing his own strong "Nightwatch."

Learning to Accept Life's Gifts

I was living in Nashville, a single lady again, when I went and made one of the biggest mistakes of my life. I don't know what it proves. That I was lonely? That I was a glutton for punishment? That I was a hopeless romantic who could never quite give up on love? It was during the winter, and Nashville had been hit with a big ice and snowstorm. Tommy, still managing to insert himself in my life, came to Nashville to see the kids. Lord, he was all honey and pie, sweetness and purity. He told me he'd changed his ways and his life. He said he'd been awful to me and knew that I'd never take him back. But, he said, at least we could part like friends. Oh, he was smooth. He loved up on the kids all the time he was there, took them out for ice cream and movies and generally acted just like a fine husband and daddy, something I'd never seen before.

The snow came down harder, and pretty soon we were housebound. That night, he came into my bedroom. There were tears in his eyes. "Baby, baby, I've been so bad to you and I've missed you so much," he whispered. And what was I doing? Letting him get away with it. Letting him into my bed. And back into my heart. But only for a few crazy hours. He started drinking heavily before noon the next day, and his entire personality shifted. It was clear that he hadn't meant any of those things he'd said to me the night before. I always had deep feelings for Tommy and wanted so badly to believe he was telling me the truth. But, oh how I hated myself for what I had done.

Six weeks later, I woke up to find that I was pregnant again. I guess that was absolutely the lowest moment of my life. I went into a depression that was so mean and low I thought I'd die. Finally, in a frantic moment, I called up Tommy in Little Rock and told him he'd gotten me pregnant. "Well," he said, "you just take your best hold and go." That was his favorite expression, the old royal kiss-off. He even went so far as to say that he would deny he was the father and then he'd be sure to get custody of the kids.

I cried all day and night. I felt like I'd been thrown out and stranded at the dark end of the world's loneliest road. The only one I knew to turn was to my brother. It killed my soul to tell J. E. what I'd done. But he was wonderful to me. He kept comforting me and telling me that everything would be all right. He even offered to help me get an abortion. But I couldn't do that, no matter what.

Too ashamed to go to any doctor in Nashville, I flew home to Little Rock and my own doctor. I didn't even tell my folks that I was coming home; I couldn't bear for them to know about the awful fix I'd got myself in. They never knew I was in town. Dr. Gillespie gave me a thorough examination, and when he was finished, he had that old familiar smile on his face. "Maxine, I don't know what you've got yourself so upset over," he said. "You're not pregnant at all. So you can stop worrying."

I was never so relieved in my whole life. Dr. Gillespie told me that I was suffering from a bad case of nerves. He gave me a pill to start my period, and before I got back to Nashville, I had started. I called J. E. from the airport and told him the good news. I think he was as relieved as I was.

As relieved as I was, though, my depression didn't lessen. For the next several weeks I was caught between two horrible emotions: a growing hatred for my ex-husband and a deep sense of guilt for what I'd done with him. For the longest time, I swore that I would never have anything to do with a man again. From my experience they couldn't be trusted, they always let you down and they put scars on you that lasted a lifetime.

• • •

J. E. and I continued doing the *Grand Ole Opry.* Most of the time now, it was just the two of us. Bonnie didn't want to leave her family in Dardanelle, Arkansas. Occasionally she'd come and sing with us, and it was like old times. But by now those moments of exhilaration were growing fewer and farther between.

I took my kids to the *Opry,* especially Tommy and Jimmy, and they grew to love that place almost as much as I did. They loved to see their Momma performing on stage. The kids each had a favorite song by the Browns, and they begged us to sing them at the *Opry*. So we'd sing "The Three Bells" for little Jimmy, "That Little Boy of Mine" for Tommy Jr., and "Scarlet Ribbons" for Alicia. After a time, my kids got to be regulars at the *Opry* themselves. I must say that this time was probably the most contented I ever had in my singing career. "This is the way it's supposed to be," I kept telling myself. But I should have known that you can't have the best of both worlds, not in this crazy business.

I never got to take my children on a real vacation. If we happened to be singing at a vacation resort or somewhere else for an extended period of time, then usually I'd take my children with me. One of those places was Calloway Gardens, Georgia. Since we were going to be there a week, J. E., Bonnie, and I took our families. You must remember, this was long before artists had tour buses, so we had to travel in three cars.

One day we took all the kids to the beach, and it took all of us to keep an eye on them. But we didn't watch closely enough. I suddenly noticed that my little four-year old daughter was missing. I have never known such fear as I experienced those next few hours. I imagined all sorts of things happening to my baby. Then, after what seemed like an eternity, we heard this voice over the loudspeakers, "Would the mother of Alicia Russell please come to the platform? We have your daughter."

On the lighter side, if you want to call it that, we took all the kids on a tour of some underground caves. At some point during the tour, we had to squeeze through some rocks to get to the other side of the caves. Since Bonnie was so amply endowed, she got stuck between those damn rocks. At first we thought it was funny, but then we got afraid. There seemed to be no way that Bonnie could get out from between those rocks. She was stuck! Her little girl, Kelly, started crying and screaming at the top of her lungs. We were all pushing and pulling and damn near panicked. Then, J. E.'s wife, Becky, came up with the idea of pouring suntan lotion all over Bonnie's arms and shoulders. We used all we had on Bonnie and the rocks until we were finally able to push her out. Later on that same week, two of my children developed big boils on their little butts and we had to take them to a doctor. All in all, this vacation turned into a nightmare for all of us. My children learned early in life that there's no place like home.

• • •

Something was happening to me. I began to have terrible back-aches, so bad sometimes that I couldn't even walk. I got to the point that I had no feeling from my waist down. Sometimes I'd slide right off the bed, and I had no control of my bladder. My Aunt Maggie couldn't stand the thought of someone else taking care of my babies. She had grown to love them so much that she moved back in with me to take care of them when I had to go on the road. One night, she called J. E. and Becky and told them to get over to my house immediately because I was completely out of it. They took me to the hospital.

For six weeks, I was in and out of the hospital. The doctors couldn't find out what was wrong with me. I'd get a little better and then a whole lot worse. Finally, one of the specialists suggested a myelogram, a rare test back in those days, so rare that a whole team of medical professionals from Vanderbilt University School of Medicine came to observe. During the test, the doctors found that three discs in my back had exploded and settled on the nerves of my back. I lay paralyzed for months. No one knows the agony a person suffers under such conditions—unless you've been flat on your back without being able to move even a little toe. I gave up. I knew I'd never be able to get out of that bed. And the worst wasn't over. During the myelogram, the doctors also discovered that I had cancer of the uterus. I had to be operated on right away.

"You're lucky," said one of the doctors.

"Uh huh. I'm lucky I didn't get killed riding all over the country in a cramped car doing one-night stands or crashed in one of those chartered airplanes," I said. "I needed to wait for this."

"No, Maxine. If we hadn't done the test, we wouldn't have found the cancer until it was too late. You're going to beat it, and you're going to get back on your feet again. I guarantee it."

His words didn't reassure me one damn bit. But do you know what? He was right.

It wasn't easy. Most of the staff at the hospital didn't give me a chance. If I didn't die of cancer, they thought, I'd be in a wheelchair for the rest of my life. So I went through with the surgery for the cancer. I went home to heal up, and after six months of barely being able to move, I went back in for the back surgery. Everything went smoothly. I had a good prognosis on my cancer surgery, and the doctors were confident I would be able to walk again and lead a normal life. I was one of those rare one-in-a-million cases. I was lucky after all.

• • •

Momma and Daddy came to take me home from the hospital after my back surgery. They were real happy I was coming along so well, but I could tell they had something on their minds. They hadn't wanted me to know the bad news until they were sure I could handle it. I was going to lose my home in North Little Rock. Tommy had been living there for about twenty-four months, with the understanding from my attorney that he would keep up the house payments. Of course he didn't, and my damn lawyer hadn't even bothered to check up on Tommy. I never got the child-support money Tommy had promised to pay, but my lawyer just shrugged and said that I had forfeited that right by moving my children out of the court's jurisdiction. To make matters even worse, I was facing monumental hospital and doctor bills because Tommy hadn't kept up the insurance policy as he had also promised. I know I was a fool for letting it all happen to me, but somehow I didn't seem to care. I was alive, I wasn't going to die of cancer, and I had feeling back in my legs and back again. I was still lucky. Or maybe I was blessed by the good Lord, who was showing me now how to live and accept life's gifts.

• • •

While I was going through the painful day-to-day process of teaching myself to walk again, I never gave up trying to prove to all those skeptics at the hospital that I'd make it all the way back. Daddy bought me a beautiful white piano so I could sit down and write songs again. He also bought me a Wollensak tape recorder so I could record everything I wrote (I don't know how many songs I'd lost over the years by not recording them when they started popping out of my head.)

By the time I got back on my feet, the Browns had a backlog of show dates and I was eager to get back on stage. If I thought things would be the same again, I was in for a rude awakening. I tried but I just couldn't get that old, magical feeling back. Not quite. Bonnie did not perform with us now except for the bigger shows. J. E. and I did a few shows by ourselves and got other girl singers to stand in for Bonnie from time to time. Bonnie still came for the *Opry* and recording sessions, but she was occupied full time with Brownie's career and her two beautiful little girls, Kelly and Robin.

J. E. and I hit the road again. It was hard work and not too profitable, and it certainly didn't have the old magical madness it used to. One night, as we were riding along out in the middle of nowhere, I thought I heard Jim Reeves's voice talking to me. I knew it couldn't be, but I sure felt like it was Jim. He sang a lullaby, he talked in that silky smooth voice and he made me want to cry forever. All the things that had happened to me came flooding into my mind: our first big hit and getting cheated out of it, our first big recording contract, our great songs, our friends getting killed in car wrecks and plane crashes, my folks' nightclub burning down three times, my Momma's stroke, loving a man who turned out to be a mean alcoholic, the threat of death hanging over me.

After a minute Jim's voice faded. When I turned the radio on, the deejay was saying, "Here's a song from yesteryear. It's an old one but a good one, and I hope you remember it." He started playing "The Three Bells." An "old one"? Has it really been all that long, I asked myself? Yes, I guess it had. A chill went down my spine. Sweet Jim Reeves's voice had come to me like an omen. I wasn't sure what it meant, but I could guess. The time was coming very soon when all this madness would have to end. I should have been relieved or happy, I guess, but all I could do was cry.

"I Can't Quit, I'm a Star"

Bonnie finally decided she'd had it with all the road trips. She wanted to stay home with her family. I had three kids of my own but no husband. I think I would have quit on the spot if I'd had any means of support. But I had to keep singing to pay the bills.

So the Brown Trio went on for a little while longer. We took on a singer named Fern Harden as part of the Trio, and we managed to keep up the old Browns image. Fern was a good singer whose voice blended well with ours. We helped her move into an apartment in Nashville, got her set up with some of the in crowd, bought her a new wardrobe of stage clothes to match mine and took her completely under our wing. Her husband, Jim, was not working at the time, so he stayed home to care for their daughter while we toured. Everything seemed fine. For about a year.

We had another overseas tour planned that would take us all over Europe. When it came time for us to leave, Fern announced that she couldn't make it. Just like that. Never mind that the whole tour had been set. Never mind that we'd be left without the vital third part of our trio. "I can't make it," Fern said flatly. Later, we found out why. She, her brother, and her sister, who performed as the Harden Trio, had gotten themselves a record contract, and she hadn't told us about it. (In the Harden Trio, Fern used the name Robbie.) We didn't mind Fern going out on her own. That happens all the time in the music business. But she left us in a bad fix by not giving us enough time to find a replacement. They had booked their session the very day we were to leave for Europe. Bonnie would have gone with us, but it was too late for her to get the necessary shots and an up-to-date passport.

The Hardens, who were also from Arkansas, did get a big hit the first time out. It was a song called "Tippy Toeing," and it sounded great. This was in early 1966. They were always good harmony singers, even back in the *Barnyard Frolic* days. Anyway, we had to cancel the tour, and that hurt us big time. All the artists who did go on the tour drew large crowds and made lots of money.

J. E. and I had to start doing one-night stands again by ourselves. Norma could no longer act as a substitute because she had also gotten married and now had two little babies, Amanda and Jack, to take care of. We were caught in one big squeeze after another. We were still billed as the Browns, which to most people meant three singers. When J. E. and I worked a date in Meridian, Mississippi, the promoter refused to pay us after we finished, which he justified by saying only two singers showed up. Things like this happened over and over. We had one show cancelled after another. It felt like our career was coming apart.

• • •

Then Bonnie got caught up in our problem. She knew she should stay at home with her own family, and yet she felt like she was letting us down. She and I got together and decided to do something about the problem. We went to Chet Atkins and convinced him that RCA should start recording J. E. as a solo act.

"All right, I'll do it," Chet said. "But you know that this will likely be the end of the Browns."

We knew it. But we felt bad for J. E. With Bonnie gone and me having all my physical problems, it just wasn't fair to our brother. Besides, we knew that he had a smooth velvet voice like Jim Reeves. He'd be a great solo artist. When we told J. E. what we'd done, the three of us just sat around staring at the walls to keep from crying.

J. E. had it as rough as anybody back then. He had a lovely wife and two sweet kids, Buster and Kim, to support with a career that seemed at a standstill. He had to sit back and watch others climb high up the ladder. But he never complained, and I think it broke his heart when the Browns split up. Still, he went to work trying to make a name as a solo artist. For a long time he had little success. In his first two years of recording alone, J. E. charted six singles, but none of them made it into the Top Ten. Our good friend Eddy Arnold took him along on several personal appearance tours, as did some of our other *Opry* friends. But he hardly made enough to pay his expenses and feed his family. Then Nat Stuckey came along.

Nat was a tall, lean, good-looking cowboy in the truest sense. In those days, Nat looked a lot like the roguish character Robert Redford played in that fine little movie called *The Electric Horseman*. Although he was a good singer and musician, Nat's first love was writing songs. Around 1967, he gave one he'd written called "Pop A Top" to J. E.'s producer, Bob Ferguson. Bob thought it might be a good song for J. E. So all three of them went into the studio to try it out. Nat was as nervous as a kitten. However, when J. E. sang the song, everybody in the studio was just knocked out. The word spread quickly around town that Jim Ed Brown finally had a big hit on the way. And he did.

"Pop A Top"—complete with beer-can-popping sound effects— hit the *Billboard* chart on May 20, 1967, and rolled quickly all the way up to number three. But J. E. had more than a radio hit to feel good about—he had also cut one of the great jukebox classics of all time. It gave voice to the feelings of every guy who'd ever been dumped and was seeking relief at a bar. From then on, J. E. would have pretty smooth sailing. And so would Nat, who would go on to write many other fine songs.

J. E. told an interviewer later that when "Pop A Top" came out he had a total of eight dollars in his pocket and a bank account that was as dry as a South Arkansas slough in July. Bonnie and I were so happy with J. E.'s success that we felt we'd done the right thing in giving him a shove. Now everything was going to be great for the Browns. J. E. was on the road to sure success, and Bonnie had a beautiful family and the love of a fine man and good provider. And me? Well, I'd make it work for me too somehow. I'd still sing with J. E. on the *Opry* and do some road shows. I'd make it, I kept telling myself.

I think my life and my career, though, could be summed up in a painfully funny story Hank Locklin used to tell. Although a great singer and entertainer, Hank wasn't known as a comedian. But I used to think he was the funniest man alive. He told us of how he went to a shrink to help straighten out his head over the many failures he'd had trying to make it big in show biz. "I went up to this psychiatrist and told him I had to have some help or I was going to crack up," Hank explained. "So the shrink says, 'Lie down on the couch and tell me all about it.' And so I do. I say, 'Well, doc, I make records that don't sell and which the deejays won't even play on the radio. I go out and do a show and the people don't "pat" for me. There's something bad wrong with me, doc.' And the doctor looks me in the eye and says, 'Well, why don't you just quit?' 'Quit!' I say. 'Quit? I can't quit. I'm a star.'"

• • •

In October 1965, we did a tour of Japan. Bonnie came along, and we had the greatest time. Also on the tour with us were Chet Atkins, Skeeter Davis, and the always funny and loveable Hank Locklin. Since RCA was sending us to the Orient to promote what was coming to be called "the Nashville sound," Chet brought along the town's best musicians. That group included Jerry Reed, Henry Strzelecki, Hank Wallis, and Kenny Buttrey. The Tokyo Grand Ole Opry had just been started. Introduced by the occupation troops after World War II, country music was getting to be very popular in Japan. This turned out to be the best-planned, most-publicized tour we had ever been on. Using Tokyo as our base, we journeyed by train to every major city in Japan for a whole month. The Japanese couldn't understand what we were saying, and we couldn't understand them. But it didn't matter. We played sold-out shows in every city and did several TV shows to promote our concerts and explain the Nashville sound. Chet was a master at this.

RCA hired a young geisha girl as our interpreter. She practically lived with us night and day, explaining restaurant menus and telling us the prices of items when we went shopping. We would never have made it without her help. One time I ran out of stockings, and since Japanese women have such small feet (or I have such big ones) there wasn't a pair in all of Tokyo that would fit me. So she arranged for us to go to the Navy PX to shop for the things we couldn't get in local stores. Better than that, she even got permission for us to have lunch in the Navy mess hall. We were all in hog heaven! You can only eat so much rice. I had never developed a taste for Japanese food, and I couldn't for the life of me learn to use chopsticks. We were so starved for American food that Hank and some of the other musicians tried to teach the chef in our hotel how to make hamburgers. By the time I got back home, I was as skinny as a rail.

While we were in Tokyo, Chet played a funny joke on Hank. He told Hank about those famous massages the beautiful Japanese girls offered. He said that those girls could get a guy so worked up it would be his biggest thrill of a lifetime. We knew Hank would try it out, and sure enough he did. But every time Hank called downstairs for an intimate massage, up would come one of those big old sumo wrestler types. Finally, Hank gave up. He never knew that Chet had fixed it with the hotel people that Hank would always get an ugly man and never a beautiful girl.

Hank came down to breakfast one morning, rubbing his arms and hands, and announced to Chet, "Hoss, I'm just sick and tired of baby powder."

"What are you talking about Hank?" Chet asked, finding it hard to keep a straight face.

"I've been trying to get me one of those massages you told me about," said Hank.

"You mean you didn't get one of those beautiful geisha girls?"

"If you call a three hundred pound fat guy a geisha, yeah, hoss. I ain't having no more massages. I don't care how horny they're supposed to make you."

I thought Chet was going to crack up over that one.

A few years later, when I was having a hard time trying to make it as a solo singer myself, I recorded a song entitled "Sugar Cane County." It never did much in this country, but it was a number one hit in Japan. I have always had a warm place in my heart for that country and those gracious people. Maybe I should have stayed over there.

If I had stayed in Japan, I would have spared myself from almost getting raped on my first night back in Nashville. I was in a dead sleep in my motel room when I felt something take hold of me. I looked up to see a man I knew well. His sister was a pretty big time singer, and he was kind of a hanger-on. He'd flirted with me on several occasions before, and I'd always managed to ignore him. But now he was insistent. So I had to fight. And I did, for all I was worth. I managed to knock him off and get myself out the door. I ran down the hall with only a sheet around me and got Bonnie up. We called the security guards and told them what had happened. They started a search and, sure enough, caught him trying to sneak out of the motel. They brought him to my room, and he argued that I'd given him the key to my room. Of course, every one knew this wasn't true. Pretty soon he was begging me not to have him arrested. What was the use? I was so anxious to get back to Little Rock to see my babies that I didn't want to stay over for court. Word did get around however, and he became *persona non grata* in Nashville. Maybe I should have pressed charges. Skunks like that need to be hung out to dry.

One year, J. E., Bonnie, and I took part in a big show in Memphis that Mary Reeves had instigated. She called it "A Tribute to Jim Reeves." A whole host of stars were there, so many, in fact, that they had to divide the program into two shows. Momma and Daddy had driven over to Memphis with us, and after the first show we all went out to dinner at a swanky Polynesian restaurant. Momma loved that kind of food, and we all had a few of those exotic drinks. I must admit that I had my share. We never drank before a show or a recording session, but here we made an exception. It proved to be a big mistake because it gave me a little too much courage to face a nasty situation that happened later that evening.

When we got back to the auditorium, the owner of a Little Rock radio station was standing backstage. We were ready to go on again and were standing in the wings waiting for our intro. That radio guy wormed his way right in behind me and reached down and pinched me on the rear. I'd known him only casually for a few years, but I knew he was one of those vulgar-mouthed grabbers who thought he could get away with anything. He leaned right into my ear and said something really sickening. Then he pinched my butt again.

I wanted to slap the hell out of him. Instead, I stormed around and gave him a piece of my mind. "Don't you touch me again, you goon!" I warned.

"Aw, come on, Maxie, baby," he purred. "I can't help it if you've got the ripest ass in town. Come on now, let ol' boss have a little. You've been around."

I guess I would have tried to scratch his eyes out right then and there if we hadn't had to go on stage and sing. I yelled at him that he was the filthiest old hog I'd ever seen and assured him he'd be the last man in the world I'd ever let touch me. The booze I'd drunk at dinner only served to make my blood boil.

After we finished our part of the show and were walking offstage, that sorry bum was still standing there. He said in a loud voice that everyone could hear, "OK, Miss High and Mighty. I just called my radio station and told them to break every record you Browns ever made."

It was one of those strained, pointless, and totally humiliating situations—for him, not us. Most people who hang around backstage are all right. They just want to get close to famous people they admire. But some are downright rude and pushy, and a few can be obnoxious and troublesome. I thought no more about the incident until later. I guess I'd injured his fragile little macho image, for his radio station did indeed put a boycott on all our records. To make matters worse, that guy even campaigned against our records with other radio stations in Little Rock. Despite having had dozens of top records, our sales in Little Rock were about the lowest of any place in the country.

I knew better than to pop off. I had let myself get out of control, which is a cardinal sin for a performer. It was those drinks I'd had that night, I told myself, and I even gave some thought to going and apologizing to the bum. But I just couldn't do it. There was just no way I could stomach it, no way I would tolerate that kind of insult, no matter how many record sales it cost us. It wasn't until after that radio station was sold and new deejays were hired that they started playing our records again. But the damage had already been done. Just because I wouldn't let a masher insult and intimidate me, the Browns suffered from a campaign of lies and slurs in our own hometown. It's a sweet business.

• • •

Lord knows I'm no prude I love a good practical joke and a smooth-talker's line. While that radio station bum was about the lowest of male skunks, I've been privileged to know some of the greatest and nicest men in the world. I wouldn't dare rank them, but I'd have to put on the top Jim Reeves, Tom T. Hall, Johnny Cash, Tex Ritter, Jimmy Dean, Eddy Arnold, Whispering Bill Anderson, Mel Tillis, Ralph Emery, Jimmy C. Newman, the great George Jones, and my all-time best friend, Tom Perryman.

Images of them from long ago float through my mind at odd times. Driving along a country road or zipping around the frenzied freeways of the glitzy new Nashville, I see those images, hear those voices and either cry or break into hysterical laughter. Just imagine Jimmy Dean seeing Dolly Parton for the first time and saying, "I think I'm gonna go bowling." Or the young Tom T. Hall, coming into Nashville in a shiny new Cadillac and looking for a parking meter with time left on it because he didn't have a dime in his pocket. Tom T. may be the greatest storyteller in song that Nashville has ever known. Can anyone listen to his "Homecoming" and not feel what country music is about at its sweetest and saddest?

I remember Johnny Cash at the airport in San Diego, looking drawn and washed out, too many one-nighters, too many pills, too much of everything bad happening to one of the finest singers and warmest country boys. Thank God Johnny finally got it all straightened out and put the demons behind him.

I remember George Jones, the time we sang to each other all night long in a lonely old motel room. It was amazing how the Browns' harmony affected him and how he would cry with each song, especially when we sang with him his hit "Window Up Above." We never could get through the whole song, no matter how many attempts we made. When George would start crying, we'd all cry. But there is one thing for sure: the more George drank, the better he sounded. No one can ever fill those shoes!

I remember Tex Ritter, the perfect gentleman. There in Centennial Park in Nashville, back in the '60s, Tex and the Browns performing before one of the biggest outdoor crowds in music history, long before the world heard about rock concerts and "happenings." Then there was the time we had equal billing with Tex, set an all-time attendance record and took him and his band down to my Momma's house in Pine Bluff. We just sat around Momma's table, talking, laughing, and harmonizing just for the sake of the song that simple Sunday afternoon.

And I remember Billie Perryman, who put up with me and Bonnie and allowed her husband, Tom, to be our chauffeur on those numerous occasions in Nashville when we were in a partying mood. We owe so many apologies to Tom: for jumping out of his car and running inside J. E.'s house to hide at four in the morning, for the night his car horn went off the minute we turned into J. E.'s driveway and woke up the whole neighborhood and for all the trouble he went through later that morning, trying to find his way back home to Murfreesboro with a flat tire and the horn still honking. Thanks partly to us, he ruined a tire and had to rip wires out to stop the horn, which by then had also awakened his wife and kids.

We were always pulling some sort of practical joke on our friends. And then there was the particularly memorable one played on me. We were doing a telethon in Nashville with some other singers and Hollywood stars. I was in my dressing room, standing there in only my panties and bra, when in walked the tall, handsome actor James Drury, the one who played the title role in *The Virginian* television series. I wasn't immediately aware of this, though. I had my back turned when I heard the door open, but I thought nothing about it. A lot of girls had been coming in and going out of the room. Drury had stripped to his briefs to get ready for his part in the show when we sort of backed into each other. When I saw him, I let out a shriek. Somebody apparently thought it would be funny to assign us both to the same dressing room. I don't know how it affected him, but I was flabbergasted.

"Why hello there, young lady," Drury said, cool as the other side of the pillow. "Can I bum a cigarette?"

I recognized him instantly and got as nervous as a whore in church. Instead of reaching for my clothes, I grabbed my purse and tried to find him a cigarette. I stammered and stuttered and apologized for being in his dressing room. But he was a total gentleman. After we both got dressed, we checked up, and sure enough someone had deliberately put our names on the same dressing room door.

Lord, what if someone had caught us half-naked in that room? Today, I'm sure the tabloids would splash some big screamers about us across their front pages. But Jim Drury turned out to be about the nicest star I'd ever met. A few days later at the Nashville airport, someone tapped me on the shoulder and said, "Young lady, can I bum a cigarette?" It was him, headed back to Hollywood. He gave me a big hug and kiss on the cheek and kept right on walking. Our paths never crossed again. The other day, I saw a rerun of *The Virginian,* and once again I felt his kiss on my cheek. And I'm still smoking!

"Old Hat"
Maxine

The Browns, who have won virtually every award in the business, no longer will record as a group. The three Browns, Jim Ed, Maxine and Bonnie, have performed as a successful trio for more than a decade . . . "The Three Bells" was the biggest Browns record. It was a million seller gold record. "Scarlet Ribbons" and "Old Lamplighter" were two other million sellers. The trio began in the music business at the Barnyard Frolic in Little Rock. Chet Atkins brought them to Nashville and the late Jim Reeves helped them in their climb.

This quotation is from the October 27, 1967, issue of *Billboard* magazine. It summarized in one paragraph the long road that brought us to our final performance together at the *Grand Ole Opry* as members. Though we would appear together on a few occasions in the future, we were no longer thought of as a trio. Bonnie went home to Brownie and the girls in Dardanelle, J. E. continued his climb as a solo artist, and I went my separate way into whatever future I could make for myself. Even with years of hard experience to light my way, I still didn't realize at this point how perilous the journey ahead would be.

In our home state paper, the *Arkansas Gazette,* a feature columnist tried to summarize our career as a trio, saying that "Success didn't come overnight but once it started, it never stopped. Their biggest hit came in 1959 with 'The Three Bells' and they joined the Grand Ole Opry in 1963 and immediately became an even bigger hit. . . . The

Browns have appeared on television and radio shows and 32 weeks out of the year at the Grand Ole Opry ever since. . ."

The papers all reported that Bonnie and I were "retiring" to stay home and raise our children. But I had no husband to retire to who would support me and my kids. And show business was the only profession I knew, the only way I had of earning a real living. I was trapped in the middle. When Bonnie quit, we still had several months remaining on our recording contract with RCA. We still had a few unreleased songs in the can, including two particularly promising ones called "I'll Bring You Water" and "Big Daddy." I was hoping and praying they would become successful; I sang lead on both the songs and desperately needed for at least one of them to become a hit. If it did, it might give me a way to stay in the business. J. E. was still going great guns with "Pop A Top." Well, neither song took off. So I was left dangling.

Pat Kelleher, one of our closer friends at RCA, tried to help. I ran into him one day during the annual Country Music Association festivities in October. He told me RCA was having promotional pictures taken of all their artists but that for some reason my name wasn't on the list. "Have you ever done any solo work?" Pat asked me. As usual I couldn't think fast enough and all I could utter was, "I'm sure there's been a few solos on our albums."

Pat said he'd try to get something going for me, and he made all the arrangements for me to meet with the RCA photographers for a series of pictures. When I got to the studio, they were waiting for me. I was the last one on the schedule. The make-up girl had already gone, so I was on my own. Those photographers were kind of clowning around, and they had me do all kinds of different poses and even change costumes. I got a funny feeling about it all. I had the strangest feeling that they didn't have any film in their cameras. To this day I have never seen one of those pictures.

What happened next has burned a hole in my mind. Not a day has gone by that I haven't thought about the way those VIPs and studio bigwigs would treat one of their artists, especially since I had helped bring megabucks into the RCA coffers during our high ride with the label.

I had talked to Pat and Chet Atkins about my remaining with

RCA. I could record some by myself and some duets with J. E., who was now signed to the label on his own. Chet told me one day that the RCA big wheels were having a special meeting all about me. He also said that he was not going to be a part of the meeting since he was too personally involved. I got the distinct feeling that Chet had been asked not to go to the meeting. He said that the new RCA talent executive would conduct the meeting and tell me the decision.

I was much too nervous to wait by the phone. Chet suggested I wait at the RCA building so I could find out right away. I got all dressed up and went down there. I had such high hopes that I would be given the chance to prove myself, if not as a soloist then maybe teaming with another artists on the label. After all those years, I was confident RCA would dangle some kind of plum in front of me.

I had just walked to the back of the building to get a Coke when I saw the talent executive coming down the hall. "Oh, is the meeting already over?" I asked.

"Yes, it is," he replied in a voice as bland as pabulum.

"Well," I kind of laughed, "did you all decide what to do with me?" I'll never forget that cocky, smug, arrogant look on his face.

"Yes," he said, "we have, and its been agreed by all. Maxine, you're old hat as far as RCA is concerned." Then he turned and walked off, smiling like Lord High and Mighty.

I wasn't stunned. I wasn't even shocked. I had just turned numb all inside, as though all the blood had been drained from my body. Just then, Chet came walking along right by me. With him was Perry Como. I had always loved but had never met Perry Como. But at that moment, I couldn't have cared less. Chet stopped and introduced me to Perry. I couldn't even say anything to Chet, much less Perry Como, for I was fighting back tears. Chet sensed that something was wrong. He reached out for my hand and said, "Come by the office tomorrow and we'll sort things out."

When I was able to regain my composure, I got into my car for what seemed the longest drive of my life. The tears flooded then as I drove to J. E.'s house. Those words, "old hat," kept ringing in my ears. I began to cry out and curse RCA. I was like a little kid. Not only had my toys been taken away, so had my whole playground. Old hat . . . old hat. If RCA didn't want me anymore, there were at least a hundred different tactful ways they could have told me. But that SOB seemed to take delight in turning my life upside down. His words will remain with me the rest of my life. Old hat.

• • •

Sometimes old hats come back in style. The next day I set out with determination to prove myself all over again. I went to Chet's office. From his initial reaction, I could tell he didn't know what that talent executive had done to me. Chet did know, however, that RCA had decided not to keep me on the label. Ever the optimist and wise friend, Chet had already gone to bat for me. He said I should go over to Chart Records and talk to its owner, Slim Williamson. Chart was a young company then, and Chet said he thought I had an excellent chance with it. He also promised to get Felton Jarvis, RCA's best producer, to work with me if I signed to Chart.

"You'll shine through, Maxine," Chet said in that great, comforting voice of his. He made me feel alive again.

In a matter of days, I had fallen from the very top of the ladder to rock bottom. I knew I had no choice but to try to hook up with a company that wouldn't have had a chance to sign the Browns. Pride is one thing, but supporting three children is another. So I had to start another climb. I walked out of the RCA building that day with the heaviest of hearts. I had been a part of the label's "hall of greats," but I knew that day that I'd never be one again.

In January of 1968 I did my first single for Chart Records. In that first recording session as a solo artist, I was more nervous than I'd ever been before. Everybody in the studio could tell it too. On the first cuts, my breathing was so heavy that it was messing up everything. I had gotten to know Slim Williamson by then, and I begged him to let me over-dub the cuts. But he said no. I don't know why, because those songs could have been good ones. The title of my first single was "Under the Influence of Love." The flip side, my favorite, was called "Never Love Again," a haunting little melody that seemed to fit my life in those days.

Felton Jarvis, my producer, got all excited over a "perfect" song he'd found for me, "The Easy Part's Over." He said the song was just made for me. And I agreed as soon as I sang through it the first time. I felt a deep-down excitement. Did I dare hope I'd have a big song my first time out of the chute as a soloist? We got all set to record it—and then Slim came in. He saw the song and started shaking his head. "No, that song's not for you, Maxine," he said. "It's all wrong."

Felton and I both argued with him. But he wouldn't listen. Slim and I hadn't gotten off to a good start anyway. He had his own publishing company and insisted that I record only songs it published. This reminded me of the chains old Fabor Robinson wrapped us in. I was determined that I wouldn't go through that again. So I told Slim I wouldn't agree to that restriction. He backed off a little, but his hackles were up. He agreed that I could record other material with his approval. But he wouldn't approve Felton's and my choice.

Charley Pride's recording of "The Easy Part's Over" came out a few months later—and went to number two on the *Billboard* charts. I certainly didn't begrudge Charley's success with the song. He's such a great singer and fine person. But that song was supposed to have been mine, and it could have given my career the lift it needed. Instead, I was headed in the other direction and, like a habitual gambler on a downward spiral to doom, there was nothing I could do to stop it.

I made some more records for Chart, and they did just OK—just enough to keep my name alive. As was so often the case with owners of small record labels in those days, Slim pushed only the side of my records on which he owned the publishing rights, no matter how good the other sides might have been. I also learned that RCA was handling all of Chart's distribution, and I already knew what RCA thought of "old hat" Maxine. They might as well have put *Hitler's Greatest Hits* on the label for all the promotion I could expect to get.

It's funny too, because my first solo record, "Never Love Again," was a sweet, sad song, one that became my Momma's favorite—and that lady had impeccable taste when it came to music. I could always depend on her to tell me when I was good and not so good. Later that year, RCA stopped handling Chart's distribution. And so continued the slow and steady decline of Maxine Brown's career.

• • •

Back in those days, I may have lacked confidence because I'd never had to go it alone, but I did truly believe I had the voice to make it as a soloist. Some other people thought so too, including Bill Williams, the leading columnist for *Billboard*. Bill had always liked the Browns, and he liked my voice. He sort of took me under his wing and made sure I got some publicity. He wrote about me often in his column. Every record I had with Chart got good reviews both in *Billboard* and *Cashbox*. But I never did get a hit. I recorded "Take Time To Know Him." It got rave reviews in the trades, but Slim would push only the other side, "I Want To Thank You," which, of course, his company owned.

I had only one solo album for Chart, *Sugar Cane County*. *Cashbox* and *Billboard* praised the whole album. ("Sugar Cane County," the single from which the album took its name, charted in *Billboard* on December 14, 1968, but made it only to number sixty-four. That was my only chart record as a soloist.) I had to assign the publishing rights to the songs I had written to Slim's company.

Later, Slim took over as my producer. He may have been a good businessman, but he was no producer. He tried to team me with Gordon Terry for duets. Gordon was one of the best fiddle players and entertainers around, but I was unable to harmonize with him. I'd had enough of Slim and Chart. I decided it was better to be out pounding the pavement than stay hooked up with an outfit that was dragging me to the bottom. I walked.

J. E. was working with his own band now. He found me some show dates with his group. He'd put together a good little band with such pickers as Corky Tittle, Dave Barton, Ray Nix, and Steve Chapman. J. E. also got himself his first tour bus. It wasn't one of those fancy, home-on-wheels cruisers like you see these days. It broke down just about every time he took it out. With the added expense of the bus, J. E. went into the hole lots of times after he paid everybody else off. I told him not to worry about paying me, that I knew he was taking me along just so I could establish myself as a solo act. So there we were, after more than fifteen years in the business, having to count every dime and dollar again.

J. E.'s agent, Delores Smiley, had agreed to get me some bookings, and I assumed that they'd mostly be on the same tours with J. E. and his band. Then one day, out of the blue, she booked me on a date way up in Topeka, Kansas. I remember opening the letter and seeing that contract with me listed as a single. J. E. and his band were not on the show. It scared me to death. I called Delores and told her I just couldn't do it by myself. She explained to me that J. E. was still trying to establish himself as a solo act and that if he continued working with me, then everyone would think the Browns were back together. She said if I intended to stay in the business, I would have to go it alone. I couldn't accept that, and it broke my heart. But Delores tried to build up my confidence. She said I should go to Topeka alone and that maybe this show would be the break I needed to send me back to the top.

Since the Topeka show was weeks away, I was able to work myself half to death getting ready for it. Day and night, I tried to learn to play the guitar again—and developed the biggest and hardest calluses I'd had on my hands since I first started playing. When the time came for me to take off, I was as ready as I'd ever get. But I couldn't get rid of my brand new case of stage fright.

I'd never traveled alone. I'd never been on stage alone. I got to Topeka a day early so I could get used to everything. I was hoping that the show would be in some intimate little nightclub. Instead, it was a huge ballroom. When I came out of my dressing room, I felt like running straight up the aisle and all the way back to Arkansas. The promoter of the show was a very kind gentleman who told me he'd always been a big fan of the Browns and that he was really looking forward to hearing me sing. That little pep talk helped me get on that stage.

I went through a medley of our old songs, got some decent applause, and then went into some of the new songs from *Sugar Cane County.* I closed with one of the Browns' favorite songs, "Big Daddy." The crowd actually cheered. I couldn't believe it. Later, Delores said she received some good reports on me. I knew I was still green and had made some mistakes, but I thought that just maybe I'd be all right after all. Deep down inside, though, I sensed that I was just dreaming and that she was telling me all this good stuff to spare my feelings. I couldn't play the guitar well enough to teach a new band my material, and I couldn't afford to take along a guitar player. Also, I knew that unless I got a hit solo record I might as well forget it. Hell, I was a harmony singer.

Momma was sick a lot now. She was in and out of the hospital so much that we knew her illness was serious. I refused to let myself think that Momma might not live much longer—she was too strong, too full of life and too much my essential source of strength. But every time I went back to Nashville to look for new material to record, I'd get a call saying that Momma was worse and in the hospital again. I'd drop everything and rush back home. Then they put Momma in intensive care; after that I mostly lived in the hospital. I couldn't even think much about continuing my career. But Momma was still stronger than any of us thought. More than once, she pulled herself back into life. Each day she survived was a blessing to me.

One day, Momma raised up from her sick bed and said, "Maxine, I want you to get out of here now and go find you a song to sing." Such a surge of emotion flooded through me that I wanted to burst into tears, but I only smiled and held her close to me. She was right, of course; I had to work at whatever I could find.

Bonnie, Norma (substituting for Maxine), and Jim Ed at the
Louisiana Hayride in 1958. *From the collection of Maxine Brown.*

This is my favorite of the publicity photos we did for RCA.
Courtesy of RCA.

THE BROWNS
featuring Jim Edward Brown

Exclusive RCA Victor
Recording Artists

Various poses we did for RCA in 1958. Courtesy of RCA.

I love this pose of the three of us, especially the expression on Bonnie's face. This picture shows off the six hundred dollar dresses we bought at Sydell's in New York and wore for the first time on the *Arthur Murray Show. Courtesy of RCA.*

Above: Listening to playback of "Scarlet Ribbons" with Chet Atkins in May 1959. *Courtesy of RCA.*

Left: Chet Atkins, our A&R for RCA and our good friend. He produced 346 singles and twenty-two albums. *Courtesy of RCA.*

"Three Bells Overhead." We were appearing in Texas somewhere and RCA wanted us to have our picture taken under
the bells. It was going to be used on an album cover, but this
never happened because RCA said I was "squinting" my eyes
too much; we were looking right into the sun. I have always
loved this picture anyway. *Courtesy of RCA.*

The Browns as they appeared on the *Ed Sullivan Show* on
May 8, 1960. Bonnie and I bought our dresses at Sydell's in
New York. It's interesting to note the extra piece of material on
the front of Bonnie's dress. In those days, you could show no
cleavage, and certainly no movements. Bonnie was sent back to
their alteration department to correct this problem. *From the
collection of Maxine Brown.*

Norma (substituting for Bonnie), Maxine, and Jim Ed at a
record shop in Cleveland. *From the collection of Maxine Brown.*

Jim Ed, Maxine, Bonnie, Billy Deaton, Jim Reeves, and Tom
Perryman. This picture was taken after a show in Henderson,
Texas, for the Jim Reeves homecoming celebration. The dresses
that Bonnie and I are wearing were made by our new designer,
Helene, of Fort Smith, Arkansas. They were not allowed on the
Grand Ole Opry. Courtesy of Tom Perryman, Tyler, Texas.

Taken by WSM's the *Grand Ole Opry* to be hung backstage at the Rymon Auditorium, along with pictures of all the other *Opry* performers. These are also the costumes we wore when we were inducted into the *Opry* on June 3, 1963. *Courtesy of Les Leverette, Nashville, Tennessee.*

The Browns were guests of the Minnesota Twins for a game around 1964. *From the collection of Maxine Brown.*

The Browns were the very first artists to record in the new RCA studio. Chet Atkins is at the controls. *Courtesy of RCA.*

Learning to use chopsticks in Japan, 1965: Skeeter Davis, Chet Atkins, and the Browns. *From the collection of Maxine Brown.*

This is my favorite picture of Mom and Dad. It looks just the
way I remember them. It was taken at a Brown family reunion.
From the collection of Maxine Brown.

All the artists on the *Opry* in 1966. Can you name any? First row: Sonny Osborne, Bobby Osborne, Archie Campbell, Jim McReynolds, Jesse McReynolds, Bill Carlisle, Hank Snow, Skeeter, Guy, and Vic Willis, Bobby Lord, and Billy Walker. Second row: Ray Pillow, Roy Acuff, Cousin Jody, Bill Monroe, Dottie West, Porter Wagoner, Stoney Cooper, Wilma Lee Cooper, Curley Fox, Stringbean, Norma Jean, Grandpa Jones, Margie Bowes, Lonzo and Oscar, Bonnie, Maxine, and Jim Edward Brown. Third row: Chuck,

Tompall, and Jim Glaser, George Hamilton IV, Marion Worth, Lester Flatt, Earl Scruggs, Maybell, June, Anita, and Helen Carter, Roy Drusky, Hank Locklin, Bill Anderson, Teddy and Doyle Wilburn, Justin Tubb, and Skeeter Davis. Fourth row: Minnie Pearl, Bobby Bare, Bob Luman, Del Wood, Ernest Tubb, Jimmy Newman, Ernie Ashworth, Loretta Lynn, Marty Robbins, Del Reeves, Charlie Louvin, Jean Shephard, Tex Ritter, Connie Smith, Billy Grammer, and George Morgan. *Courtesy of Les Leverette, Nashville, Tennessee.*

Above: Publicity picture of Maxine Brown made for Chart Records in 1969. *Courtesy of Fabry Photography, Nashville, Tennessee.*

Right: Publicity picture of Maxine Brown made for Chart Records. *Courtesy of Fabry Photography, Nashville, Tennessee.*

Losing Momma

Delores booked me on a series of "hillbilly park" dates, four or five in succession in and around West Virginia. She had also booked a band I'd never heard of to accompany me on all the dates and arranged for me to ride the circuit in one of their cars, since I was alone and flying in to begin the tour.

It was the most vulgar band I ever saw. They were not only bad pickers, they dressed sloppy and smelled like a brewery. They drank constantly from one date to the next. I didn't want to travel with them and tried every way to get out of it. But there were no planes or buses traveling that route. We got through the first two shows and began the long trip to the next park. It was obvious we would have to drive all night.

We hadn't gone many miles when those geeks started making suggestive and insulting remarks to me. "Hey Maxine, when are you gonna cut loose and show us your stuff?" "Baby, I'll give you the ride of your life." "Come on, woman you've been on the road, you're an old pro, you can take us all on."

Then one of them started running his hands over me, really getting fresh. They were drunk as coots, and I began to get scared. I could tell what they had in mind, and they were not kidding. All of a sudden, the drummer, who was driving, pulled the car off the road. It was dark, and all I could hear were those SOBs laughing and whispering. The guy next to me tried to take hold of my knees. I rammed my fist into his gut and jumped out of the car, yelling and screaming. I started running back down the road as fast as I could.

"Come on back, Maxine!" they yelled. "We was just kidding!"

I ran on. I prayed for a car or truck to come along so I could get away. The road was dark as pitch. I ran until I was out of breath. I just stood there trembling and crying. This is it, I thought. I was going to get raped and beat up and left in some ditch in West Virginia.

Their car came cruising along slowly. I was exhausted by now, and all I could do was limp along. One guy leaned out the window and tried to smooth things over. "We were just kidding with you. We only wanted to see how far you'd go." I'd rather have died than get back in that car with them, but they had my guitar, all my costumes, and my purse with all my money in it. So I got back in. They didn't try anything else the rest of the trip, but I didn't close an eye either.

Hap Peebles, one of the biggest concert promoters in the country, was at the next park. He came up to me and said, "Your brother and his band are playing about twenty miles down the road." I was never so happy to hear anything in my life. I told Hap what had happened to me and that I wasn't going to work the next date with that bunch of creeps. I called J. E. and told him to pick me up. He said he had a new girl singer, Jamie Ryan, on the bus and that there wasn't room for me. I told him I'd sit on the floor if I had to. So he agreed to pick me up as soon as they finished their last show.

I had to tell J. E. what happened to me. I was a physical and an emotional wreck by the time his bus pulled in that night. I prayed to God all those miles back and vowed that if I got back home to my babies and family I'd never do another show by myself as long as I lived. My children needed me and I needed them. I would find some other way to make a living; I'd done it before, and I could do it again.

I came home and it was like crawling into a hollow log. I didn't want to see anybody or anyone to see me. I felt like my life was over. I know now that I was in dire need of professional help. My nerves were shot. I was about as emotionally sure-footed as a mountain goat in high heels. I became a recluse. My mind simply wouldn't hold a thought. Finally I was able to face the mirror and tell myself, "You don't have the will to put up that almighty front any longer." How unkind, cruel, and unyielding show business had become. "Give it up," a small voice kept saying. "Give it up." At that moment, a terrible melancholy and sadness came over me. So I got a paper and pencil and began to write a song.

• • •

J. E. had named his band the Gems. They were booked for an extended engagement at Lake Tahoe in 1968 and decided to stop at our folks' house in Pine Bluff to spend a few hours. I went down to see them off, and J. E. had a surprise for me. It was a copy of his new single, "The Cajun Stripper." After we listened to it, he played the flip side. To my utter surprise the song was "(You'll Never Know) The Thrill of Loving You," a song I had written. This was a thrill. I knew he had the song, but I never dreamed he would actually record it. After a little while J. E. took me aside and said, "Pack your bag. You're going with me to Tahoe and be part of the show."

There was no way I could do it. I'd given it all up. I'd made my separate peace. But my heart was beating a mile a minute, and I knew I'd give anything for another chance. Even though I hadn't sung on stage in over a year and had let myself go physically, I couldn't resist.

"I've gained weight and I don't have anything to wear on stage," I argued—with myself as much as with J. E.

"You're going," J. E. said. "We can stop somewhere along the way and get you a dress."

So I made up my mind to go back, just like that. They waited for me while I ran back to Little Rock, packed and said goodbye to my kids yet again. The road pulled me like a magnet. It was on that trip, I guess, that I started drinking, more out of habit than for relaxation. J. E. got on to me one night after I ordered a double. He said he didn't allow his band members to drink on tour and that I was setting a bad example. I was so embarrassed and ashamed that I almost died, and I resented his jumping me. I wasn't a drunk. That little scene should have served as an omen to me, but I forgot about it quickly.

I sang a few solos in Tahoe and did some medleys with J. E. We got a great reception from the crowds out there. But when I came back home, I told myself that there wasn't enough on the road to drag me back to that tough old life. I stayed at home, took care of my ailing mother, and tried to make feeble ends meet. I found myself hitting the bottle a little bit more. It wasn't enough to hurt me, I rationalized, just enough to ease me through these meager days.

A year passed, and I still stayed away from the stage. I took care of my children and eked out a living as best I could. I was sure it was all over for me, but something inside wouldn't let me quit completely. I found that I missed my old friends terribly. So when the Country Music Association Awards show rolled around in the fall of 1969, I decided to go to Nashville and see what was going on.

For so many of those past years, we had invitations to every function at the convention. And we were up for awards just about every year. This time, I was going as an outsider and a freeloader. I didn't get invited to one single event. But that was OK. I just wanted to be there. I got a ticket to the CMA Awards show through the *Grand Ole Opry*, but no one bothered to explain to me the procedure for getting in. I stood outside in line for two hours with the fans, waiting to get inside and mingle with the greats. I found out later that the *Grand Ole Opry* artists were all guests of honor and seated in a special roped-off section of the auditorium. All my *Opry* friends came right by me, while I just stood there like a whipped animal, fighting the hurt and the tears. I wasn't even old hat anymore—I was a has-been.

Bob Jennings, the great all-night deejay at WLAC in Nashville, came by, saw me and stopped. "Why, Maxine Brown! What are you doing out here in this line? You're supposed to be with all the other *Opry* stars."

"I'm not an *Opry* star any more," I said.

"The hell you're not."

He took hold of my hand and led me inside and found me a seat. That little act of kindness braced me and lifted my spirits, and I'll always be grateful to Bob Jennings. Still, I felt like such an outsider, even though I'd been gone for less than a year. The old saying that you're only as big as your last record was painfully true. I began to feel as though the Browns had never existed, that we had never made it off that poor dirt farm in south Arkansas, and everything that had happened—the excitement of hoping and the depression of losing it all—was just a dream.

The next year Bonnie and I went back and experienced the same thing together. No invitations. No parties. No nothing. We felt completely left out, and it hurt us badly. It would be a long time before I could pull enough self-esteem together to be an onstage performer. I went back to live at home in Little Rock and tried to forget that I had ever dreamed of being a singer. I had yet to learn that even if you give up the business, it seems to come back to you.

At the end of the '60s, Herb Shucher, our former manager, was doing some publicity work for Shelby Singleton of Plantation Records. Herb called me one day and said that Shelby was interested in signing me if I hadn't committed to anyone else. I'd just gotten loose from Chart. This seemed like just the break I was looking for. I'd known Shelby from the old *Louisiana Hayride* days, and his label was doing quite well, having just come out with Jeannie C. Riley's "Harper Valley P.T.A.," which my old friend Tom T. Hall had written. I jumped at this new chance.

In 1970, I had my one and only record for Plantation. It was called "Is That All There Is" and was a cover of the pop hit Peggy Lee had had out the year before. I think it is one of the best songs of all time. And it was Peggy Lee at her best. But my country version of it was probably the best thing I'd ever done, too. When my version came out, the trade magazines all praised it to the heavens. One deejay even went so far as to say my version was in many ways better than Peggy Lee's was.

I was thrilled when all the reviews came out. It was getting great play on the country music stations and had already started climbing up some of the charts. Then all of a sudden, nothing. Nothing. It was as though my version was struck by lighting, killed, and buried. No one could understand it. All the radio stations that reported their playlists to the trade magazines were still giving it high marks. Then everything stopped, as if a boycott had been put in place.

I've wondered all the years since what actually happened to my song. And I've heard all sorts of dark rumors. One person high up in the music business told me my version was killed because it was threatening the sales of Peggy Lee's version. While I never really believed that rumor, since Peggy Lee was on a different label, I had no reason to dismiss the word of the reputable person who told me the story. An artist can always find excuses for their record not hitting. The fact that the song was over four minutes long probably had something to do with it since deejays didn't like to program singles that ran more than three minutes. Whatever the reason, the song was dead—along with the usual bouquet of my high hopes. I never had a chance to record a second session for Shelby. Shortly after my song died on the charts, Plantation Records went completely out of business. Instead of "Is That All There Is," it was "that's all there was."

J. E. and the Gems had been a big hit out at Tahoe in 1968, and early in 1970 they were invited back for a longer engagement. The booking agent asked that I be a part of the show, too. Again I was flattered and again lured to the bright lights. So back I went. This time we were in taller cotton. We worked the Sahara Casino and Hotel, along with the popular *Laugh-In* TV cast that featured Rowan and Martin and Goldie Hawn and a good group called the Four 3 Cheers.

Because we were booked in Tahoe for six weeks, we got the great idea to fly Momma and Daddy out for the first real vacation of their lives. But Momma couldn't talk Daddy into leaving his sawmill, so she decided to come by herself. Besides having never flown alone before, she also had a bad heart condition. I was anxious every minute of the time she was in flight until we picked her up at Reno. She was carrying a large overnight case full of her medicine, and when I picked it up I noticed how heavy it was. She was tired from the trip, and she looked weaker than ever. But she was one tough trooper. I'm glad now that she got to take the trip, for she had the greatest time of her life. She loved those big shows and casinos. She got up early every morning and went to play bingo, her favorite. I swear she was the luckiest gambler alive. She bingoed three or four times a day and once hit a six hundred dollar jackpot.

J. E.'s wife Becky came out to join him too, and after our shows we all lived it up. J. E. and Becky went skiing a lot, and we toured historic old Virginia City. Momma didn't miss a beat. She'd summoned up so much energy she amazed us all. When Momma and I were on our way back home, we had a layover in Dallas. We were strolling around and window shopping in some of those nice stores. At one of them, Momma stopped me, pointed to a dress in the window and said she was going to buy it for me. She was always doing something for her children. As we walked out of the shop with the new dress, she tried to take her heavy overnight case that I was carrying.

"You're not carrying this, Momma," I said and pulled it back.

"But it's too heavy for you," she argued.

There she was, a woman whose hard life had tried to beat her down, and she was still worried about one of her children. This little scene, which seemed almost trivial and insignificant at the time, would play in my mind again and again in the years to come.

• • •

In June of 1970, Momma saw us on stage for the last time. J. E. and I were booked as separate acts at the big Robinson Auditorium in downtown Little Rock. This was where J. E. and I had started our career on the old *Barnyard Frolic*. As I went on stage that night I couldn't help but think of the scores of times Momma had sat out there in the audience watching her kids perform. That night she was thrilled to see us again where it all started.

It was a special moment, and I know now that it made up to her for a lot of the bad times we'd gone through. There was a glow about my mother that night, and it was more than just pride in her kids. There was a peacefulness in her eyes and a sweetness in her voice that even her relentless pain could not blot out.

Then, on July 3, 1970, J. E. and I were working a show in Maryland. (I still wouldn't work with anyone but J. E. and his band.) That night, Blake Emmons, who would soon become the co-host with J. E. on the popular TV show *Nashville On The Road,* was working with us. We put on a good show, but we felt bad that we couldn't be home for the Fourth of July; it had always been a family-reunion day for the Browns. I talked to Bonnie on the phone the next day. She said that she and Norma and their families had spent an old-fashioned Fourth with Momma. It made me terribly homesick.

A week later I was home again with Momma. I helped her put up two whole bushels of peas, and that night for supper she cooked some of her special Mexican food for me. It was one of those balmy, still, July nights when people sit out on the front porch and look off into the deepening, starry night. It was the last time I ever saw her.

My mother died the next day, July 12, 1970. She was in her kitchen, as always, and had a seizure. Her heart just stopped. She was only fifty-seven years old. I actually think she died from overwork.

It isn't enough to say that I loved my mother. It was so much more than that. In the end, I was thankful and grateful to her for being my greatest friend and for teaching me, above all, the power of loving kindness.

Chicken Today, Feathers Tomorrow

Nobody knew how hard the next few years would be for me, the rough times I would have simply keeping food on the table for my children. After my marriage went to pieces and my singing career started downhill, my folks made sure my kids didn't go without the necessities. As long as Momma was alive, she saw to it that her grandchildren had the best clothes, the most expensive toys, and about everything else that their hearts desired.

I hated to take money from my folks; it was the most shameful and humiliating thing I ever did. Many a time I lied and told Daddy that Tommy had sent me money for the kids. But I was constantly having to track him down to get the money due. Every month was a war. Even when he gave me a check, I couldn't be sure it would clear. His favorite slogan was, "Take your best hold and go." I never knew quite what that meant, but it pretty much translated into "Take care of yourself, because I'm not going to help you one little bit." I got tired of eating his crow, but that's all I had at the time. So I had to swallow all the pride in me and beg him every month, even while he was taking big vacation trips and sporting a harem of women around. Every now and then I would hear Tammy Wynette singing "Stand By Your Man," and I'd just laugh until I cried.

When insurance and tax time rolled around, I'd hold a garage sale. I'd almost give away the many valuable items I'd picked up on my travels as a big-time recording star. Some star I was now! I was living out that old saying: "Chicken today, feathers tomorrow." Times got so hard that I wondered if I'd ever have chicken again.

And then I got a phone call from J. E. I was back in show business.

• • •

J. E. was very excited on the phone; he said he had found a big hit, another "The Three Bells" for sure. He wanted me to come to Nashville as soon as I could get there—and Bonnie too. But Bonnie and Brownie were attending a medical convention in California.

"The recording session is in two days," J. E. said. "Can you make it, Maxine?"

"I'll be there with bells on."

I don't know how I arranged everything, but somehow I made it to Nashville the next day. Just walking back into a recording studio again with purpose was almost as big a thrill to me as having that first hit. All my old session friends were there and welcomed me back royally. The song J. E. had found was "Morning." This was in the fall of 1970. After we ran through it the first time, I agreed with J. E. that it was a special song, every bit as good as "The Three Bells." During the session I sang both my part and the one Bonnie would have sung. This gave us that true "Brown sound." Everybody connected with the recording of the song thought the same thing—that the Browns were back and better than ever.

When the record came out, it got rave reviews. It went to number four in *Billboard,* J. E.'s highest charter since "Pop A Top" three years earlier. I was thrilled. What an amazing and wonderful comeback, I thought.

I didn't get any credit for my work on the record, however. My name wasn't on the record anywhere, and the deejays who were playing it now were simply saying that Jim Ed Brown had a smash hit on his hands. I must say, though, that many of the deejays were asking out loud if this wasn't the Brown Trio at work again because the sound was so much like that of those great songs we'd done in the past. Still, my name wasn't mentioned on the credits, not even in tiny print. It was J. E. who was signed to the record company—still RCA—and naturally they were going to promote his name, not mine.

I thought that maybe I'd reestablish myself in the business after the great success of "Morning," but it didn't happen. I never went on tour again. It was right after "Morning" that J. E. hired the Cates Sisters as part of his act. They were the first in a succession of girl singers who would try to fill the gap Bonnie and I left. But try as they might, none of these substitutes could ever quite duplicate our voices, at least that's what all the deejays said. I was trapped in the middle of things, with neither the option of going forward with my career or backward into being a supported housewife. In music, what I had to settle for, when I could get it, was singing backup on someone else's records for union scale.

J. E. came up with what he though was another hit song, "Butterfly," fast on the heels of "Morning." I went back to Nashville, this time with Bonnie, for the recording session. Like it or not, the record company and the producers had to work with "the Brown sound" again. "Butterfly" went beautifully, I thought. Bob Ferguson, a great producer, had already laid down the instrumental tracks before we ever got to the studio. That's the way they were doing things then, and my oh my, how things were changing. Bonnie and I understood that we'd be working for only union scale. But we didn't care. It was good enough for us that we were singing as the trio once more. We rehearsed and rehearsed to get ready for the session. When we finished overdubbing our voices, we knew we had matched the very best we had ever done in making a record.

We went back home to Arkansas thinking that "Butterfly" would be another "Morning" for J. E. Our satisfaction was in knowing we had been reunited and had taken part in his triumph. It turned out that we did too good a job. The record company people weren't at all satisfied. We heard that the bigwigs were afraid that the old Browns' sound was just too dominant on the record. So they ordered some last-minute fixing. When the record came out, Bonnie and I got the shock of our life. We couldn't hear our voices on it at all. The studio had gone back and covered our voices with those of other background singers.

What the label managed to do in all its corporate wisdom was totally ruin a song that could have become a classic. "Butterfly" got lukewarm reviews and never got on the charts. J. E. finally had to include it in one of his albums. It was a pity too, and J. E. was awfully depressed about it. If anybody at the label had ever bothered to listen to and release the original tracks, they would have had a big hit on their hands. At least Bonnie and I had the satisfaction of knowing we could still make a great record. It's still there, brilliant but silent, gathering dust in the label's musty archives.

• • •

So my return to the business was short-lived. My financial circumstances did finally begin to improve, though. One day, I received a sizable check from RCA. It seemed that the Browns, after so many years of being in the red to the label (despite our string of hits), had finally moved into the black. Our records were still selling briskly and showing a profit. The check wasn't nearly as large as the first one back we got when we started making it big, but it was enough to help pay my mounting bills and buy my children the things they needed. Getting that official statement of royalties from RCA lifted my spirits tremendously. It was almost like a scene out of a movie, where you're saved just in the nick of time.

All of a sudden, I felt much better. I had gone back to Nashville and helped make a great song, and now I had a slice of RCA pie. It was such a good feeling that I kept waiting around for something even bigger to happen. I'm still waiting.

Back home, things sort of drifted along. Since my Momma's death, I hadn't seen much of my dad. I heard he was going out with women and spending a lot of his money on the kind of high living Momma seldom got to taste. I saw him a time or two with a young woman from near Redfield. Pretty soon the whole family became upset with the way he was carrying on, spending big money on gifts and trips for that young floozy. All of the family felt he was committing an unpardonable sin against our Momma's memory. It took the whole family to convince him that his lady friend was playing him for a fool. He finally dropped her, but it wasn't long until he took up with some others just as bad.

My dad and I hadn't gotten along well for the past several years. For one thing, he had such a double standard when it came to the girls in the family. We argued a lot of the time, and it was very difficult for me—and the whole family—to go through what happened next. Though we hadn't gotten along too well all those years, I didn't think that he was a bad man. Overall, he was truly a good man. He helped people all his life and would give the proverbial shirt off his back to a friend in need. He was also the strongest man I ever knew. That's why it hurt so much to see what happened to him the last few years of his life.

Back when I was a young girl, sneaking away to a show in Little

Rock, I had caught my daddy with another woman. That awful day stayed hidden deep inside me for years. There were times when I knew Momma wanted to talk privately to me about something that had always bothered her. I always managed to put her off and refuse to listen. I knew what she wanted to say, just as I knew Momma and Daddy had once had some pretty bad fights over a certain woman.

Not long after Momma died, Daddy was seen again with this same woman. Momma had told me a few weeks before she died that she was getting calls from an unidentified woman asking for "Floyd." Surely to God it wasn't the same woman they'd always fought over? But it was. Some men are plagued all their lives by the wrong woman.

In a strange way, I was kind of happy that Daddy was seeing other women, even though they were just tramps after his money. I just didn't want him to be with *that* woman. For a while, everything seemed to go along smoothly. We thought Daddy had settled down after getting some of that sunshine out of his ass. Then he stopped coming to my house to visit with his grandchildren and me. He was treating my sister Norma the same way. One day Norma dropped in on him at his home, and there sat that one woman we all knew. Well, all hell broke loose in the family, and for the next six years it was pure, unadulterated torture.

We had to sit back and watch as Daddy slowly sank from being a millionaire to the level of a pauper. He sold off everything he and Momma owned: their home, his lumber and sawmill business, the club, and all his other holdings. He built his new woman an elegant new home and gave her new cars, jewelry, and fine clothes. They took trips to the horse races all over the country and lived, for a time, like the rich and famous.

J. E. was filming his TV series, *Nashville On the Road,* in Biloxi, Mississippi, and he called Bonnie and me to see if we'd like to come down and do a show with him. We jumped at the chance. I promised Daddy that we'd stop off to see him on our way down to the coast. But for some reason or another—maybe we were running late—we didn't do it. I've always regretted that, for while we were in Biloxi, Norma called and said that Daddy was in the hospital.

"What's wrong?" I asked. "He was feeling fine when I saw him the other day."

"He went into the hospital," Norma said, "because he got a crick in his neck that was giving him fits." She said his condition was growing worse by the hour and that it wasn't just from a crick in his neck. "The doctor says he's real bad off." She told me that Daddy was crying and asking for us and that he was going on and on about wanting our forgiveness for the bad things he'd done.

J. E., Bonnie, and I rushed back home. But by the time we got to the hospital, Daddy had suffered a stroke. They let us go in to see him. We tried to talk to him, but he really didn't understand what we were saying. The next day he slipped into a coma that he never came out of. He lingered for a few hours, but there was no hope. He died on June 6, 1976, at the age of sixty-six.

There's an old saying, put in a song by Waylon Jennings, that what goes around comes around. Nobody in the wide world will ever make me believe that old saw. I've seen too many evil people, in and out of show business, prosper and never answer for it. There's a bigger meaning or reason to life, I guess, in the way we choose to be. Still, I'm sure in the memory of my daddy's good works that the Lord doesn't want that bad woman, just as I'm sure the devil ain't through with her.

The Browns' Recording Studio

It's funny how people who know you were a star think you retired on top. I hadn't retired at all. The country music business just sort of sloughed away from me piece by painful piece. Though I was getting along better financially, I was always on the lookout for some way to stay in touch with that crazy world I'd been in love with since I was a little girl listening to the *Grand Ole Opry*. I know Bonnie felt the loss too.

We got the idea of starting up our own recording studio in Little Rock. Beginning such a venture would be a major undertaking, we knew, but we were very idealistic. We wanted to offer our experience in the business to good artists, new and old, without them having to experience the shoddy treatment and thievery we'd been subjected to. Even if we didn't make a million, we told ourselves we'd run the best and most honest recording studio in the business.

With much encouragement and financial assistance from Bonnie's husband, Brownie, we started Brown's Recording Studio. For our grand opening, we threw one hell of a party. We invited every local celebrity and politician we could think of. The spanking new studio was a beautiful sight, and we wanted to show it off. Bonnie thought it would be nice to have someone from Nashville so she decided on our friend, Leo O'Rourke, who was a hypnotist. Leo brought along two of Nashville's finest songwriters, Hank Cochran and Red Lane. All three were hits of the party, especially Leo.

A few months after our studio opened, Bonnie and I started getting complaints about the sound quality. We contacted our friend Scotty Moore, to see if he would come to Little Rock and give us his expertise. He had his own recording studio in Nashville and was living there since his days of traveling with Elvis were over. "I'll be there as soon as I can make the arrangements," he assured us.

Scotty worked with me, Bonnie, and our engineer, Gary McVay, one full day until about ten o'clock, and we couldn't find one damn thing wrong with the sound. So we decided to take a break and go downtown to one of the clubs. There was a new band playing that Scotty wanted to hear. It was a band Gary played with when we didn't have a session booked. He was very talented and could play just about every instrument there was.

Gary had just bought a big, black hearse to transport his instruments in, so instead of taking one of our automobiles, we decided to go in Gary's new hearse. Gary had white stripes painted all over the sides, front, and back to make it look like a zebra. Everything had been removed except the front seat and the rollers for the caskets. To tell the truth, we were all about three sheets in the wind or else we wouldn't have dared to climb into the hearse. I rode up front with Gary, while Bonnie and Scotty rolled around in the back on those rollers. Scotty had brought along a young girlfriend to the studio, and she got mad as hell because we went off and left her. There she stood, watching as Bonnie and Scotty waved bye-bye, laughing like two hyenas.

I think she was so mad that she was the one who called the police on us (no telling what she told them). I kept telling Scotty that we ought to go back and get her, but he said, "Hell, she's got my car and she can go on back to the motel."

We went on to the club, but the band was taking a long break. So we had a few drinks and left. We had almost made it back to the studio when all of a sudden there were blue lights everywhere. There must have been fifty police cars.

"Gary, what in the world do they want?" I shouted. "There ain't no dope in here, is there?"

Gary assured us there wasn't. "I think I was weaving too much," he said. "But it's all Bonnie and Scotty's fault for rolling around like that. Why, those policemen have probably never seen two people rolling around in the back of a hearse, not live ones anyway."

Two police officers came around to my side and ordered us all out to be searched. One of them told me to throw out my purse and get out with my hands up.

I said, "Look, you son of a bitch, I'm not about to throw out my purse."

Well, this was the unpardonable sin. I called the bastard an SOB. They took us all down to the police station and booked us. After about three hours they let everybody go except me. They kept me all night long. They weren't about to turn me loose. I told Bonnie to go to my house and stay with my kids.

Scotty said, "Bonnie, I think you better get a lawyer for Maxine."

Bonnie woke up a judge and every lawyer she knew, all to no avail. It wasn't until about noon the next day that I was allowed to make a phone call and find someone to "go my bail" and get me out of that stinking place. That was an experience that none of us will ever forget, especially me.

Bonnie and I tried running the studio. But after Gary left to play in a band full-time, we discovered how impossible it was to find a dependable replacement in the Little Rock area, someone who knew how to operate a sixteen-track board. We found another young man who was interested in learning the board and sent him to Nashville to learn everything he could about recording. Everything was fine for awhile, but then he started drinking. If we had a recording session booked he might show up or he might not.

The recording studio was a flop for us and a financial disaster for Brownie. It took Bonnie and me a long time to get over it. By then we had pretty much decided that there wasn't a single place for us in the music business. Oh, we got a few slim opportunities as time went by. We recorded some tracks at J. E.'s house and worked our butts off. But nothing came of it. Later on we cut two demos in Tom T. Hall's studio. Tom Perryman was always our finest friend and supporter. He maintained that some of our old Brown songs could become hits again if we recorded them with a new beat and better equipment. I remember being snowed in once for fourteen days, and during that time I went through every album and single the Browns ever made, looking for a comeback song.

I had a jug of Old Charter stashed away in the house, and when I couldn't stand the drudgery any longer, I started in sipping on it. After a while I found the song all right. It was "The Last Thing I Want," written by Ira Louvin. The more I drank, the better the song got. I must have called everybody I ever knew because my phone bill was outrageous. Tom Perryman kept calling, wanting to know if I wanted him to drop me in a young stud by helicopter. I was damn near ready for anything, young stud or old dud, didn't matter, after staring at four walls for two weeks. At least I had found a hit song for the Browns. The trouble was, no one thought so except me.

• • •

A lot of my friends have wanted to know why I didn't continue to write songs after my early successes. Actually, I wrote often, but only for my own satisfaction and enjoyment. I believed that if my Daddy saw some of my lyrics, he would have thrown me out of the house—or worse. He loved to accuse me of all sorts of sneaky things anyway. I think it was because he was so guilty himself and knew that I was aware of some of his shenanigans. He was probably trying to get something to hold over my head since he was always afraid I'd tell Momma what I knew about his many women friends.

Writing songs became an escape for me, but by the time I started writing again seriously, the old magic was gone. I could never write another one I really liked for the Browns. After signing with RCA, I never seemed to have time to write. Then, after my divorce, I was too bitter to even think about it. Perhaps if I'd have had a real good juicy love affair I could have written another "Here Today." But that never happened.

After the Browns broke up, I wrote quite a few songs. J. E. put some of them on the B-side of his singles. That was upsetting, because I thought mine were better than the A-sides, especially one entitled "If Wishes Were Horses, Beggars Would Ride."

I sent some of my songs to various publishing companies with notes indicating which artists they might be good for, but they'd send them back saying, "We are not soliciting material at this time." It was as though they were dealing with a "wannabe" songwriter instead of someone who'd actually written country hits. Pretty soon, I didn't even care to try. When you never get paid for the songs you have written, what's the use? To this day, I have received very few royalty statements from publishing companies and certainly very little money. On a few occasions, they literally paid me in postage stamps.

When Bonnie and I opened our recording studio, we realized we needed to start our own publishing company. To get us started, I wrote one hell of a song called "Too Many Yesterdays." We sent a demo to a female artist in Nashville who has since made a big name for herself. She loved the song but said she would record it only if we assigned her all the publishing rights and give her one-half of the writer's credit. I flatly refused. Looking back, I'm sorry I didn't do what she asked. One-half would have been better than nothing. I have never tried to get it recorded again.

Things had changed drastically in the music business. Back when the Browns were busy recording, we never once asked a songwriter to split royalties with us. Now, most of the big-time writers have to "cowrite" with an artist to get their songs recorded. And generally they're willing to do it. Things aren't like they were back in our heyday. Today it's a billion-dollar business, and a wise writer can retire on one big hit. With artists demanding a share and publishing companies having staff writers, an outsider doesn't stand a chance of getting his or her songs recorded. So forget it. My trunk is full of what I call "good old outdated country songs."

•　•　•

Nothing stays the same. Not only have publishing companies changed, so have the record labels. Today, an artist might take months to record a song. It's all done in pieces by electronic overdubbing. Digital editing has gotten so precise that they can take a word out of one session and transplant it into another to improve the sound. Often the singer and the musicians are in the studio at different times.

Back during the '50s and '60s when we were recording, you could cut four songs in a standard three-hour session. You sang one or two run-throughs so the musicians could write down the notes. You did a run-through so the engineer could get a balance. And that was it. Then you started taping the song. Session musicians had original ideas and creative minds. We had the best in the business. Chet saw to that. No one had an ear for music that matched Chet's. He was a genius. If he heard a musician hit a certain lick he liked, then that is what he would have him play on the record. Songs recorded in this manner became classics we still listen to today because they were created from the heart.

There were many excellent musicians in Nashville. Chet tried giving each of them a chance to shine, not only with us but with his other artists as well. He was that kind of person. We usually had the same musicians on all our sessions so there was never a problem of getting them to tune their instruments to match our voices. They all knew the Browns sang "tempering harmony" and that Bonnie and I would often bend our notes. Chet taught all of them exactly how to tune so we would never sound flat or sharp.

Floyd Cramer played piano on almost every record the Browns ever made. Jerry Reed, Ray Stevens, Jerry Kennedy, Charlie McCoy, Buddy Harman, Bob Moore, and Junior Huskey also played on a lot of our sessions. Hank "Sugarfoot" Garland played guitar on every one of our sessions until he was severely injured in an automobile accident. From then on, he was so incapacitated he couldn't even remember how to play the guitar. We missed him terribly when we recorded his famous "Sugarfoot Rag" in October 1963. It was one of the songs on our album *Grand Ole Opry Favorites,* which was nominated for a Grammy in 1964.

Another great musician was Bill Walker. Jim Reeves had brought him from Australia to Nashville in 1964 to produce, arrange, and conduct his concerts. It wasn't until he landed in New York that Bill learned of Jim's death. He didn't even know Jim's plane was missing. After the memorial service in Nashville, Chet told Bill that he would use him on RCA sessions. Bill played vibes on his very first session with the Browns on August 6, 1964. After that, he played on almost every record we made.

Chet had stopped playing guitar himself on most of the recording sessions so he could concentrate on producing. There had been entirely too much demand put on him to play, and he decided it wouldn't be fair to play on one artist's session and not on another's. But Chet loved playing on our records. What a thrill it was to see him slip out of the control room and sit in with the other musicians. He even played on our biggest record, "The Three Bells."

Shortly before his death on June 20, 2001, Chet recorded an interview with Eddie Stubbs, the scholarly and award-winning disc jockey on radio station WSM. He told Eddie that the artists he loved recording and producing the most were Jim Reeves and the Browns. In country music, there can be no higher praise than that. Thank you, Chet!

• • •

It was a little after Daddy died that Bonnie decided for sure that she wanted to return to show business full time. We drove over to J. E.'s house in Brentwood, intending to walk in and tell him, "We're back, both of us. We're ready to start recording again, if RCA will have us." J. E.'s own records weren't doing very well at the time, and he was in bad need of a career lift. We thought our return would be that lift.

When we got to J. E.'s house, he met us with a great big smile. "Hello sis and sis," he said. "Am I glad to see you!"

"We've got some news for you," Bonnie said, intending to tell him we were ready to form the trio again and start making personal appearances.

But J. E. said, "First, I've got some news for you. Come on downstairs and let me play you something."

Well, we followed him downstairs, and before we could say another word, he started playing us his new record It was a duet with a new girl singer named Helen Cornelius. The song was entitled, "I Don't Want To Have To Marry You." If you're a country music fan, or even a serious pop music fan, I needn't say more. The song J. E. was playing for us would go on to become one of country's all-time smash hits and make Jim Ed Brown and Helen Cornelius the hottest duet around. As Bonnie and I stood there listening, we knew we were just a little too late.

When J. E. asked Bonnie what she wanted to tell him, she just said, "Oh, well, whatever it was has just been shot out of the saddle. Forget it."

• • •

Our next-to-last hurrah in the recording business was with Tom T. Hall. Back in the '60s, when Tom T. came to Nashville to make a name for himself as a writer, we'd met him several times and loved the songs he was pitching to artists. Though our harmony didn't fit his songs then, we always knew that there was something extra special about that young man. Tom not only had a keen and unsentimental way of looking at things, he also had the perfect way of saying in his lyrics precisely what he saw. He called himself "the Storyteller," and, in my mind, no one has ever come close to taking that title away from him.

Tom T. will never know what a thrill it was for Bonnie and me when, almost out of the blue, he asked us if we'd mind recording an album with him. Would we mind? We were ecstatic! It was in 1977, and except for a few impromptu guest appearances on the *Grand Ole*

Opry and J. E.'s TV show, Bonnie and I were strictly on the sidelines. During the days leading up to our session, Bonnie and I were as nervous as preachers at a horse race. We practiced a lot, dieted, walked, and generally went into combat training. It was hard as hell getting our voices back in shape, but we loved every minute of the effort.

Tom T. had his own recording studio (which he called the Toy Box), so he didn't have to worry about the cost of studio time. Bonnie and I arrived in Nashville early on the day we were to start recording. We were worried about how we'd sound trying to harmonize with Tom T. since we'd not rehearsed a single minute with him. When Bonnie called to let him know we were in town, Tom T. must have anticipated that we were nervous.

"Don't worry about a thing," he said. "We'll have plenty of time to rehearse everything before the session ever starts." With that kind of calming reassurance, we knew we couldn't fail. That old-time spirit we used to take into our recording sessions started coming back.

Tom T. wrote all of the songs we did with him, two of them the very day before the session. They were all great songs. The title of the album was *New Train, Same Rider.* In keeping with the Tom T. Hall style, it had some knockout stuff on it.

Prior to the session, Tom T. had ordered yellow T-shirts for the production staff and everyone who played on the session. In big black letters the shirts said, "The Browns' in Town and Tom T.'s Got 'em!" I mean, he was treating us like we had just won a dozen Grammys! I don't think we've ever been around a more thoughtful person in the business. Some years before, he and his brother Hillman had come to dinner at my house and afterward he sent me a dozen yellow roses. Lord knows how many pickers and singers I've fed over the years, but only Tom T. ever sent flowers.

The session came off without a hitch. It wasn't arduous or backbreaking or one bit tedious. We loved every second of the work. When we were done, Tom T. hosted a big party in our honor out at his and Miss Dixie's home at Fox Hollow. The party came as a big surprise to us. At the end of the session, we were beginning to feel the letdown that inevitably follows the ending of a project you've really enjoyed, but Tom T. said, "Hey, the fun's just beginning." Tom T. and Miss Dixie had arranged to have many of our old Nashville friends come to the party to surprise us. There was Ralph Emery, Bobby Bare, Dee Kilpatrick, and dozens of others we hadn't seen in years. It was the bash of the year in Music City U.S.A. During the party, Tom T. played the album, just hours after it had been cut. Man, we were on Cloud Nine.

Naturally, there's a bittersweet ending to this story. Tom T. had gone to a world of trouble to have Bonnie and me on the album. He believed, like everybody connected with the production, that the album would be a hit and spawn two number one singles. It was Tom T.'s very first album for RCA, and it did yield two number thirteen singles, "May the Force Be with You Always" and "I Wish I Loved Somebody Else." Our vocals were credited on both. But in my opinion, RCA hardly lifted a finger to promote Tom T. or the album. He couldn't understand it. After the album was finished and delivered to RCA, the mixing sounded weak, half-hearted, and well below the high technical standards of Tom T.'s earlier records. Bonnie and I were disappointed both for Tom T. and for our own prospects of returning to recording. But personally and artistically, working with Tom T. Hall was as good as it gets!

Bonnie and I didn't do much in show business after that album. I guess it just proved what some people were saying—that we were has-beens. Still I couldn't stop dreaming. After all those years, I could never quite convince myself it was over. I quit going to see many of the shows my old friends performed when they came through Little Rock. They all had so much security that it was impossible for anyone to get backstage. Once I went to see Willie Nelson, an old and dear friend with whom we'd played many dates. When I tried to go backstage and say hello, his drummer and road manager, Paul English, stopped me.

"I'm Maxine Brown," I told him, and he said, "Oh, yeah? And I'm Jesus Christ." He wasn't about to let me backstage. I'm not sure Willie ever found out about my embarrassment, but maybe he did. When he came to Little Rock the next time, he had me escorted backstage and then led me out on stage to sing "Looking Back To See" with him.

Another time, Waylon Jennings was in town, and I tried to have a note delivered to him. A guy took my note backstage and came back to say, "Waylon doesn't know anybody by the name of Maxine Brown."

Love of God! I'd known Waylon ever since the first day he darted in the doors of RCA, and we'd been the best of friends ever since. I'm sure my note never reached him.

A few years later, George Jones, Conway Twitty, and Merle Haggard, all three our long-time friends, came to Little Rock for a concert. By then every artist had a tour bus and didn't have to resort to waiting in a backstage dressing room. They would remain on their bus until time to go on stage then be escorted in by an army of security guards. Bonnie and I were standing outside Conway's bus, talking to Pork Chop Markham, who had been his drummer for as long as we could remember. We wanted to see Conway in the worst kind of way. But Pork Chop told us that Conway had a new wife who allowed no one on board, not even the band members. Merle must have had other things on his mind too. We couldn't get within a mile of him.

We were so hurt that we said "to hell with it" and started to leave. Then all of a sudden, someone came up behind us and gave us a big old bear hug. It was George Jones. He led us back to his bus, and we had a nice long visit with him and his wife, Nancy. Later, during his show, George introduced Bonnie and me from the stage. This goes to show what a caring and thoughtful person he was—and has always been. He never forgets his friends. Bonnie and I will never forget, either.

I was feeling pretty low down on the totem pole about this time. So I got my pen and paper and wrote:

> I'm looking for the world of the has-been
> Where too many are forgotten too soon
> A place I can reminisce with old friends
> And the sun never comes up till noon . . .

The song goes on to ask about old friends and family ties that time has pushed aside. I showed the song to several artists and friends, and they all seemed to like it. But I could never get anybody to record it. I'm sure it hit too close to home for too many of them.

Legends of Country Music

In 1985, Bonnie and I got another chance to make a comeback as the Browns. On a visit to Nashville to see J. E. and Becky, we went to watch the taping of his show, *You Can Be A Star.* Then we went with J. E. to the *Grand Ole Opry*. He called us on stage to sing with him, and we were called back for several encores.

Opry announcer Charlie Douglas, who was also a disc jockey on WSM, came up to us after the show all aglow. He told us we ought to get the Browns back together because we sounded better than ever—good enough to make a big come back. We thought he was just being nice, but he went on with it.

"I'm putting together a big show in June," Charlie told us. "It's called 'Legends of Country Music.' I'd like all the Browns to be a part of it."

We loved the idea. Since the show wasn't happening until June, Bonnie and I would have time to rehearse and get our voices (and bodies) back up to performance level. And when June came around, we were more than ready. I guess it showed too, because if we ever created magic on stage, it was that night. Of all the great artists who performed that night, only the Browns got a standing ovation and an encore. That old-time adrenaline was pumping harder than ever. Just knowing we could still sing well and still had a world of fans just about overwhelmed us. I looked over at Bonnie as we were performing and saw tears streaming down her face.

It was rough coming back home after that, a terrible let down. We knew we could still do it if only we could find the right label to start recording us again. In the next few weeks, I made several trips to Nashville looking for material we could use on a comeback album. I went through hundreds of tapes in J. E.'s office. I checked with all the writers and publishers I knew. But I discovered that no songwriter or music publisher will ever give you their best songs to record unless you're hot and already selling lots of albums. We were neither. And about all we ever heard from the recording companies was, "We're looking for young, fresh talent and we're reducing our roster."

I found out that about half the artists on the *Grand Ole Opry* had been dropped by their record labels. So it didn't matter much to anyone but us that we had lots of fans and could still be a hit in front of audiences. This was also the dawning of the age of music videos. Now you were expected to look good (that is, young) as well as sound good. A kind of depression had hit country music. It was especially hard on those who had been in the business for a long time. And it was next to impossible for those trying to replant some old roots.

Bonnie and I tried staying in shape while J. E. tried to find us some new connections. In January of 1986, he called to tell us he was about to sign with a new record label. He said it was picking up a lot of good artists who were no longer under contract. That sounded like a description of us. J. E. signed on and asked us to come to Nashville to do an album with him. So we did. We quickly realized that the people who worked for the new label were not of the caliber of those we'd worked with before. Their producer couldn't hold a candle to Chet Atkins. Still, Bonnie and I were happy just to be back in a recording studio. Since only J. E. was under contract, Bonnie and I would receive no artist royalties. But we didn't care. We saw this as an opportunity that could lead to better things.

After we'd finished recording, one of the engineers, a nice guy, made us a tape of our songs. He'd mixed it perfectly, and we left the studio convinced that something good was again going to happen to us. However, just before we walked out, the producer told us he might do some over-dubbing and maybe add some other stuff, such as harmonica and bongo drums. We thought he was kidding.

In April, we returned to Nashville to have photos taken for the album cover. Having been told that the final mix was to be finished later in the week, we stayed over to hear how it all was going to sound. When we went to the studio, we saw a different engineer from the one we'd worked with sitting there and doing the mixing. Something was wrong and we knew it. The sound coming out of the speakers wasn't us. There was no blend at all. We suggested that the engineer and producer listen to the reference tape we were still carrying with us, the one the first engineer had done. But they didn't pay a lick of attention to us.

The mix kept getting worse. Bonnie noticed that the engineer had her name on my track and my name on hers. When she pointed this out, the producer went into a rage. He ranted and raved and finally ordered us out of the studio. We left in tears.

From the studio, we drove straight to J. E.'s house and told him what was going on. He tried to calm us down. He said he'd go down to the studio and straighten it all out. Well, J. E. came back about an hour later, all sour-faced and down. He and the producer had gotten into it and the producer kicked *him* out. J. E. did find out that the control board had broken down and couldn't be repaired in time to get our master recordings out as scheduled. Our album, of course, was the last one they were working on. So they were trying to make do with what they had. This resulted in some of the tracks being left off completely.

The album came out in June, and it sounded so awful that I was ashamed to let anyone know about it. Because of its inferior sound quality, radio stations couldn't play a single cut from it. It was a disaster, and it hurt like hell. We'd been in the business twenty years, and it all came down to this pile of dung.

Meanwhile, newspapers and magazines all around the country were writing about the Browns' comeback. We were getting all kinds of publicity in anticipation of our return with a major album. In the Nashville daily, the *Tennessean,* Thomas Goldsmith wrote, "For nearly 20 years, fans have never stopped asking about a reunion of the sweet-singing Brown Trio . . . [T]hey had a sound that's never been duplicated." The *Memphis Commercial Appeal* carried a full-page headline, "The Browns Comeback Bound to Happen." The *Oakland* (California) *Tribune* headlined us with, "Dream Comes True for Famous Browns." And in another article, the *Tennessean* called our upcoming album "historic."

The articles kept pouring in. We were more famous than we'd ever realized. But the album sent us back into obscurity. We never could understand why the record company would treat artists so poorly, but after all we'd been through, we shouldn't have been surprised.

Still Singing

It's not over until it's over. And it wasn't over yet for the Browns—not by a long shot. Nostalgia for older music had gotten so strong in the '90s that many groups that had disbanded years earlier were getting back together and drawing huge crowds. One reason for this was that radio had stopped playing songs by the classic country artists who'd built the business. But long-time fans still wanted to see the stars and listen to those great old songs again.

By now, our children had all grown up and flown the nest. We were free to leave home any time we wanted to. If we had a worry, it was only about who was going to take care of the dog. Bonnie and I began going to Nashville more often to perform with J. E. on the *Grand Ole Opry*. It seemed like the Browns were going over better with live audiences than we'd ever done before. I can't recall a time we didn't get an encore or a standing ovation.

Our appearance on the *Opry* on October 7, 1990, was awesome. The audience wouldn't let us leave the stage. We did all our hits and they still wanted more. When we finally did leave, Bonnie and I were so excited we couldn't stop crying. Only another performer could know how good it make us feel to be accepted in such a tremendous way after all those years.

Our voices were in excellent shape for this performance because we had been rehearsing with J. E to sing for the ROPE (Reunion of Professional Entertainers) awards show and banquet in 1989. Gordon Terry, then president of ROPE, had invited us to perform at this gala event along with Little Jimmy Dickens. What an honor it was to sing for our peers and see them give us a standing ovation. Happily for us, the press was there to witness it all. In the next day's *Tennessean*, critic Robert K. Oermann enthused, "The family trio, the Browns, reunited especially for the show. Jim Ed and his sisters Maxine and Bonnie practically breathed in harmony as they flawlessly recreated 'The Three Bells,' 'Scarlet Ribbons,' 'The Old Lamplighter' and their other classic hits."

I should say something here about what ROPE is and why it's always been important to us. Because the country music industry was getting so big, impersonal and forgetful of its roots, a bunch of "old timers" got together in 1983 and founded ROPE. Among the founders was our good friend and former manager, Tom Perryman; Patsy Cline's husband, Charlie Dick; and legendary disc jockeys Smokey Smith, Len Ellis, and Ramblin' Lou. A main purpose in establishing the group was to show some respect for the people who had helped make country music into a billion-dollar business. Many of these talented and still-active folks had been cast aside and forgotten, no longer nominated for awards or invited to the big industry social functions. ROPE gave us a place of our own.

Apart from restoring our dignity, ROPE had two other goals— providing financial assistance to entertainers in need and building a retirement home for entertainers. (I've always joked that I'd probably be the first one to move in.) We did a repeat performance for ROPE in 1990 to help fund these two goals. On the show with us were Bill Monroe, Faron Young, and Justin Tubb, all of who have since died.

• • •

The scariest show for an artist is performing to an audience of his or her peers. I was almost quaking with fear when ROPE invited us back again to sing at its annual banquet and awards show in 1999. Even though we had entertained for them twice in the past, this show somehow seemed to be the most important of all. Maybe it was because we were older then and wanted so badly to do a good job.

J. E. hired a TV crew to tape the entire show. I think he wanted to have a full hour on film in case something happened to one of us. After all, the Browns were no spring chickens. Bonnie and I thought we should rehearse, and we did. For two weeks we practiced with the Browns' records until we could sing them all with ease. Then, after arriving in Nashville, we practiced some more with J. E.'s band to master the new material we'd be inserting in the show.

All our finger-crossing and planning paid off. We could tell that as soon as we hit the stage. As usual, my jitters were for nothing. The crowd loved us, and we felt like young stars again. Some of my apprehension, I'm sure, grew out of the informal way we prepared. During all those years of recording for RCA and traveling all over the country, the only time we ever rehearsed was in the car. J. E. would ride in the back seat with his guitar and we would practice as the road flew beneath us. Our main aim in these on-the-run rehearsals was to find a key we liked and which helped us sound the best. I never rehearsed "The Three Bells" until we were on our way to record it.

• • •

I swore I'd never put my voice on another record without having a contract that gave me control over what the final product sounded like. But, oh, what a singer won't do for a chance to sing "one more song." There's a saying among country music people that a singer will drive one thousand miles just to hear himself sing for nothing.

Mabel Birdsong, who owned Master's Touch Recording Studio and Angel Song Music in Nashville, told us she had a telemarketing deal with CBS and that they wanted the Browns to record two religious albums. J. E. called me and said, "Come on up. We'll pick out some songs, rehearse them and if the deal don't work out, we'll pay for the master tape and release it ourselves."

Mabel hired the musicians and engineers and booked the studio time. We recorded ten old-time gospel songs, and when we finished, Bonnie and I asked Mabel about the union contracts we needed to sign for the session. She didn't have them. But we had to come back in a couple of weeks to overdub a big, crucial flat note I sang on "The Family Bible," and Mabel agreed she would have the contracts ready for us to sign then.

Since it was my birthday, April 27, Mabel had ordered a big cake. After the session was over, we were listening to the playback and enjoying our cake and ice cream when in walked this holy-roller preacher from Atlanta, accompanied by two men and two women he identified as his "church quartet." They were all falling-down drunk and as "countryfried" as they come. They said they wanted to record an album—and they wanted to do it now. Mabel pointed out that it was late and that her crew was much too tired to do any more recording that day. But when the preacher pulled out a big old wad of sweaty hundred-dollar bills, Mabel purred, "How soon can you start?"

They began warming up, and I'll swear if this wasn't about the funniest thing we ever saw. The drunker they sang, the longer they got! I've often wondered where they came up with all that money and how many offering plates they had passed. We wanted to stick around and watch those clowns but we had to leave to do the Friday night *Opry*. We heard the next day that they recorded way into the night and kept shelling out those sweaty hundred dollar bills. The engineer promised to send us a copy of their session. He said it was hilarious. Of course we never got it—or the promised contracts.

Two weeks after we returned home, Bonnie's husband, Brownie, had a major heart attack and had to have a quintuple bypass. He was in critical condition for a long time. So we put our gospel album on the back burner. Then we learned that Mabel had filed for bankruptcy, leaving us in limbo. Some months later, J. E. managed to buy back our master. But it would stay untouched on the shelf for another six years.

When Ralph Emery heard we had recorded a gospel album, he asked us to preview some of the songs from it on his television show, *Nashville Now.* We did the show on July 31, Bonnie's birthday. Bonnie's husband was still recuperating from heart surgery, so he came to Nashville with us. Later, we all went with J. E. to the *Opry.* The guest on J. E.'s segment of the show that night was Dottie West. But when it came time for her to go on, she wasn't there. The *Opry* manager asked if Bonnie and I would take her spot, and we agreed. We sang "The Three Bells" and got an encore.

Finally, Dottie arrived, and they let her sing on another segment. I knew she needed the money, but I didn't know just how bad until she invited me into her dressing room. We talked about some of the financial hardships she was facing and how much she still loved Bill, her first husband. She even said, "I wish I could be more like you Maxine—just love 'em and leave 'em and not feel I have to marry everyone who turns me on. But I can't." In spite of all the talk of troubles, we had a few laughs, and then I told her goodbye. That was the last time I saw her. She died in 1991 of complications from a car accident she had on her way to the *Opry.* When I had lived in Nashville years earlier, Dottie was the only one who ever invited me and my children to her home for Sunday dinners. I've always been grateful for her kindness to my children and me.

And the gospel album? Well, years later, after we'd all pretty much forgotten about it, our friend Tom Perryman convinced Step One Records, a small independent label, to release it. Before they could do that, though, we had to pay all the musicians and take care of all the union red tape that Mabel had neglected. *The Browns Family Bible* came out on February 15, 1996, with my still-uncorrected flat note sticking out like a sore thumb.

• • •

In the early '90s, Connie Smith introduced me to a new announcer for WSM and its flagship show, the *Grand Ole Opry*. The announcer's name was Eddie Stubbs. Not only was he one of the nicest young men I'd ever met, he also knew more about country music and country artists than anyone else I've ever known. When I first met him, he asked, "What song of the Browns do you like best?" When I told him my all-time favorite was "Ground Hog," he was flabbergasted! I'm sure he expected me to say "Just As Long As You Love Me" or "I Take the Chance" or one of the pretty ballads from our early years. Then I explained that it wasn't our singing that made me like "Ground Hog" but Chet Atkins's fantastic picking on the record.

I don't know if Eddie was there to see it or not, but one night on the *Opry*, I lost my teeth. Right on stage and right in the middle of the plaintive "Scarlet Ribbons," my upper partial fell completely out of my mouth and down on my tongue. It may have been because I was nervous and my mouth was dry as a bone. Anyway, I had to turn my back to the audience and push the partial back into place. I know everyone must have wondered what in the world I was doing. When the *Opry* crew found out about it, they just roared!

Somehow, word of how well the Browns were doing on the *Opry* spread to Ed Gregory, the owner of United Shows of America. At that time, his company booked several big shows a year, some of which featured as many as forty acts. In early February of 1996, Ed asked Bonnie and me if we would like to go to Tampa for the Florida State Fair and sing with J. E., who was already booked on the show. Ed said he would pay for our plane fare and for our performance. Of course we'd go. What made his offer even more attractive is that it would give Bonnie a chance to see her daughter, Kelly, who lived in Florida, and her new baby.

Strictly speaking, this would be the first concert the Browns had performed in twenty-eight years. Of course we had performed on the *Grand Ole Opry* and the ROPE banquets, appeared on several TV shows, at the ROPE events, and sung on a few other stage shows in and around Nashville. But they hadn't been full-fledged concerts. We had dreamed of having one for many years, and we will always be grateful to Ed and Jo Gregory for giving us this golden opportunity. It was such a pleasure to have Kelly introduce us on stage to 27,000 people. It was awesome. We got a standing ovation, and the applause was deafening. Since there were forty acts on the show, our stage time was limited, but the way we were accepted gave us a huge high.

None of Bonnie's children or mine had ever seen us in concert. Tampa was a first for Bonnie's daughter, Kelly. When Ed invited us to appear at the Arizona State Fair in Phoenix the following October, it was my turn to have a special delight. My oldest son lived near Phoenix, so this gave him the opportunity to finally see his mom in concert. We brought the house down, and I was so happy Tommy got to see it. I wanted to make him proud, and we did!

Ed always referred to Bonnie and me as "his girls." We loved it! He asked us to do the same circuit again in 1997: Tampa, West Palm Beach, and Phoenix. There was no way we'd turn him down. It wasn't just that the money he paid helped me handle a lot of bills, it was also the chance his bookings gave us to see a lot of our old friends, such as Freddie Hart, Hank Thompson, Leroy Van Dyke, and artists from the west coast we hadn't seen in years. Ed started bringing in Eddie Stubbs to help emcee the show. He was so brilliant and such a joy to listen to. He's the type of person you'd like to put in your pocket and take home.

Brownie and our younger sister, Norma made the next trip with us to the *Opry*. We stopped off in Tunica, Mississippi, for a little relaxation and gambling before going on to Music City. No use to hurry. J. E. wouldn't be back in town until that Saturday afternoon. So we couldn't rehearse. During the night, I awoke with the most excruciating pain I ever had in my life! Thank God our doctor—Brownie— was with us. I was having a gallbladder attack. Brownie thought we should go back home, but I wouldn't hear of it. I had been seeing commercials on TNN advertising our appearance on the *Opry*. Since I didn't know if TNN had any clips of us singing "The Three Bells" that they could substitute for our live appearance, I had to do the show. Having decided this, we drove on to Nashville.

On Saturday morning, the day of the *Opry*, Bonnie and I did an interview with Eddie Stubbs on WSM. Since J. E. was still out of town, we did it by ourselves. But we must have done all right because calls came in from all over the country. And one was from our long-time friend, George Jones. That made our day!

After the *Opry*, I went back home and had my gallbladder removed. I started thinking that I needed some mechanical insurance to cover all my worn-out body parts. As soon as I healed, we went back to Nashville. Besides playing the *Opry*, we were booked on a lot of locally produced shows—seven in four days. One of them was TNN's popular variety series, *Prime Time Country*. We had never done this show before and the guest host was one of our friends from long ago, Brenda Lee. Neither Bonnie nor I had seen Brenda since our *Ozark Jubilee* days. She was just as spunky and as much fun as ever. We did two shows on both the Friday and Saturday night *Oprys*, *Ernest Tubb's Midnight Jamboree*, Opryland Park, and two interviews. I must say we tore 'em up on every show we did. This was especially true on the *Opry* shows, where we sang every song we could think of. We did "Here Today and Gone Tomorrow" and "I Take the Chance" without even having a chance to rehearse them. And the crowds loved us. They never got tired of hearing "The Three Bells."

I would have to say that 1996 and 1997 were the most spectacular years we had since our retirement. Bonnie and I began feeling like stars again. The excitement of knowing our music was still in demand and that country fans still accepted us was the greatest thrill we could imagine. *Opry* star Jeannie Seely once asked us "How do you just walk away?" Well, you can be sure we'd given that question a lot of thought. If you're a woman entertainer and you've got kids, the answer is simple. You don't walk away. You run. I can still feel the pain of coming home from a trip and seeing the wants and needs on the faces of my children and then watching the tears stream down their little faces when Momma had to leave again. It was heartbreaking.

I've been asked several times over the years what advice I would give to a young girl just starting out in show business. My answer: Don't get married. If you can't give a hundred percent of yourself to your home life, then it's best to remain single. You can't have the best of both worlds. But if you insist on marrying, try to marry someone in the business who understands the demands that will be made on you. But even a show business marriage is no guarantee of satisfaction or permanency. I've seen too many of them fail.

• • •

It was January of 1998 when we next went back to Nashville. We did the *Grand Ole Opry Live* segment, which Bill Anderson hosted. Bill has always been one of my favorite songwriters and entertainers. He wrote one of the early songs we recorded, "Alpha and Omega." For reasons I still don't understand, it never became a hit. But I think it still could be a smash! Bill has so much charm, dignity, and class that it's easy to understand why he is a superstar. We were proud we finally had a chance to be on his show.

Earlier that Saturday morning, I noticed I couldn't see well enough to read the morning paper. I wasn't too alarmed, though. I thought it might be the medication I was taking for an infected tooth that caused my vision to blur. By the time we got back to Little Rock, I couldn't read the road signs or even see to unlock my front door. Five years earlier I lost my left eye to a disease called macular degeneration, which destroys your central vision. Since that time, Bonnie had been my chauffeur on the numerous trips to Nashville. At airport terminals, she was my guide. I know it was hard on her having to do all the driving, but she never did complain. She loved the spotlight as much as I did.

The diagnosis on my remaining eye was that I was losing it to the same disease. The doctors said it might be tomorrow, next week, or next year, but I would eventually go blind. The news was devastating! Two weeks later, some of my sight was restored, and I know it was the Great Physician who did it. I'm trying hard as I possibly can to keep the faith. I refuse to sit around and wait for the inevitable. So long as Bonnie is able to chauffeur, we'll go back and sing every opportunity we get.

Because of my impaired vision, we had to cancel the West Palm Beach and Tampa shows Ed Gregory had arranged for us. That hurt like hell! J. E. took his duet singing partner, Helen Cornelius, to take our place. That hurt like hell too! Helen made the statement one time that the only reason Bonnie and I came around was just so we could sing. She doesn't know how right she was. Of course, that wasn't the only reason, but it's the best one I can think of. We will always want to sing—and we will—as long as the good Lord allows us. It's not over till it's ALL over. I have yet to hear the fat lady singing.

Last Song:
Still Dreaming
the Dream

Finally it came time for me to accept the fact that the music world was a cloud I'd been riding for too long. I had experienced enough setbacks and frustrations to stay bitter for the rest of my life. Even today, it's hard for me to understand why the Browns haven't been accorded more recognition within the country music industry. The fact that we sold so many records, filled so many concert halls and still have so many songs in those "greatest hits" packages you see advertised in magazines and on TV is proof that we made a huge impact.

But I long ago outgrew that old dead-end of self-pity. I have been able to recognize that most of the bad things that happened were beyond my control. J. E. has always said that we should never look back. And that seems wise. That's where the pain is. But I think we must look back now and then, if only to find the meaning of things, good and bad.

"To everything there is a season," sang sweet old Pete Seeger. I haven't said much about the trials and tribulations of my sons' growing up. Their father, Tommy, still relatively young, died just a few years ago. I hold no enmity toward his memory. Tommy was a wild, crazy fire that scorched everything in his path, and he burned himself out way too soon (or not soon enough, depending on how you look upon the tumult that was his life) My children had no father to provide guidance during their critical years, and their mother, I confess, was not the typical apple-pie mom, either. I truly believe that the good Lord had a hand in leading my two sons, Tommy Jr. and Jimmy, through the troubled times of youth. My daughter, Alicia, never needed much guidance, and she was the strength I myself came to depend upon.

I finally realized the turmoil my sons were going through. They were in high school when marijuana became the in thing with teenagers. Old stupid me, I thought Jimmy was growing those beautiful, green pot plants outside his bedroom window because he had become interested in horticulture. I knew I had no choice but to withdraw from show business and stay home with my children. I have never regretted that decision for one moment, even though I missed performing and being with my friends. My kids meant more. They have made me the proud mom I am today.

Tommy Jr. majored in English at Hendrix College in Conway, Arkansas; Jimmy majored in business at the University of Arkansas at Little Rock; and Alicia received her bachelor's degree in business administration from the University of Arkansas at Fayetteville. Tommy Jr. lives in Payson, Arizona, with his wife, Colleen. He is an insurance broker and owns his own corporation that helps clients with advanced estate strategies. He also trains salespeople. Jimmy and his wife, Mary, have two children, Patrick and Katherine. Jimmy is a successful businessman and president of his own home-improvement company in North Little Rock, Arkansas. Alicia lives in Maumelle, Arkansas, with her husband, Curtis, and children Caitlin, Daniel, Meredith, and Eva. She seems to be content with being a wife, mother, and home-school teacher. Alicia is the most devoted and caring mother I have ever known.

I have six beautiful, well-adjusted grandchildren who keep me busy, happy, and young. I think the reason I enjoy them so much is because I was able to watch them grow. I missed out on all those cute little things my own children did—taking their first steps, saying their first words, losing their first teeth. Each of my grandchildren has his or her own identity. Caitlin plays the piano and guitar, sings, and stars in theatre/art productions. She does Irish dancing with her younger sister, Meredith, and her mom. They have won medals for their performances in Arkansas, Missouri, Texas, and Tennessee. Eva is only five years old, but it looks as though she will make the dance troupe a foursome in the near future. Oh yes, Meredith also excels in ballet, tap, and jazz. Daniel is a star pitcher and hitter for the Central Arkansas Baseball Club. Patrick's basketball skills will no doubt get him a scholarship to college, and Katherine also plays basketball for her school. All my grandchildren are talented, thanks to their parents who completely turned their own lives around on their behalf. Not only did they become leaders in their churches, they also have developed into pillars of their communities.

Many people have asked me why I never remarried. The answer is quite simple: no one ever asked me. No one wanted a ready-made family to start with. Besides, I never met a man who was willing to shake hands first. I wish I could have patterned my life after my favorite motto: "In order to have a good life, we need someone to love and be loved, something to do, something to look forward to, and a good BM every day."

I realized how short life really is on Super Bowl Sunday, January 28, 2001. That was the day we lost our little sister, Norma. She was only fifty-seven. Norma died in her sleep from a massive heart attack. She never believed in herself as an artist, but she had more talent in her little finger than any of the rest of us has in our entire body. She was known for her beautiful artwork. Not a day goes by that I don't look at one of her paintings and remember how talented, loving, and unselfish she was. I will always miss my "buddy."

My lifestyle these days won't seem too exciting for most people. But I enjoy it. I still live in Arkansas and try to keep a very low profile. I like being myself without having to worry about trying to impress somebody. I love working in my yard and shopping at Wal-Mart. I can't seem to accomplish as much as I used to. I don't know if I'm mellowing with age, slowing down or what. I just know that what I used to do all night now takes me all night to do.

I'm in all my glory when Bonnie and I return to Nashville and sing with J. E. on stage at the *Grand Old Opry*. We still entertain at such functions and places as the ROPE awards show and banquet, the Texas Hall of Fame, the Florida State Fair, and the Golden Voice Awards Show. In June 2000, the Browns won the Golden Voice Award as the Legacy Group. On June 13, 2002, we returned to Nashville to entertain for the Golden Voice Awards Show during Fan Fair Week. It was awesome! The fans gave us a standing ovation when we finished singing "The Three Bells." As long as the Browns are recognized and accepted this way, we will keep entertaining until the good Lord gets ready to call one of us home.

We have had a great career in spite of all we had to endure. The Browns are proud to be recognized as legends of country music. Oh, I've never quite given up on the dream that one day, J. E., Bonnie, and I will still make the biggest Browns' hit of all time. That would be a tall order, but I hope I never stop dreaming the dream. So I'm always looking back to see. Sometimes it all blends together back there—like looking into a kaleidoscope of many-colored glass that is first bright and too shiny, and then deep and darkened and so pretty in one instant that you can't bear it, but ever-changing, as elusive as life's joys.

Sooner or later, all those sorry, sad, and sweet lines you hear in country songs do seem to come true. Hard, ain't it? We never set out to conquer the world or even to shoot for that big ball of wax called success. We had our share of triumphs, but all that we ever really needed or wanted was a good song to sing and good people to sing it to. Our song started out with three poor-as-dirt country kids dreaming wildflower dreams; the chorus took us all over the world; and the last verse brought us right back home to the fire and the hunger of our strong beginnings.

Performing at the *Grand Ole Opry* in 1989. *From the collection of*
Maxine Brown.

Maxine's family on board the Commodore Cruise Line in
1989 after we did one of our shows. Jim Ed, his wife Becky,
Maxine, Norma, Bonnie, and her husband Brownie. *From the
collection of Maxine Brown.*

On stage at the Florida State Fair in Tampa in 1996. This was our first big concert together in twenty-eight years, and it was in front of 27,000 people. We were introduced by Bonnie's daughter, Kelly, who is a TV anchor for Fox News in Tampa. Our performance was awesome; we received encore after encore and several standing ovations. *From the collection of Ed Gregory, Nashville, Tennessee.*

Performing at the *Grand Ole Opry* in 1996. One of our fans took this. *From the collection of Maxine Brown.*

Entertaining at the ROPE (Reunion of Professional
Entertainers) Banquet in Nashville in 1999. *Courtesy of
Hope Powell, ROPE photographer, Nashville, Tennessee.*

Performing at the *Grand Ole Opry* in 1999. *From the collection of Maxine Brown.*

The Browns onstage at the Texas Country Music Hall of
Fame in Carthage, Texas, in July of 2000. *From the collection
of Maxine Brown.*

Backstage with Ralph Emery at the Texas Hall of Fame. Ralph was the MC. *From the collection of Maxine Brown.*

My home in North Little Rock, where I raised my three children. *From the collection of Maxine Brown.*

My three children: Tommy, Alicia, and Jimmy. *From the collection of Maxine Brown.*

APPENDIX A • ALBUMS

ALBUMS RECORDED BY THE BROWNS
RCA albums unless otherwise noted

Jim Ed, Maxine and Bonnie Brown (1957)
Sweet Sounds By the Browns (1959)
Town and Country (1960)
The Browns Sing Their Hits (1960)
Our Favorite Folk Songs (1961)
Songs From the Little Brown Church Hymnal (1961)
Grand Ole Opry Favorites (1964)
This Young Land (1964)
I Heard the Bluebirds Sing (1965) (Camden)
Three Shades of Brown (1965)
When Love Is Gone (1965)
Our Kind of Country (1966)
The Old Country Church (1967)
The Browns Sing the Big Ones From the Country (1967)
A Harvest of Country Songs (1968) (Camden)
Sugar Cane County (1969) (Chart—Maxine Brown solo recording)
Rockin' Rollin' Browns (1984) (Bear Family)
Browns Family Bible (1996) (Step One)

COMPILATIONS

The Best Of the Browns (1966)
20 of the Best (1985)
Looking Back To See (1986) (Bear Family)
The Three Bells (1993/eight CD set) (Bear Family)
Essential Jim Ed Brown and the Browns (1996)
Sweet Sounds By the Browns / Grand Ole Opry Favorites (2000)
    (West Side)

APPENDIX B • HITS AND AWARDS

SINGLES THAT CHARTED IN *BILLBOARD*, *CASHBOX*, *MUSIC REPORTER*, AND *MUSIC VENDOR* MAGAZINES

1954
"Looking Back To See"

1955
"Draggin' Main Street"
"Here Today and Gone Tomorrow"

1956
"I Heard the Bluebirds Sing"
"I'm in Heaven"
"I Take the Chance"
"It Takes a Long, Long Train with a Red Caboose"
"Just as Long as You Love Me"
"Money"

1958
"Beyond the Shadow"
"Would You Care"

1959
"The Old Lamplighter"
"Scarlet Ribbons"
"Teen-Ex"
"The Three Bells"
"The Whiffenpoof Song"

1960
"Brighten the Corner"
"Ground Hog"
"Lonely Little Robin"
"Margo, the Ninth of May"
"Send Me the Pillow You Dream On"
"Shenandoah"

1961

"Alpha and Omega"

1963

"Oh No"

"The Twelfth Rose"

"They Call the Wind Maria"

1964

"Everybody's Darling Plus Mine"

"Meadowgreen"

"Then I'll Stop Loving You"

1965

"You Can't Grow Peaches on a Cherry Tree"

1966

"Big Daddy"

"Coming Back To You"

"I Will Bring You Water"

"I'd Just Be Fool Enough"

1967

"I Hear It Now"

1969

"Sugar Cane County" (Maxine Brown)

AWARDS

1954

Up and Coming Vocal Group (*Cashbox*)

Best New Singing Group (*Country Song Roundup*)

Most Programmed Vocal Group (*Cashbox*)

Citation of Achievement (BMI)

1955

Most Promising Male, Jim Ed Brown (*Cashbox*)

Most Promising Female, Maxine Brown (*Cashbox*)

Most Promising Vocal Group, Jim Ed and Maxine Brown (*Cashbox*)

1956

Number One Vocal Group (*Cashbox*)

Number One Up and Coming Group (*Country Song Roundup*)

Number One Most Played (*Billboard*)

Number One Favorite Record of the Year, "I Take the Chance"
(*Cashbox*)

Favorite Girl Singers, Maxine and Bonnie Brown (Disc Jockeys of
America, *Cashbox*)

1957

Best Vocal Group (*Cashbox*)

Best Vocal Group (Jamboree)

Number One Vocal Group (Juke Box Operators of America,
Billboard)

Favorite Vocal Group (Country and Western Disc Jockeys, *Billboard*)

Number Ten Favorite Female Singers, Maxine and Bonnie Brown
(Country and Western Disc Jockeys, *Music Reporter*)

1958

Number One Vocal Group (*Billboard*)

Best Vocal Group in England (United Kingdom Country–Western
Express)

1959

Best Country Vocal Group (National Academy of Recording Arts
and Sciences)

Favorite Vocal Group (*Cashbox*)

Most Promising Pop Group (National Academy of Recording
Arts and Sciences)

Nomination for Best Performance by a Vocal Group (National
Academy of Recording Arts and Sciences)

Nomination for Best Recording of the Year (National Academy
of Recording Arts and Sciences)

Number One Vocal Group (United Kingdom)

Certificate of Achievement for the Longest Consistent Run by a
Vocal Group on the Official Hit Parade (*Music Vendor*)

1960

Favorite Vocal Group (*Cashbox*)

1964

Nomination for Best Performance by a Vocal Group, *Grand Ole Opry Favorites* (National Academy of Recording Arts and Sciences)

Favorite Singing Group (*Billboard*)

Favorite Vocal Group (*Cashbox*)

1965

Favorite Singing Group (*Billboard*)

Most Programmed Vocal Group (*Cashbox*)

1966

Favorite Singing Group (*Billboard*)

Favorite Group (*Country Song Roundup* reader's poll)

1967

Most Programmed Vocal Group (*Cashbox*)

Nomination for Best Sacred Performance, *The Old Country Church* (National Academy of Recording Arts and Sciences)

Favorite Vocal Group (*Country Song Roundup*)

Most Programmed Vocal Group (*Cashbox*)

1973

Citation of Achievement Award to Maxine Brown, "Looking Back To See" (BMI)

1998

Inducted into the Arkansas Entertainers Hall of Fame

2000

Golden Voice Award, Favorite Singing Group (voted on by recording peers)

Inducted into the Walkway of the Stars, Hot Springs, Arkansas

2001

Proclaimed Outstanding Arkansans (Eighty-third Arkansas General Assembly)

APPENDIX C • GLOSSARY OF NAMES

ACUFF, ROY—(1903–92) Born in Tennessee, Roy Acuff was best known in his long-standing role as the elder statesman of the *Grand Ole Opry*. He first became known when his singing of the gospel standard "The Great Speckled Bird" for the *Opry* in 1938 generated sacks of fan mail. He enjoyed greatest popularity in the World War II era, but kept his association with the *Opry* right up to his death. He was inducted into the Country Music Hall of Fame in 1962.

AMERICAN BANDSTAND—*American Bandstand* began in 1952 in Philadelphia, Pennsylvania, as the *Bob Horn* show with Bob Horn acting as host. In 1956, Dick Clark became the host, and in 1957 the ABC network picked up the show, renaming it *American Bandstand*. The show featured musical artists and a regular group of unpaid teenagers who were shown dancing to the music.

AMES BROTHERS—The Ames Brothers were a Massachusetts-born quartet (Joe, b. 1921, Gene, b. 1923, Vic, 1925–78, Eddie, b. 1927) famous as a nightclub and television show act in the 1950s. In 1956 they starred in their own *Ames Brothers Show*. The group disbanded in the 1960s.

ANDERSON, BILL—(b. 1937) Born in South Carolina, Bill Anderson was dubbed "Whispering Bill" for his style of vocal delivery. Equally successful as singer and composer, in 1958 he wrote "City Lights," which became a hit for Ray Price. Continued success as a songwriter in the 1970s was coupled with his role as TV host for several shows in the 1980s. He is a regular performer on the *Grand Ole Opry*.

ARNOLD, EDDY—(b. 1918) Born in Tennessee, Eddie Arnold was first known as "The Tennessee Plowboy." Arnold was a hugely successful singer from the 40s through the '60s who also found success in the pop markets from the 1960s onward. He was inducted into the Country Music Hall of Fame in 1966. One of his most famous songs is "The Cattle Call."

ATKINS, CHET—(1924–2001) Born in Tennessee, Chet Atkins was an influential guitar player and, later, producer, whose playing style continues to influence contemporary players across many genres. He first gained success as a studio guitarist, part of Nashville's early "A-team" of session musicians. He was inducted into the Country Music Hall of Fame in 1973.

AUSTIN, BOB—(dates unavailable) Bob Austin was editor of *Cashbox* magazine.

AUTRY, GENE—(1907–98) Born in Texas, Gene Autry became known as "America's Favorite Singing Cowboy." Autry first found success as a depression-era singer of early country standards. He became a full-fledged pop icon in his role as a film cowboy atop the white steed Champion; he would make over ninety films between 1931 and 1957, paving the way for Roy Rogers and Tex Ritter in the "singing cowboy" movie genre. The smooth, relaxed baritone delivery of his recordings appealed to a wide mainstream audience. He fulfilled a lifelong fantasy by acquiring the California Angels baseball team in 1960 and was inducted into the Country Music Hall of Fame in 1969.

BARE, BOBBY—(b. 1935) Born in Ohio, Bobby Bare was a singer and songwriter. He first came on the country scene with the song "All-American Boy" in 1958, which became a hit after Bare was drafted for the Army. His long-lasting career spanned genres, including folk, outlaw country, and humor. His reputation for having a great instinct for songs has led to associations with many of country music's greatest songwriters.

BARNYARD FROLIC—The *Barnyard Frolic* was a 1950s radio music program produced by Little Rock station KLRA.

BATES, SHIRLEY—(dates unavailable) Shirley Bates had her success on west coast radio and—later—television program, the *Country Barndance.* She became known as the Sweetheart of the *Country Barndance.* She eventually signed a contract with Fabor Robinson but dropped out of country music to be with her young sons.

BARTON, DAVE—(dates unavailable) Dave Barton played guitar for Jim Ed Brown during his solo career and later worked in promotion for various artists.

JACK BENNY SHOW—After twenty-three years as a radio program, the *Jack Benny Show* had its television debut in 1950 and continued airing until 1965. Benny developed a humorous character who perpetually claimed to be thirty-nine years old.

BIG D JAMBOREE—Established in Dallas, Texas, in 1948, *Big D Jamboee* was an important regional broadcast that served as a springboard for artists like Sonny James, as well as for regional stars like Hank Locklin. The show continued in some form into the mid-1960s.

BILLBOARD MAGAZINE—*Billboard Magazine* began in 1894 and featured carnival entertainment news; however, the music portion of the magazine quickly took center stage. In 1936, *Billboard* published its first *Hit Parade,* and in 1940 it added its first "Music Popularity Chart." It currently publishes charts of the top 100 songs in various categories and is usually accepted as the standard measure for ranking music popularity in the United States.

BLACK, BILL (1926–65) Born in Memphis, Tennessee, Bill Black, a.k.a. Blackie, was Elvis Presley's bass player until 1958. Bill Black, Scotty Moore, and Elvis Presley formed the trio that took Elvis to the top; they were joined later by D.J. Fontana.

BLACK, LOU—(dates unavailable) Lou Black booked talent on the *Ozark Jubilee* with Red Foley.

BLOCH, RAY (MARTIN)—(1902–82) Born in the Alsace-Lorraine region of France, Ray Bloch had his start in vaudeville and radio but eventually became maestro for the Ed Sullivan and Jackie Gleason shows in the early '50s.

BLOCKER, DAN—(1928–72) Most famous for his role as Hoss Cartwright on the television western *Bonanza*, Blocker was born in

Texas. He turned down a chance to play professional football in order to act and also served in the Korean Conflict. He died in 1972 from a blood clot in his lung.

BOBBY AND SONNY—*See* the Osborne Brothers

BOWMAN, DON—(b. 1937) Born in Lubbock, Texas, Bowman is a humorist and songwriter. His first charted record was entitled "Chit Atkins, Make Me a Star."

BRASFIELD, ROY (ROD)—(1910–58) Born in Mississippi, he was the *Grand Ole Opry*'s premier humorist from 1947 to1958. He frequently teamed with Minnie Pearl in routines that humorously poked fun at country life.

BRYANT, ANITA—(b. 1940) Born in Florida, Anita Bryant became Miss Oklahoma in 1958 and was second runner up in the Miss America Pageant of 1959. She had several hit songs in the late 1950s and early 1960s before she became the spokeswoman for Florida orange juice. She is famous for her 1977 campaign that lobbied against extending civil rights to homosexuals.

BRYANT, FELICE AND BOUDLEAUX—(Felice 1925–2003; Boudleaux 1920–87) Husband and wife team who were among the first to make a career of songwriting. Wrote many hits for the Everly Brothers, including "Bye, Bye, Love" and "Wake Up, Little Susie." Also wrote "Rocky Top," the official Tennessee state song. They entered the Country Music Hall of Fame in 1991.

BUTTREY, KENNY—(dates unavailable) Kenny Buttrey is a legendary drummer, and one of Nashville's premier session players. He has recorded with such stars as Elvis Presley, Bob Dylan, Gordon Lightfoot, Joan Baez, and Waylon Jennings.

CAMPBELL, ARCHIE—(1914–87) Born in Tennessee, Campbell was a popular country comedian best known for his writing and performances for the TV show *Hee Haw*.

THE CARLISLES—(Clifford 1904–83; William 1908–2003) Born in Kentucky, the Carlisles were a brother singing duet during the '30s and '40s. Clifford popularized the dobro and steel guitar for country music. They were regularly featured stars on *Midday Merry-Go-Round, Tennessee Barn Dance,* and the *Grand Ole Opry.* William was also known as Jumpin' Bill Carlisle and recorded several songs with his children, including "No Help Wanted." He was a member of the *Grand Ole Opry* until his death, and always maintained he could still jump as high as always, he just couldn't stay up as long. In 2002, William was elected to the Country Music Hall of Fame.

CARSON, MARTHA—(b. 1921) Born in Kentucky, Martha Carson's most famous song was "Satisfied." She sang rockabilly gospel music during the late '40s and early '50s. Her energetic performing style influenced many later artists such as Elvis Presley and Brenda Lee.

THE CARTER FAMILY—(Maybellle 1909–78; A.P. 1891–1960; Sara 1899–1979) All three members of the Carter Family are Virginia-born, with A.P. and Sara being husband and wife and Maybelle, Sara's cousin. The Carter Family is known as the first family of country music. Their signature song was "Keep on the Sunny Side." They produced many hit records from 1927 to 1941 in genres ranging from blues to gospel to ballads and parlor songs. Although they were extremely popular, and entered the Country Music Hall of Fame in 1970, they never achieved great financial success.

CASH, JOHNNY—(1932–2003) Born in Arkansas, Johnny Cash is known as The Man in Black. His lengthy career in country music spanned five decades with many crossover hits such as "A Boy Named Sue" and "Ring of Fire." He was inducted into the Country Music Hall of Fame in 1980 and the Rock 'n' Roll Hall of Fame in 1992.

CASHBOX—*Cashbox* was a weekly music-industry publication running from 1942 to 1996. It charted top-selling country music records.

THE COUNTRY MUSIC ASSOCIATION—Established in 1958, the CMA was formed to boost popularity of country music and secure airtime on radio and television for country artists. The association created The Country Music Hall of Fame in 1961, which opened in 1967 in Nashville.

THE CASUALS—The Casuals were a short-lived '60s group that had a few singles that did well. They won a band competition in mid '60s and landed a contract with Panorama label, but their vehicle crashed on the way to a performance and two members, Tom Blessing and Larry Evans, were killed.

CATE SISTERS—(Marcy and Margie) Born in Missouri, the Cate Sisters were in demand as session singers and musicians beginning in the '70s. They debuted on the *Jim Ed Brown Show* in 1972.

CHANCE, LIGHTNIN'—(dates unavailable) A staff musician on the *Grand Ole Opry* for many years, Lightnin' Chance worked with Ernest Tubbs as one of his Texas Troubadours.

CHANDLER, JEFF—(1918–61) Born in New York City, Jeff Chandler was known as the "Silver Fox." He was a movie star during the '50s and early '60s, playing roles such as Cochise in *Broken Arrow*, which won him an Academy Award nomination. He also had some success as a recording artist, songwriter, and owner of Chandler Music, a publishing company. He died at age forty-two during a botched back surgery.

CHAPMAN, STEVE—(dates unavailable) Steve Chapman played steel guitar for many artists, including Jim Ed Brown.

CLARK, DICK—(b. 1929) Born in New York, Dick Clark has become an American icon. Clark became the host of *American Bandstand* in 1956. When the show went national, Clark's career was launched. He has since had a successful career in the television, film, and music industries. He is now famous for his annual New Year's Eve show. *See also* American Bandstand

CLARK, ROY—(b. 1933) Born in Virginia, Roy Clark was the host of *Hee Haw* throughout its entire twenty-five-year run. A talented musician, achieving recognition in jazz as well as country, he is best known for his guitar and banjo playing. He has helped to establish Branson, Missouri, as a prime country-music destination.

CLINE, PATSY—(1932–63) Patsy Cline was one of country music's biggest stars. Born in Virginia, her biggest hits were "Walkin' After Midnight," "I Fall to Pieces," and "Crazy" (her version of "Faded Love" is also well known, but it was released after her death). Cline died in an airplane crash in 1963 and was inducted into the Country Music Hall of Fame in 1973.

COCHRAN, HANK—(b. 1935) Born in Mississippi, Hank Cochran was an influential songwriter during the 1960s, contributing songs to Eddy Arnold, Jim Reeves, Patsy Cline, and George Jones, among others. One of his most famous songs was "I Fall to Pieces," performed by Patsy Cline.

COKER, SANDY—(b. 1940) Born in California, Sandy Coker became one of western swing's greatest musicians. He began playing the fiddle at a young age but also became an established guitar player.

COLLINS, TOMMY—(1930–2000) Born in Oklahoma City, Tommy Collins, whose given name was Leonard Sipes, was an influential songwriter contributing many songs to Merle Haggard.

COMO, PERRY—(1912–2001) Born in Pennsylvania, Perry Como became one of America's most famous crooners. After a series of hit songs throughout the 1940s, Como began his career in television. *The Perry Como* show began on NBC in 1955 and aired until 1963. His Christmas programs were also well received.

COOPER, SHELBY AND SARAH JANE—(dates unavailable) Members of the *Barnyard Frolic*, Shelby and Sarah Jane Cooper also performed on the first live show for KRTV television.

CORNELIUS, HELEN—(b 1941) Born in Missouri, Helen Cornelius collaborated with Jim Ed Brown in 1975. Their first song together, "I Don't Want to Have to Marry You," reached the top of the charts in 1976. They had several subsequent hits during the late '70s and early '80s. She also joined forces with Brown to host the *Nashville On The Road* television series.

COVINGTON, PAPPY. *See* Louisiana Hayride

CRAMER, FLOYD—(1933–97) Born in Louisiana, Floyd Cramer was a pianist accompanying many country artists such as Jim Reeves and the Browns. He went on to sell millions of records for RCA; including the hit single "Last Date." He was inducted into the Arkansas Entertainers Hall of Fame in 1998.

CRUM, SIMON—Simon Crum was Ferlin Husky's comic alter-ego. Husky recorded comic songs under this pseudonym.

DARIN, BOBBY—(1936–73) Born in New York City, Bobby Darin started his career as crooner but became a popular '50s rocker and later a folk artist. His most famous songs include: "Mac the Knife," "Dream Lover," and "Splish Splash.

DAVIS, JIMMIE—(1899–1963) Born in Louisiana, Jimmie Davis was a successful politician and movie actor as well as a well-known recording star. He served two terms as governor of Louisiana, acted in western movies, and made hundreds of recordings between 1929 and the 1960s. He remains well known for "You Are My Sunshine" and is a member of the Country Music Hall of Fame, having been inducted in 1972.

DAVIS, SKEETER—(1931–2004) Born in Kentucky, Skeeter Davis's given name was Mary Frances Penick. She was a member of the Davis Sisters but then went on to tour with RCA's *Caravan of Stars.* She maintained successful solo career throughout the '60s and continued to perform regularly until her death. She was a member of the *Grand Ole Opry* for 45 years. Her biggest crossover hit was "The End of the World." She also published an autobiography, *Bus Fare to Kentucky,* in 1993.

THE DAVIS SISTERS—Skeeter Davis and her best friend Betty Jack Davis formed the Davis sisters in the early '50s. Their song "I Forgot More Than You'll Ever Know" stayed on the charts in 1952. Betty Jack was killed in a car crash in 1953.

DAY, JIMMY—(1934–99) Born in Alabama, Jimmy Day was a steel guitar player who played on the *Louisiana Hayride* throughout the 1950s. He later played for Ray Price and Willie Nelson.

DEAN, JIMMY—(b. 1928) Born in Texas, Jimmy Dean became famous for his dramatic narrative songs; his most famous was "Big Bad John." He later became a television personality, hosting *The Jimmy Dean Show* and acting in several made-for-TV movies. He is currently known as the spokesperson for the Jimmy Dean Foods.

DENNY, JIM—(1911–63) Born in Tennessee, Jim Denny was the manager of the *Grand Ole Opry* artist service. He went onto become one of the most successful talent agents and song publishers in country music history.

DEVINE, OTT—(1910–94) Born in Alabama, Ott Devine was a prominent radio executive for WSM radio in Nashville, retiring in 1968. He became the manager of the *Grand Ole Opry* in 1959.

DICKENS, LITTLE JIMMY—(b. 1920) Born in West Virginia, Little Jimmy Dickens became popular in the late 1940s with humorous novelty songs like "Take an Old Cold Tater (and Wait)." His short stature (4"11') and big voice won him fame within country music circles. He continued to record into the early 1970s and remains a performing artist at the *Grand Ole Opry* and joined the Country Music Hall of Fame in 1983.

DISKIN, TOM—Tom Diskin was Col. Tom Parker's top assistant and one of Elvis Presely's managers.

DONAHUE, TROY—(1937–2001) Troy Donahue was born Merle Johnson. He was a 1950s teen idol and film and television actor. He co-starred with Sandra Dee in the 1959 film *A Summer Place*.

DRURY, JAMES—(b. 1934) Born in New York City, James Drury became a successful film and television actor in the 1950s. He starred in many westerns and is most famous for his role in *The Virginian*.

EMERY, RALPH—(b. 1933) Born in Tennessee, Ralph Emery was a famous radio and television personality. He hosted *The Ralph Emery Show* from 1972 to 1991, but his greatest success was hosting *Nashville Now* from 1983–93.

EMMONS, BLAKE—(dates unavailable) Blake Emmons played steel guitar for various artists.

EMMONS, BUDDY—(b. 1937) Born in Indiana, Buddy Emmons is one of the most famous steel guitarists in country music history. As a session player, he contributed to songs by Faron Young, Ray Price, and the Everly Brothers.

THE EVERLY BROTHERS—(Don b. 1937; Phil b. 1939) The Everly Brothers are famous for their smooth harmonies. Their first number one hit was "Bye, Bye, Love" in 1957, which they followed up with "Wake Up Little Suzie" that same year. Between 1957 and 1962, they were rivaled only by Elvis Presley and Pat Boone for number of records sold. Although considered a country act, The Everly Brothers achieved great success on the pop-music charts. They were named to the Country Music Hall of Fame in 2001.

FABIAN—(b. 1943) Born in Philadelphia, Fabian was a singer and teen idol during the late 1950s. His most famous songs are "Tiger" and "Turn Me Loose." He pursued a film career in the 1960s, with mixed success.

FAIRBURN, WERLY—(1924–85) Born in Louisiana, Werly Fairburn was known as the "Singing Barber" and later as the "Singing Deejay." He never produced a hit during his lifetime, but he managed a successful singing career during the 1940s and 1950s. He was a member of the *Louisiana Hayride* and wrote "I Guess I'm Crazy for Loving You," which was a hit for Jim Reeves and was included on the Browns' first album.

FAUBUS, ORVAL—(1910–94) Orval Faubus was an Arkansas governor for six terms. He was best known for resisting school integration at Little Rock's Central High in 1957, causing President Eisenhower to send in the National Guard.

FERGUSON, BOB—(1927–2001) Born in Missouri, Bob Ferguson was a producer for RCA during the '60s and early '70s. He was also a successful song writer; among his most famous songs is "Wings of a Dove," which was recorded by Ferlin Husky.

FLATT, LESTER—(1914–79) Born in Tennessee, Lester Flatt was a member of the band the Foggy Mountain Boys, which included Earl Scruggs. Together, Scruggs and Flatt wrote the theme song for *The Beverly Hillbillies* television show and were influential in the development of bluegrass music. They joined the Country Music Hall of Fame in 1985.

THE FLEETWOODS—The Fleetwoods (Barbara Ellis, Gary Troxel, and Gretchen Christopher) are a famous pop-rock trio of the '50s and '60s. Among their most famous hits are "Come Softly To Me" and "Mister Blue." Their harmonizing made them a favorite in country circles as well.

FLOOD, DICK—(b. 1932) Born in Pennsylvania, Dick Flood was a singer/songwriter during the late '50s. He performed on CBS's The *Jimmy Dean* show in 1957 with Billy Graves. He had one hit record, "The Three Bells", in 1959, but his recording was overshadowed by the Browns who took the song to number one that same year.

FOLEY, RED—(1910–68) Born in Kentucky, Red (Clyde) Foley had a continuous succession of hits through the '40s and '50s. Among his most famous songs are "Old Shep," "Tennessee Saturday Night," and "Chattanooga Shoe Shine Boy." Red Foley made his acting debut costarring with Tex Ritter in the film *The Pioneers* and entered the Country Music Hall of Fame in 1967.

FONTANA, D. J.—(b. 1934) Born in Louisiana, Dominic James (D. J.) Fontana started his career as the drummer for the *Louisiana Hayride*. Elvis Presley performed for the *Louisiana Hayride* in 1954 and was impressed by Fontana's ability. Fontana became Elvis's drummer the following year and remained with Elvis for fourteen years.

THE FOUR FRESHMEN—A long-enduring (with changing members) jazz vocal group, the Four Freshmen originated in Indiana in the late 1940s. Their biggest hit was "Graduation Day" in 1957. They were nominated for a Grammy (along with the Browns) in 1964 and they also received a Grammy nomination in 1986 for their forty-first album.

FRANKS, TILLMAN—(b. 1920) Born in Arkansas, Tillman Franks became manager of the *Louisiana Hayride* in the 1950s. Franks also had success in a songwriting team with Johnny Horton. They cowrote songs such as "Honky Tonk Man," "When It's Springtime in Alaska," and "Sink the Bismark." He was injured in the Texas car crash that killed Johnny Horton in 1960.

THE FRIDAY NIGHT FROLIC—WSM Radio's country music show that aired every Friday night 7–9 p.m. The show featured country artists such as Patsy Cline, Jim Reeves, Ferlin Husky, and all the members of the *Grand Ole Opry*.

FRIZZELL, LEFTY—(1928–75) Born in Texas, Lefty Frizzell was an influential singer known for his "vowel-bending" style. He became a star in 1950 with two hit songs "If You Got the Money, I've Got the Time" and "I Love You a Thousand Ways." He topped the charts again in early 1964 with "Saginaw, Michigan." He was inducted into the Country Music Hall of Fame in 1982.

GARLAND, HANK "SUGARFOOT"—(b. 1930) Born in South Carolina, Hank Garland was one of Nashville's eminent studio guitarists in the 1950s. He played guitar on a number of hits by Patsy Cline, Elvis Presley, The Everly Brothers, and Red Foley. He was earning acclaim for his jazz performances when his career was cut short when he was injured in an automobile accident in 1961.

GARROWAY, DAVE—(1913–82) Born in New York, Dave Garroway became the popular host of the *Today Show* in 1952 and remained host until 1961. He also hosted the *Wide World of Sports* from 1955–58. He characteristically signed off his shows by saying "Peace."

GATELY, JIMMY—(1931–85) Born in Missouri, Jimmy Gately was a song writer who wrote classics like "The Minute You've Gone" and "Bright Lights and Country Music." He was a fiddle player for the *Ozark Jubilee* with Red Foley's troupe from 1954 to 1963.

GATLIN BROTHERS—The Gatlin Brothers (Larry b. 1948, Steve b. 1951, and Rudy b. 1952) were all born in Texas and achieved success in the 1970s; their biggest hit song was "All the Gold in California." Larry Gatlin has also made a songwriting career, writing songs covered by artists such as Elvis Presley, Barbara Streisand, Charlie Rich, and Johnny Cash.

GIBSON, DON—(1928–2003) Born in North Carolina, Don Gibson was responsible for writing three famous songs in country music— "Sweet Dreams," "Oh Lonesome Me," and "I Can't Stop Loving You." He was named to the Country Music Hall of Fame in 2001.

GLASER BROTHERS—The Glaser Brothers (Tompall b. 1933, Jim b. 1937, and Charles b. 1936) were a family group whose performance career spanned from the 1950s to the early '70s. They made their mark in Nashville with a publishing company and an historic recording studio known as Hillbilly Central. Tompall also became famous as one of the "Outlaws" along with Waylon Jennings and Willie Nelson.

GRAND OLE OPRY—*The Grand Ole Opry* was established in Nashville in 1925 and is the longest running radio show in the United States. Its parent station is WSM radio of Nashville. Although it suffered due to the rising status of television, it has continued to serve as a premier venue for country music. In 1974 it moved from the Ryman Theater to its current location at the Grand Ole Opry House at Opryland.

GREGORY, ED—(1938–2004) Ed Gregory was the owner of United Shows of America, which oversaw a series of state carnivals and fairs as well as owning memorabilia and royalty rights to country artists Jim Reeves and Faron Young. Ed Gregory was pardoned by President Clinton in 2000 from bank fraud convictions. United Shows of America filed for bankruptcy in 2002.

HAGGARD, MERLE—(b. 1937) Born in California to parents who had moved to escape the dust bowl, Merle Haggard ran away from home at age fourteen, spent three years in prison for breaking into a bar, and worked as a ditch digger before he made it big in country music. His real success in country music began in 1966 when he had three hit songs: "Swinging Doors," "The Bottle Let Me Down," and "The Fugitive." His popularity continued throughout the '70s and early '80s. Among his most famous songs are "Okie From Muskogee," "Rainbow Stew," and "Are the Good Times Really Over." He joined the Country Music Hall of Fame in 1994

HALEY, BILL—(1925–81) Born in Michigan, Bill Haley and the Comets's recording of "Rock Around the Clock" marked the beginning of the rock era. The song topped the charts for eight weeks in 1955. Haley continued to be popular throughout the '50s with hits such as "Shake, Rattle, and Roll" and "See You Later Alligator."

HALL, TOM T.—(b. 1936) Nicknamed "The Storyteller," Tom T. Hall was born in Kentucky and began his career as a songwriter. He quickly added success as a performer to his list of achievements. He hit the Top Ten in the late '60s and continued to be popular throughout the '70s. Among his most famous songs are "Watermelon Wine," "Homecoming," and "Country Is." He has since hosted a syndicated television show, *Pop Goes Country,* and written several books.

THE HARDEN TRIO—The Harden Trio [Robbie a.k.a. Fern, Arleen (b. 1945), and Bobby—all three born in Arkansas] began performing at the *Barnyard Frolic,* the *Ozark Mountain Jubilee,* and the *Louisiana Hayride.* They had moderate success with a song called "Poor Boy" in 1965, but in 1966 they produced the song "Tippy Toeing" which was a major crossover hit. They were unable to duplicate the success of "Tippy Toeing," producing only moderate hits before disbanding in 1967. Bobby Harden continues to be a successful songwriter.

HARMAN, BUDDY—(b. 1928) Born in Tennessee, Buddy Harman was Nashville's first full-time session drummer in 1955. By the mid-'60s he was working close to six hundred sessions a year.

HARRIS, EMMYLOU—(b. 1947) Born in Alabama, Emmylou Harris has had continued success since she made it big in the late 1970s. She has recorded seven number one and twenty Top Ten country hits. Her 1995 album *Wrecking Ball* received critical acclaim for its ground-breaking alternative sound.

HARRIS, TED "CURLY"—(dates unavailable) Curly Harris was a fiddle player for Faron Young.

HARRIS, WYNONIE—(1920–69) Wynonie Harris was an early rhythm and blues singer from Nebraska, best known today for her late '40s hits later covered by rock 'n' roll singers in the 1950s. Most prominent among these is 1947's "Good Rockin' Tonight," the Harris cover of a Roy Brown hit that inspired Elvis Presley's version.

HART, FREDDIE—(b. 1926) Born in Alabama, Freddie Hart achieved his greatest success with the song "Easy Loving," which received the CMA Song of the Year award in 1971 and 1972.

HART, DICK—(dates unavailable) A member of *Barnyard Frolic*, Dick Hart hosted a radio show on KLRA in Little Rock in the early 1950s.

HAWKINS, HAWKSHAW—(1921–63) Born in West Virginia, Hawkshaw Hawkins had established a name as a colorful stage performer before his first record success in 1948 for "Doghouse Boogie" and "Pan American." He joined the *Grand Ole Opry* in 1955. He died in the 1963 plane clash that also claimed Patsy Cline.

HAY, GEORGE D.—(1895–1968) Born in Indiana, George D. Hay is given credit for founding the *Grand Ole Opry*. He started his career in Memphis as a newspaper reporter where he wrote a column called "Howdy, Judge" (from which his nickname, the solemn old judge, derives) and worked at several radio stations across the country promoting country music. He was an announcer for the *Opry* from 1927 through the 1940s and was named to the Country Music Hall of Fame in 1966.

HEE HAW—Considered the most successful country television show of all time, *Hee Haw* aired from 1969 to 1994. The initial hosts were Buck Owens and Roy Clark. The show featured musical performances and comical skits. Some of the regular cast members were Minnie Pearl, Grandpa Jones, and String Bean.

HELMS, BOBBY—(1933–97) Born in Indiana, Bobby Helms's greatest success came in 1957 with his three hits, "Fraulein," "My Special Angel," and "Jingle Bell Rock."

HILL, GOLDIE—(b. 1933) Born in Texas, Goldie Hill appeared with her brother Tommy on the *Louisiana Hayride* and had a hit, along with Justin Tubb, with the Browns' "Looking Back To See."

HOMER AND JETHRO—(Homer Haynes 1920–71; Jethro Burns 1920–89) Both born in Tennessee, Homer and Jethro were one of the most successful comedy acts in country music history. They recorded several parody songs that reached the Top Ten; some of their more famous songs are: "Baby It's Cold Outside," "Tennessee Border No. 2," and "How Much is that Hound Dog in the Window." Their song, "Battle of Kookamonga", their most successful record, lampooned Jimmy Driftwood's "The Battle of New Orleans." They were named to the Country Music Hall of Fame in 2001.

HORTON, JOHNNY—(1925–60) Born in California, Johnny Horton hit the country charts with his number one hit "When Its Springtime in Alaska" in 1958. His follow-up recording of "The Battle of New Orleans" topped both the country and pop charts. He also achieved varying degrees of success with songs like "Sink the Bismarck" and "North to Alaska." He was killed in a car crash in 1960.

HOUSTON, DAVID—(1938–93) Born in Louisiana, David Houston had one of the widest vocal ranges of any country singer. He had several successful records in the '60s and '70s; among his most famous songs are "Mountain of Love" and "I Was Almost Persuaded."

HOWARD, HARLAN—(1927–2002) Born in Michigan, Harlan Howard is considered one of country music's greatest song writers, writing songs such as "I Fall to Pieces" (co-written with Hank Cochran), "I've Got a Tiger by the Tail," and "It's All Over (But the Crying)." He joined the Country Music Hall of Fame in 1997.

HUSKEY, JUNIOR—(1928–71) Born in Tennessee, Junior Husky was one of Nashville's first-team session bass players, recording on such artist's albums as Loretta Lynn, George Jones, and Tammy Wynette. He appeared weekly on the *Grand Ole Opry* during the '50s and '60s.

HUSKY, FERLIN—(b. 1927) Born in Missouri, Ferlin Husky—a.k.a. Simon Crum—was a mainstay on the country music charts during the '50s and '60s. Among his most famous hits are "Dear John Letter" and "Gone." His recording of "Wings of a Dove" is the most recognized version of this classic.

JACKSON, WANDA—(b. 1937) Born in Oklahoma, Wanda Jackson was a singer and song writer who crossed over easily between county and pop music. She had a number of hits in the 1960s and early 1970s. Among her most famous songs are "Let's Have a Party," "Right or Wrong," and "In the Middle of a Heartache."

JAMES, SONNY—(b. 1929) Born in Alabama, Sonny James (James "Sonny" Hugh Loden) became known as "the Southern Gentleman" because of his fine manners and congenial personality. He holds the record for the most consecutive number one country hits during the '60s and '70s, with twenty-one of twenty-five singles released from 1964–72 hitting number one. Some of his hit songs include "Young Love," "Need You," "Heaven Says Hello," "Running Bear," and "Here Comes Honey Again."

JARVIS, FELTON—(1934–81) Born in Atlanta, Felton Jarvis was an RCA producer from 1965 to 1970. He left RCA to focus exclusively on Elvis Presley's career. He remained Elvis's producer until the artist's death in 1977. Jarvis started suffering from health problems in 1971 and died ten years later of a stroke at the age of forty-six.

JEAN, NORMA—(b. 1938) Born in Oklahoma, Norma Jean Beasley got her start on *Ozark Jubilee* with Red Foley in 1958. In 1960, she became a featured vocalist on the *Porter Wagoner Show.* Norma Jean had several hit recordings, her most famous being "Let's Go All the Way" and "Go Cat Go." She married in 1967 and left the Porter Wagoner Show to concentrate on her family.

JENKINS, HAROLD—*See* Twitty, Conway

JENNINGS, WAYLON—(1937–2002) Born in Texas, Waylon Jennings joined Buddy Holly's band as a bass player in 1958. He was supposed to be aboard the ill-fated airplane that crashed in 1959 and killed Buddy Holly, Ritchie Valens, and the Big Bopper (J.P. Richardson), but he had given his seat up to the Big Bopper in a coin toss. Jennings became known as one of the outlaws of country music. He had several hit songs in the late '60s and throughout the '70s. In the mid-'70s he collaborated with Willie Nelson, Jessi Colter, and Tompall Glaser on a project entitled *Wanted: the Outlaws;* this album became the first in country music history to be certified as platinum. He was named to the Country Music Hall of Fame in 2001.

JONES, GEORGE—(b. 1931) Born in Texas, George Jones has endearingly been called "the Opossum" and is one of the most recognized country artists since Hank Williams. His talents and achievements are legendary and span four decades, but his violent temper and addiction to both alcohol and drugs played a heavy role throughout his career. Somehow Jones managed to produce many hit songs during his turbulent years—songs such as "Why, Baby, Why," "The Race is On," "Love Bug," and "He Stopped Loving Her Today." Jones recovered from his addictions in the early '90s and continues to produce critically acclaimed music, and in 1992 he was inducted into the Country Music Hall of Fame.

JONES, SPIKE—(1911–65) Born in California, Spike Jones's given name was Lindley Murray. With his band, The City Slickers, Jones became famous for his novelty songs of the '40s and '50s, including "Yes, We Have No Bananas" and "Der Fuhrer's Face."

THE JORDANAIRES—At the height of their success, the Jordanaires were heard on more hit records than any other vocal group. They backed up such artists as Elvis Presley, Patsy Cline, Jim Reeves, and George Jones. They have also produced some solo albums, the majority of which are gospel. The original members of the group were elected into the Country Music Hall of Fame in 2001.

JUST US—Chip Taylor and Al Gorgoni teamed up as contract songwriters, penning songs such as "Wild Thing" and "Angel of the Morning." They had a short-lived recording career as the group Just Us with one hit song in 1966, "I Can't Grow Peaches on a Cherry Tree."

KANTER, HAL—(b. 1918) A Hollywood writer and director, Hal Kanter directed Elvis Presley in *Loving You* and cowrote *Blue Hawaii*. He was a writer, director, and producer for the television series "Julia," and executive producer of the popular '70s television show "All in the Family."

KENNEDY, JERRY—(b. 1940) Jerry Kennedy performed as a guitar player on the *Louisiana Hayride* in the early 1960s before becoming a session guitarist and producer in Nashville. He was the head of Mercury's country music division from 1969–84.

KERR, ANITA—(b. 1927) Born Anita Grilli in Memphis, Kerr was the headliner of the Anita Kerr singers, who by some estimates appeared on a quarter of all the records produced in Nashville in the early 1960s. Anita Kerr worked extensively with Chet Atkins, beginning in 1961, on vocal arrangements and as an occasional producer. She had left the country music scene to pursue other projects by 1967.

KILPATRICK, DEE—(b. 1919) Walter David "Dee" Kilpatrick was born in North Carolina. He was manager of WSM's *Grand Ole Opry* from 1956–59. He helped found the Country Music Association in 1958.

THE KINGSTON TRIO—The trio—Bob Shane (b. 1934), Nick Reynolds (b. 1933), and Dave Guard (1934–91)—formed in San

Francisco in 1957 and soon after had the smash hit "Tom Dooley." They are credited with helping to launch the folk revival of the late 1950s and early 1960s. At one time they had four records in *Billboard's* Top Ten simultaneously. Dave Guard was replaced by John Stewart (b. 1939) in 1961. The Trio lineup has been re-shaken several times, but they continue to tour.

LAINE, FRANKIE—(1913–2004) Born in Chicago, Frankie Laine's given name was Frank LoVecchio. He was a successful crooner in the 1940s with hit recordings like "Shine" and Louis Armstrong's "When You're Smiling." Laine became involved with Hollywood and sang the main themes for many cowboy films such as *High Noon, Gunfight at the OK Corral*, and the television show *Rawhide*.

LANE, RED—(b. 1939) Born Hollis Delaughter in Louisiana, Lane is recognized as one of the finest songwriters in country music. Merle Haggard alone has recorded more than twenty of Lane's songs. Red Lane had his first hit when Faron Young recorded "My Friend On the Right" in 1964, and his songs were recorded throughout the 1970s by numerous artists.

LAUGH-IN—Popular television show airing from 1968 to 1973. The show was hosted by Dan Rowan and Dick Martin and featured comedic skits, gag jokes, one-liners, news parodies, and running skits. Many famous comedic actors got their start with this show including Goldie Hawn, Lily Tomlin, and Robin Williams.

LAW, DON—(1902–82) A native of London, England, Don Law was head of Columbia Records country division in the 1950s and 1960s. Law is credited with enhancing Nashville's commercial viability during the "Nashville Sound" era (1957–72) by helping to produce country-pop crossover hits like Marty Robbins's "El Paso," Johnny Horton's "Battle of New Orleans," and Jimmy Dean's "Big Bad John." After leaving Columbia in 1967, Law worked as an independent producer into the 1970s and was inducted into the Country Music Hall of Fame in 2001.

LaRosa, Julius—(b. 1930) Born in New York City, Julius LaRosa got his start on the *Arthur Godfrey Show* in 1951. He had several successful recordings in the 1950's. He went on to become a popular disk jockey in New York in the 1960s and later joined the soap opera *Another World,* earning an Emmy nomination as best supporting actor.

Lee, Brenda—(b. 1944) Born Brenda Tarpley in Atlanta, Brenda Lee was a child prodigy as a singer who became one of the best-selling female singers of the 1960s. She had her first hit at the age of sixteen with the ballad "I'm Sorry," and had another hit later that same year with "Rockin' Around the Christmas Tree." Considered a pop artist early in her career, she changed directions in 1969 and produced a number of country hits in the 1970s. Brenda Lee continues to be in demand as a performer. She was inducted into the Country Music Hall of Fame in 1997.

Lee, Peggy—(1920–2002) Born in North Dakota, Peggy Lee was a successful jazz singer, songwriter, and actress. She began her career touring with Benny Goodman and his band in 1941. She married Goodman's guitarist, Dave Barbour; the couple wrote many songs together. She had several hit songs such as "Golden Earrings" and "Mañana." She acted in several movies and wrote and provided voices for Disney's *Lady and the Tramp.*

Leonard, Jack E.—(1911–73) Born in Chicago, Jack E. Leonard was also known as "Fat Jack" because of his rotund appearance. He was one of the inventors of the Don Rickles style of comedy, which used insulting and abrasive humor.

Locklin, Hank—(b. 1918) Born in Florida, Lawrence Hankins Locklin joined the *Louisiana Hayride* in 1949 and recorded a number of hits in the 1950s. His best success was with the song he wrote entitled *Please Help Me, I'm Falling,* which hit number one in 1960, the same year he joined the *Grand Ole Opry.* He continues to perform for the *Opry* and enjoys life as the unofficial mayor of McLellan, Florida.

LOGAN, HORACE—(1916–2002) Born in Louisiana, Horace "Hoss" Logan created the *Louisiana Hayride* in 1948. He is famous for coming up with the catchphrase "Elvis has left the building." He left the *Louisiana Hayride* in 1957. His memoir, *Elvis, Hank, and Me: Making Musical History on the "Louisiana Hayride"* came out in 1998.

LOMBARDO, GUY—(1902–77) Born in London, Ontario, Canada, Guy Lombardo and his band, The Royal Canadians, sold over one hundred million records in Lombardo's long career. In the years 1929–52 the band never failed to chart a record. Lombardo is remembered for his rendition of "Auld Lang Syne" every New Year's Eve. By the beginning of the rock era, Lombardo's time of huge record sales had passed, but Lombardo and his band continued to enjoy performing almost right up to his death in 1977.

LONG, HUBERT—(1923–72) One of the most successful music executives of his day, Hubert Long ran one of Nashville's first independent booking agencies (after doing publicity for Eddy Arnold at RCA with Col. Tom Parker). He was a founding member of the Country Music Association and was inducted into the Country Music Hall of Fame in 1979.

LOPEZ, VINCENT—(1898–1975) Born in Florida, Vincent Lopez was a famous pianist and dance bandleader specializing in jazz and swing music. He had several hit songs from 1922 to 1939, including "Nola," "I'm Just Wild about Harry," and "There's Honey on the Moon Tonight." He hosted a radio show airing from the Taft Hotel in New York.

LORD, BOBBY—(b. 1934) Born in Florida, Bobby Lord had disjointed success in his singing career, topping the chart close to ten times between the years 1956 and 1971. Lord is most noted for his television personality. The *Bobby Lord Show* was one of the most important country music shows of the mid-1960s.

LOUDERMILK, JOHN D.—(b. 1934) Born in North Carolina, John Loudermilk is the first cousin to the Louvin Brothers (their real last name is Loudermilk). John Loudermilk had some success as a performing artist, but his real contribution to country music has been his song writing. He has penned hits for artists such as the Everly Brothers, Stonewall Jackson, the Browns, Johnny Cash, Glen Campbell, and Tim McGraw. Some of his most famous songs are "A Rose and a Baby Ruth," "Waterloo," "Tobacco Road," and "Abilene."

THE LOUISIANA HAYRIDE—Known as "the cradle of the stars" and "Heaven's Gate," the *Louisiana Hayride* was established in 1948 as a country music radio program based in Shreveport, Louisiana (KWKH). It was second in popularity only to the *Grand Ole Opry,* and boasted such famous members as Hank Williams, Johnny Horton, Jim Reeves, Loretta Lynn, and Elvis Presley. It began to decline in popularity in the late sixties.

THE LOUVIN BROTHERS—(Ira 1924–65; Charlie b. 1927) Both brothers were born in Alabama and are one of the favorite brother harmony acts of country music. They had success on the country music charts during the '50s, and Ira Louvin became a successful and well known songwriter. Some of their best known hits are "When I Stop Dreaming," "I Don't Believe You've Met My Baby," and "Hoping That Your Hoping." Ira and his wife Ann were killed in an auto accident in 1965. The duo was named to the Country Music Hall of Fame in 2001.

LUX RADIO THEATER—Lux Radio Theater was a live radio program that aired from 1934–55. The show began by recreating Broadway hits shows and tunes for its listeners but moved west in order to feature Hollywood personalities and films. Cecil B. DeMille was one of the hosts of the show, which drew Hollywood's biggest names such as Bing Crosby, Judy Garland, Walt Disney, and Humphrey Bogart.

MACRAE, GORDON—(1921–86) Born in New Jersey, Gordon MacRae was a successful singer, Broadway and film actor, and television personality. He had a string of hits in the 1950s, starred alongside Doris Day, and hosted the *Gordon MacRae Show* on television.

MANUEL, DEAN—(1934–64) Dean Manuel was Jim Reeves's piano player and road manager who died with Reeves in the fatal airplane crash in July of 1964.

MARTIN, DEAN—(1917–95) Born in Ohio, Dean Martin's success in music, film, television, and stage established him as an icon in American culture. His given name was Dino Paul Crocetti and he was known as the King of Cool. He began his quest for stardom as a comic duo with Jerry Lewis, but his solo career eventually overshadowed his early successes. He was a member of the Rat Pack and enjoyed tremendous success as a crooner and film star.

MARTIN, JANIS—(b. 1940) Born in Virginia, Janis Martin was known as the female Elvis. She was hugely popular in 1956 and 1957 with several rockabilly hits like "Will You, Willyum" and "Ooby Dooby," but her career was cut short when she became a mother in 1958. She retired from the music business soon after.

MCAULIFFE, LEON—(1917–88) Born in Texas, Leon McAuliffe was a member of Bob Wills and His Texas Playboys. He is one of the most celebrated and acclaimed steel guitarists in western swing music.

MCCOY, CHARLIE—(b. 1941) Born in West Virginia, Charlie McCoy is one of Nashville's elite studio musicians and has played with such stars as Roy Orbison, Stonewall Jackson, and Bob Dylan. Apparently while recording his album *Blonde on Blonde,* Dylan stood amazed that Charlie could play guitar with his left hand while playing trumpet with his right without missing a beat.

MICKEY AND SYLVIA—Mickey Baker (b. 1925) and Sylvia Robinson (b. 1936) formed a duo in 1956 and had an immediate hit with "Love is Strange" in 1957. They enjoyed moderate success after this hit song but eventually disbanded in 1965. Mickey Baker continued his career as a session guitarist, and Sylvia had another hit song, "Pillow Talk," in 1973. She also co-founded the influential rap label Sugar Hill in the late '70s.

MONROE, BILL—(b. 1911–96) Born in Kentucky, Bill Monroe is known as the Father of Bluegrass. His bold mandolin playing and "high, lonesome" singing has shaped bluegrass music for over fifty years. His original songs like "Blue Moon of Kentucky" have become canonized classics in the bluegrass genre. His genius and accomplishments won him the Heritage Award, presented to him by the National Endowment for the Arts in 1982, and his album *Southern Flavor* was the first bluegrass album to win a Grammy. He joined the Country Music Hall of Fame in 1970.

MOORE, BOB—(b. 1932) Born in Tennessee, Bob Monroe is an accomplished country bass and jazz player. He has recorded on many famous country and pop artists records such as Marty Robbins, Patsy Cline, Elvis Presley, Roy Orbison, and the Browns.

MOORE, SCOTTY—(b. 1931) Born in Tennessee, Scotty Moore was Elvis Presley's guitar player and first manager. He and Bill Black remained with Elvis for fourteen years. Scotty Moore has since become involved as a recording engineer and has worked on many television shows for Opryland Productions. Moore also recorded an album with Carl Perkins for Sun Studios in 1992.

MORAN, DIAMOND JIM—(dates unavailable) Diamond Jim Moran operated a restaurant on Iberville Street in New Orleans. He got his nickname from all the flashy diamond jewelry that he wore. It was rumored that he would occasionally hide a diamond in a meatball for a lucky customer.

MORGAN, JAYE P.—(b. 1931) Born in Colorado, Jaye P. Morgan was born Mary Margaret Morgan. She was a successful singer in the '50s with hits such as "Life Is Just a Bowl of Cherries" and "That's All I Want from You." In the 1970s she became well known again for her role on Chuck Barris's *The Gong Show*.

MORMON TABERNACLE CHOIR—The Mormon Tabernacle Choir had its beginnings in 1847 in northern Utah. The Choir has performed for over one hundred and fifty years and now has over three hundred members. It is headquartered in Salt Lake City, Utah, and is sponsored by the Church of Later Day Saints. Ronald Reagan called it "America's Choir," George H. W. Bush had them perform at his inauguration, and George W. Bush awarded the choir the 2003 Medal of Arts.

MORRISON, HAROLD—(1931–93) Born in Missouri, Harold Morrison was a session player and played such instruments as banjo, guitar, dobro, and steel guitar. He recorded with such artists as the Browns, George Jones, Tammy Wynette, and Ferlin Husky.

ARTHUR MURRAY SHOW—The *Arthur Murray Show* first aired in 1950. It was a dance show that featured music, dance contests, and comedy. The show's cohost was Kathryn Murray, and it aired from 1950 to 1960.

NASHVILLE NOW—*Nashville Now* was a country music show hosted by Ralph Emery. The show aired from 1983 to 1993 and featured musical performances and interviews with the top artists and newest faces in country music.

NASHVILLE ON THE ROAD—*Nashville on the Road* was a country music show airing from 1975–83. The show had several hosts including Jerry Clowers, Jim Stafford, and Jim Ed Brown.

NATHAN, SIDNEY—(1903–68) Born in Ohio, Sidney Nathan was the founder and president of King Records, which was established in 1943 and became one of the biggest and most influential independent labels of its time, serving as a model for future independents. Because he encouraged his artists to blur the lines between "black" and "white" music, Nathan seemed to anticipate rock 'n' roll.

NELSON, RICKY—(1940–85) Born in New Jersey, Rick Nelson brought a clean-cut image to rock 'n' roll. He became hugely popular in the late '50s and early '60s with a brief decline before hitting it big again in the early '70s. His most famous songs are "Never Be Anyone Else But You," "Traveling Man," and "Garden Party." His father was entertainer Ozzie Nelson. He was killed in a plane crash in 1985.

NELSON, WILLIE—(b. 1933) Born in Texas, Willie Nelson is one of country music's most enduring stars. He started as a song writer, writing such legendary songs as *Crazy* (Patsy Cline) and *Hello Walls* (Faron Young). He had success as a performer as well; however, his unconventional sound kept him from really making it big as a singer until the 1970s. His hit record "Blue Eyes Crying in the Rain" hit the charts at number one in 1975. After this initial hit, Nelson has enjoyed and continues to enjoy tremendous success and acclaim for his music. In 1993, he was named to the Country Music Hall of Fame.

NEWMAN, JIMMY C.—(b. 1927) Born in Louisiana, Jimmy C. Newman is an important contributor to Cajun country music. He was a member of the *Louisiana Hayride* and is still a member of the *Grand Ole Opry*, where he performs regularly. His biggest hit was the crossover "A Fallen Star."

NUTT, HOUSTON—(dates unavailable) Houston Nutt Sr. was a basketball and football sports star at Fordyce High School in Arkansas; he went on to play college basketball for two legendary coaches, Adolph Rupp at the University of Kentucky and Henry Iba at Oklahoma A&M. Nutt became the football and basketball coach for the Arkansas School for the Deaf in the mid '50s and later the school's athletic director. He was inducted into the Arkansas Sports Hall of Fame in 2001. Houston Nutt, Jr. (b. 1957), his eldest son, is the head coach for the University of Arkansas football team.

OSBORNE BROTHERS—(Bobby b. 1931; Sonny b. 1937) Born in Kentucky, the Osborne Brothers were one of the pioneer bluegrass bands. They managed to incorporate some contemporary country instruments into their music, winning some popularity for bluegrass music. Through the '60s and '70s, the Osborne Brothers were the only bluegrass band that consistently stayed on the country charts.

O'SHAUGHNESSY, DICK—(dates unavailable) A comedian from California, Dick O'Shaughnessy frequently worked shows with Jim Reeves.

OWENS, BUCK—(b. 1929) Born in Texas, Buck Owens is noted for having brought the Bakersfield sound to country music. He reached the height of his success in the '60s and '70s with hits such as "Under the Influence of Love," "You're for Me," "Waitin' in Your Welfare Line," "Ain't It Amazing, Gracie," "Think of Me," and "How Long Will My Baby Be Gone." He became a member of the *Hee Haw* cast, which helped to solidify his popularity. He was named to the Country Music Hall of Fame in 1996.

OZARK JUBILEE—Also known as *Jubilee USA,* the *Ozark Jubilee* was based in Springfield, Missouri, and was the first network country music television program. Red Foley hosted the show, which first aired on a local station in 1952. It was accepted by the ABC in 1955. It featured guests such as Brenda Lee, Bobby Lord, and Hawkshaw Hawkins. The show ended in 1960 as a result of Red Foley's having problems with the IRS.

PARKER, COL. TOM—(1909–97) Born Andreas van Kuijk in the Netherlands, Parker served as Elvis Presley's manager from 1955–77. Parker began his career as the manager of Eddy Arnold, a position he held between 1945–53. Parker managed Presley exclusively during the latter's career. He retired from the music business after Presley's death, and in 1983 engineered a two million dollar buyout from RCA in exchange for title to all Presley-related contracts.

PARTON, DOLLY—(b. 1946) Born in Tennessee, Dolly Parton helped redefine the role of women performers in country music. She made her first appearance on the *Grand Ole Opry* at the age of thirteen. Her career began in earnest with her role opposite the host of the *Porter Wagner Show* in 1967. She has gone on to become successful as a singer, songwriter and movie actress, although her projects have slowly moved her away from country music into pop and other realms since about the mid-'70s. She was named to the Country Music Hall of Fame in 1999.

PEARL, MINNIE—(1912–96) Born in Tennessee as Sarah Colley, Pearl is the most famous comedienne appearing on the *Grand Ole Opry* and

Hee Haw. Her character Minnie Pearl was a man-hungry old maid who was easily recognized by her signature hat from which a price tag still dangles. She was inducted into the Country Music Hall of Fame in 1975.

PERRYMAN, TOM—(b. 1927) A successful disk jockey and talent promoter, Tom Perryman was the first person to book and promote Elvis Presley; he also worked with the stars of the *Louisiana Hayride.* He promoted Elvis and the Browns, and was instrumental in getting the Browns on the *Ozark Jubilee.* He owned several radio stations with Jim Reeves in Tennessee and Texas. He was once the host of the WSM all-night radio show and now works as a disk jockey for radio station KKUS in Tyler, Texas. He is a member of the Country Music D. J. Hall of Fame.

PEEBLES, HAP—(1913–93) Born in Kansas, Peebles worked as a promoter and booking agent for sixty-two years. He became the first promoter to provide country music talent to State fairs in an organized fashion.

PETER, PAUL, AND MARY—Formed in New York's Greenwich Village in 1961 by Peter Yarrow (b. 1938), Noel Paul Stookey (b. 1937), and Mary Travers (b. 1937), this trio's self-titled debut album in 1962 was a huge success; it stayed on the pop charts for three and a half years. It included the classic "If I Had a Hammer." Their recording of "Puff the Magic Dragon" was very popular in 1962, and the following year their recording of "Blowin' in the Wind" introduced the songs of Bob Dylan to a larger audience. The group disbanded in 1971, although they continue to reunite and perform periodically for special occasions.

PIERCE, WEBB—(1921–91) Born in Louisiana, Pierce broke in with the *Louisiana Hayride* in 1950, and soon became that show's biggest act. With such hits as "That Heart Belongs to Me" and "In the Jailhouse Now," Pierce became honky-tonk's biggest star in the 1950s. A successful investor, he became known later on as much for his high-profile purchases—his Nashville home included a guitar-shaped swimming pool—as for his recordings, and he was inducted into the Country Music Hall of Fame in 2001.

PREVIN, ANDRE—(b. 1929) Born in Berlin, Germany, Andre Previn is a renowned pianist, conductor, and composer. He began his career as a classical and jazz pianist, but quickly became the conductor for the London Symphony Orchestra. He started working as a musical director and oversaw the production for such leading shows as *Gigi, My Fair Lady,* and *Porgy and Bess.* As a composer, He has scored several films including *Kiss Me Kate* and *Paint Your Wagon.*

PRIDE, CHARLEY—(b. 1938) Born in Mississippi, Pride was a good enough baseball player to have had tryouts with professional teams in the early 1960s. Instead, he achieved success as a singer from 1966–89—after being heard by Chet Atkins—recording hits with songs like "Is Anybody Goin' to San Antone" and "Kiss an Angel Good Morning." His success was sometimes overshadowed by his anomalous position as a black country music performer. He joined the Country Music Hall of Fame in 2000.

PRIME TIME COUNTRY—Prime Time Country is a country music show that first aired in 1999 and remains popular. The show is hosted by Gary Chapman and features musical guests and interviews. It is recorded in several cities, including Houston, Las Vegas, and Orlando.

RAINWATER, MARVIN—(b. 1925) Born in Kansas, Marvin Rainwater was a maverick performer who had several hits in the late 1950s, including "Gonna Find Me a Bluebird." His music veered between country and rock 'n' roll, and he ultimately found a permanent home in neither market.

RANEY, WAYNE—(1920–93) Born in Arkansas, Raney had a long-running radio show with Lonnie Glosson for Cincinnati's WCKY. Raney also toured and had a hit in 1949 with his own composition, "Why Don't You Haul Off and Love Me."

REED, JERRY—(b. 1937) Born in Atlanta, Reed spent many years developing his guitar picking and singing style before scoring hits, most notably with 1971s "When You're Hot You're Hot." Reed's music career suffered when he began an acting career playing roles in a number of films, including *Gator, Smoky and the Bandit,* and *Concrete Cowboy.*

REEVES, JIM—(1924–64) Born in Texas, Jim Reeves crooned his way to becoming one of the most recognized and respected crossover country artists of the twentieth century. He was affectionately called "Gentleman Jim" by his peers and fans. His most famous songs include "Four Walls" and "He'll Have to Go." Reeves's career was cut short when he was killed in a plane crash near Nashville, Tennessee in 1964. He was named to the Country Music Hall of Fame in 1967.

REGAN, PHIL—(b. 1937) Born in Michigan, Phil Regan was signed by the Detroit Tigers in 1956. He had thirteen major league seasons, playing for Detroit (starting pitcher), Los Angeles (relief pitcher) and both Chicago teams. He managed the West Michigan White Caps in 2002 and 2003.

RILEY, JEANNIE C.—(b. 1945) Texas-born Jeannie Riley claimed overnight success with her crossover hit recording of "Harper Valley P.T.A." She had several subsequent hit singles but eventually turned to gospel music.

RITTER, TEX—(1905–74) Born in Texas, Tex Ritter was one of Hollywood's singing cowboys. His first film was in 1936; this film and subsequent films did well at the box office. Surprisingly, his success on the country music charts did not come until later when, in 1942, he signed as one of the first artists for Capital Records. He sang the title song for the film *High Noon,* which would become his signature song. He was one of the first country artists to record albums centered around a central theme. He helped form the Country Music Association, was elected its president in 1963, and was inducted into the Country Music Hall of Fame in 1964. He also ran unsuccessfully for U.S. Senate in 1970. Tex Ritter was the father of the late actor John Ritter.

ROBBINS, MARTY—(1925–82) Born in Arizona, Marty Robbins was one of country music's most successful crossover artists during the '50s and '60s. He had a total of ninety-four chart records with sixteen number one hits over the course of his career. Many of his songs were self-penned, including his signature song "El Paso." Robbins was the first country artist to be awarded a Grammy. He also received the Man of the Decade award from the Academy of Country Music in 1971. He starred in films and television series such as *The Drifter* and the *Marty Robbins Show.* He suffered a second and fatal heart attack in 1982, the same year he was elected to the Country Music Hall of Fame.

RODGERS, JIMMIE—(1897–1933) Born in Mississippi, Jimmie Rodgers is known as the Father of Country Music and was the first performer to be inducted into the Country Music Hall of Fame (in 1961). He drew inspiration for his music from folk and southern traditions, early jazz, stage yodeling, work chants, and African American blues. His style has profoundly influenced all of country music. Some of his most famous songs are "In the Jailhouse Now," "Frankie and Johnny," and "Blue Yodel." In 1933, he recorded his last twelve songs over the course of a week died two days later from complications of tuberculosis.

ROONEY, MICKEY—(b. 1920) Born in New York City, Mickey Rooney's given name is Joe Yule Jr. He became a child star in 1927 and went on to become the number-one box office actor during the years of 1939–41. He has over two hundred film credits to his name and has had success in television as well. He has won a lifetime achievement Oscar and many other awards for his acting. He remains one of Hollywood's legendary actors.

ROWLEY, JERRY—(dates unavailable) Jerry Rowley was a fiddle player who recorded with such artists as Lefty Frizzell, Johnny Horton, and Jim Reeves. He was also part of the Rowley Trio (with Evelyn and Dido), which appeared on the *Louisiana Hayride*, and he played fiddle on the Browns' "Looking Back To See."

SCRUGGS, EARL—(b. 1924) Born in North Carolina, Earl Scruggs had a great influence on bluegrass music and is noted for popularizing the three-finger method of banjo playing and developing the "Scruggs peg," which can be used to change the tuning of a banjo string while still playing the instrument. Scruggs played with Bill Monroe before resigning and joining with Lester Flatt. Scruggs, Flat, and the Foggy Mountain Boys recorded many bluegrass classics before splitting in 1969. Scruggs went on to pursue a solo career that veered more toward rock 'n' roll.

SEEGER, PETE—(b. 1919) Born in New York, Pete Seeger's parents were both professors at Julliard School of Music. Seeger rejected his parents' love for classical music, however, and developed a passion for American folk music and the five-string banjo. He left in the middle of his Harvard education to pursue his dream of being a traveling singer. He joined with Woody Guthrie and together they became singing activists. Seeger later recorded many folk classics, but his popularity was stifled by his affiliation with the Communist Party. He has had a large impact on folk music. He continues to play and is an active environmentalist.

SEELY, JEANNIE—(b. 1940) Born in Pennsylvania, Jeannie Seely had a successful singing career during the '60s and '70s and is most notably responsible for updating the image of the female country and western star by wearing miniskirts and clothes that caused a stir. She had a big hit with "Don't Touch Me," a song penned by Hank Cochran.

SHOLES, STEVE—(1911–68) Born in Washington, D.C., Steve Sholes was largely responsible for popularizing country music. In 1945, he became head of both country and rhythm and blues recordings for RCA. He signed such artists as Chet Atkins, Eddy Arnold, the Browns, and Jim Reeves. He gained much respect and power within the RCA Company when he signed Elvis Presely in 1955. He was inducted into the Country Music Hall of Fame in 1967.

SIMAN, SI—(b. 1921) Si Siman was a radio station executive with KWTO in Springfield, Missouri. He is best known for organizing the *Ozark Jubilee*, first as a local show in 1953 and then as a nationally aired program on ABC in 1955.

SINGLETON, SHELBY—(b. 1931) Born in Texas, Shelby Singleton served several years with Mercury Records where he reached the position of vice president before resigning in 1966 to set up his own independent label, SSS International. His company had a smash hit in 1968 with Jeannie C. Riley's recording of "Harper Valley P.T.A." Singleton purchased Sun Records from Sam Phillips and also managed the Silver Fox label and Shelby Singleton Music.

SMITH, CONNIE—(b. 1941) Born in Indiana, Connie Smith was a small-town housewife before her hit record, "Once a Day," topped the charts in 1964. She maintained a successful singing career until the early '70s when she dropped out of country music to devote time to her family. She resurfaced in 1985 with a hit recording of Steve Earle's song "A Far Cry from You." She is not as well known as some of her contemporaries, but she has been cited by many country artists such as George Jones and Dolly Parton as being one of their favorite all time female artists.

SNOW, HANK—(1914–99) Born in Nova Scotia, Hank Snow is the most successful country music star to come out of Canada. He played on *the Big D Jamboree* in 1948 and was successful enough to be invited to play with the *Grand Ole Opry*. His first hit was "I'm Movin' On" in 1950. His record output was remarkably consistent throughout the 1960s and '70s, and he was recognized as one of the finest guitarists in country music. In 1979, he was named to the Country Music Hall of Fame.

STEVENS, RAY—(b. 1939) Born Harold Ragsdale in Georgia, Stevens is best known for the series of novelty songs he recorded in the 1960s and '70s. His first hit was "Ahab the Arab" in 1962. He also recorded "The Streak" (1974) and "Everything is Beautiful" (1970), which was number one on the pop charts. His biggest country hit was the straightforward "Misty," which won him a Grammy in 1975.

STRANGE, BILLY—(dates unavailable) Billy Strange was an L.A. session guitarist in the 1960s. He also did some arranging work for artists such as Dean Martin. His style has been called "loungeabilly," perfect for those who want to ease into roots music.

STRZELECKI, HENRY—(b. 1939) Born in Alabama, Strzlecki was an in-demand bassist in Nashville for thirty years. He performed on hundreds of Top Ten hits, backing everyone from Fats Domino to Perry Como, along with many country artists.

STUBBS, EDDIE—(b. 1961) Born in Bethesda, Maryland, Stubbs was the fiddler for the Johnson Mountain Boys, who in the late 1970s and early 1980s helped generate a resurgence of interest in bluegrass music. After the Johnson Mountain Boys broke up in 1994, Stubbs went on to work in Nashville as a radio show host and *Grand Ole Opry* announcer. He is an award-winning scholar of bluegrass music.

STUCKEY, NAT—(1933–1988) Born in Texas, Stuckey was an announcer for the *Louisiana Hayride* for eight years. He was also a successful songwriter, writing "Sweet Thang" in 1966, and "Pop a Top," a hit in 1967 for Jim Ed Brown. He died of lung cancer in 1988.

THE *ED SULLIVAN SHOW*—*The Ed Sullivan Show* aired every Sunday night from 1948 to 1971. It was a variety television show featuring various performers. Both Elvis Presley and The Beatles made their American television debuts on Sullivan's show.

TALL, TOM—(b. 1937) Born in Texas, Tom Tall signed with Fabor Robinson and had some recording success in the 1950s.

TERRY, GORDON—(b. 1931) Born in Alabama, Terry was a singer, actor, and musician. He began his career as a fiddler for Bill Monroe's Blue Grass Boys in 1950. He went on to tour with Johnny Cash for four years, and became a respected fiddler for Nashville's studio sessions. He acted in a number of films, including the B-movie favorite *Girl From Tobacco Row.*

TEXAS TROUBADOURS—*See* Tubb, Ernest

THOMPSON, HANK—(b. 1925) Born in Waco, Texas, Thompson and his band, The Brazos Valley Boys, helped bridge the gap between western swing bands and honky-tonk country singers His long-lasting career has seen hits in four decades, and he is also known for his magnetic stage presence. He was inducted into the Country Music Hall of Fame in 1989, and his sound has influenced a new generation of country singers such as Dwight Yoakum and George Strait.

TILLIS, MEL—(b. 1932) Born Lonnie Tillis in Florida, Mel Tillis began his career in Nashville as a songwriter, penning hits like "I'm Tired," "Detroit City," and "Ruby Don't Take Your Love to Town." Overcoming a chronic stuttering problem, Tillis also began a recording career in the late 1950s, and an acting career in the 1970s and '80s. He is the father of recording artist Pam Tillis.

TITTLE, CORKY—(dates unavailable) A guitar player, Corky Tittle performed with Jim Ed Brown during his solo career.

TOBIAS, CHARLES—(1898–1970) Born in New York, Charles Tobias was a song writer and was highly active in writing music for film including several songs used in the Bugs Bunny cartoons.

TOMLINSON, TOMMY—(dates unavailable) Tommy Tomlinson played guitar for Johnny Horton and was injured in the automobile accident that killed Horton in 1960.

TOWN HALL PARTY—The most popular country music show in Southern California in the 1950s, *Town Hall Party* began as a radio barn dance on KFI Compton and became a television show in 1953. It is credited for launching the careers of Freddie Hart and Buck Owens. The show featured artists from many genres and was headlined by names like Tex Ritter, Lefty Frizzell, and Johnny Cash. The show was cancelled in 1960.

TRENT, BUCK—(b. 1938) Born in Spartanburg, South Carolina, Buck Trent was a regular on the *Porter Wagoner Show* and a well-respected banjo player. Trent played on many RCA hits, such as Wagoner's "The Cold Hard Facts of Life" (1967) and Dolly Parton's "Mule Skinner Blues" (1970). In more recent years, Trent could be found playing in the Branson, Missouri, music theater scene.

TUBB, ERNEST—(1914–84) Born in Texas, Ernest Tubb had a fifty-year career in country music and is recognized as one of the most influential performers in history. Tubb joined the *Grand Ole Opry* cast in 1943 and remained one of its major stars for the thirty-nine years he stayed with the show—he was the first to bring an *Opry* show to Carnegie Hall, in 1947. As a singer, he was influenced early by Jimmie Rodgers. In the 1960s and '70s Tubb toured with his band, The Texas Troubadours, for one hundred and fifty to two hundred shows a year. Tubb also opened a record store in Nashville in 1947, and began recording a show there, the *Midnight Jamboree*, which continues to this day. He was inducted into the Country Music Hall of Fame in 1965.

TUBB, JUSTIN—(1935–98) Born in San Antonio, Justin Tubb was the eldest son of Ernest Tubb. Justin carved out his own path in country music as a talented singer and songwriter. He had a hit in 1954 with "Looking Back To See" as a duet with Goldie Hill. He also wrote songs for artists such as George Jones, Patsy Cline, and Faron Young. Justin Tubb joined the *Grand Ole Opry* in 1955 and stayed with the *Opry* for the rest of his career.

TWITTY, CONWAY—(1933–93) Born in Mississippi, Harold Jenkins took his stage name from Conway, Arkansas, and Twitty, Texas. Conway Twitty had more number one country hits in his lifetime than any other artist (fifty-five). He started out successfully in rock 'n' roll with Sun Records, but his true calling was in country music. Once his country music career began, he charted hit after hit during the '60s, '70s, and early '80s. He was also a successful song writer, writing many of his own songs. Among his most famous hit records are "It's Only Make Believe," "Hello Darlin'," "Slow Hand," and "Tight Fittin' Jeans." In 1999 he was inducted into the Country Music Hall of Fame.

VAN, BOBBY—(1928–80) Born in New York City, Bobby Van's given name was Robert Jack Stein. He was a film actor and dancer during the '50s. After musicals went out of vogue, Van reinvented himself as a game-show host.

VAN DYKE, LEROY—(b. 1929) Born in Missouri, Leroy Van Dyke had three hits at the beginning of his career with "The Auctioneer," "Walk On By," and "If a Woman Answers (Hang Up the Phone)." Van Dyke never duplicated his early success, but he did manage to produce some Top One Hundred hits into the late 1960s.

WAGONER, PORTER—(b. 1927) Born in Missouri, Wagner enjoyed early stints with the *Ozark Jubilee* TV show and then the *Grand Ole Opry*. In 1960, he began fronting the syndicated TV show with which he is now best known. The *Porter Wagner Show* ran from 1960–81, and featured both celebrities and newcomers to the country music scene. A versatile performer, he also recorded a string of hits in the 1960s, including "Misery Loves Company" and "The Carroll County Accident." He was elected to the Country Music Hall of Fame in 2002.

WALKER, BILL—(b. 1937) Born in Sydney, Australia, Bill Walker was an arranger/conductor who steered Nashville away from "head" arrangements and popularized the written, note-for-note arrangements. By the late 1960s he was the most sought after arranger in Nashville. He had originally come to the United States to work with Jim Reeves but arrived in Nashville the weekend of Jim's fatal plane crash in 1964.

WALKER, BILLY—(b. 1929) A current member of the *Grand Ole Opry*, Billy Walker also was a member of the *Louisiana Hayride* and *Ozark Jubilee*. He had several hit records and six number one hits, including "Charlie's Shoes."

WEST, DOTTIE—(1932–91) Born in Tennessee, Dottie West was a successful singer and song writer in the '60s and '70s. Her first big hit was the self-penned "Here Comes My Baby." She had several subsequent hits including a jingle for Coca-Cola entitled "Country Sunshine," which made it to the Top Ten on the country charts. After some serious financial difficulties, she declared bankruptcy in 1990 and died from complications after a car crash in 1991.

WEST, SPEEDY—(1924–2003) Born in Missouri, Wesley Webb West began his career partnered with Jimmy Bryant. The two guitarists were so technically accomplished and fast that they became known as "the flaming guitars." The duo split up in 1958, and Speedy West went on to become one of the great session guitarists.

WHITMAN, SLIM—(b. 1924) Born in Florida, Slim Whitman is known for his high falsetto voice. He had great success as a singer in the '50s, mid '60s, and early '70s with hits like "Love Song of the Waterfall" and "Indian Love Call." Whitman enjoyed even greater success in England, being the first country artist to top the charts in the U.K. He continued to have modest hits into the '80s and is still touring today.

THE WILBURN BROTHERS—(Doyle 1930–82; and Teddy b. 1931) Both Arkansas-born, the Wilburn Brothers had several hit records in the '50s and '60s. Some of there hits songs include "I'm So in Love with You," "Roll, Muddy River," and "Somebody's Back in Town." They sang vocal harmonies with several artists and began a song polishing company and a talent agency. In 1953 they started a syndicated television show that gave valuable exposure to singers such as Loretta Lynn.

WILLIAMS, HANK—(1923–53) Born in Alabama, Hank Williams is a legend in country music and has had profound influence on the development of country music style. The height of his success came in the early 1950s. He wrote most of his songs and his performances were hugely popular with audiences. He had several number one hits; some of his most famous are "Lovesick Blues," "Long Gone Lonesome Blues," "Jambalaya," and "Your Cheating Heart." Williams, however, was an alcoholic, and his alcoholism made it difficult for him to keep engagements. He died while on tour in the back of his chauffeured Cadillac on New Year's Day in 1953. Along with Jimmie Rodgers he was named to the Country Music Hall of Fame in 1961, in the first induction class.

WILLIAMS, HANK JR.—(b. 1949) The son of a famous father, Louisiana-born Hank Williams Jr. made his own name as a country music "outlaw" in the late 1970s and early 1980s with hits like "I Fought the Law" (1978) and "All My Rowdy Friends" (1981).

WILLIAMSON, SLIM—(dates unavailable) Slim Williamson's given name was Bradley L. Williamson. He owned several independent record labels. His first label was Peach Records, which operated from 1954 to 1962. He purchased Chart Records in 1964 for three hundred and fifty dollars. Chart was successful during the mid-'60s and became affiliated with RCA records in 1967.

WOOD, DEL—(1902–1989) Del Wood played piano on the *Grand Ole Opry* from 1953 through the late 1980s. Her biggest hit was the 1951 song "Down Yonder."

WRIGHT, GINNY—(dates unavailable) Born in Georgia, Ginny Wright had two country hit songs. She sang "I Love You" with Jim Reeves, which was released in 1954, and "Are You Mine" with Tom Tall in 1955.

YOUNG, FARON—(1932–96) Born in Louisiana, Faron Young's most successful years were from 1954–62. He had several hit records such as "Sweet Dreams" and "Hello Walls" (written by Willie Nelson). He experienced a resurgence in popularity in the early to mid '70s, but by the '80s he had fallen out of favor. Young then disappeared from country music and ended up killing himself in 1996. In 2000 he was named to the Country Music Hall of Fame.

INDEX

154, 211–12; battleship christening, 118; beginnings, 68–69; benefit performance, 166; *Big D Jamboree*, 104–6; breakthroughs, 111; and Brown, Norma, 141; career summary, 233–34; car wreck, 193; Christmas record, 183–84; comeback possibilities, 260–61, 265–67; concert tours, 155–56; cross-over records, xvi–xvii, 152, 171, 180–82; dance lessons, 164–65; European tour, 129–35, 143, 223–24; financial status, 207–8; first album, 139–40; gold record, 157; gospel albums, 271–73; Grammy nominations, 154; guest appearances, 265–66, 269; "Here Today and Gone Tomorrow," 86–87; hiatus, 137–38; hit songs, 86–87, 145–46, 154–55; and the Louvin Brothers, 116–17; March of Dimes tour, 123–24; missed tour, 138–39; nightclub act, 163–66; personal appearance tours, 151–53; popularity, 141–44, 149–52, 154–72; practical jokes, 178–79, 206, 230–31; and Presley, Elvis, 96, 99–105; publicity photo shoot, 156–57; record boycott, 228–29; recording contracts, 112–13, 155; retirement, 233–34; reunion appearances, 269–70; and Robinson, Fabor, 79–85; "Scarlet Ribbons," 161–162; and Sholes, Steve, 319; state fair performances, 202–3, 273–74, 279; substitute singers, 223; television appearances, 142, 151, 157–59, 164–65, 272; "Three Bells, The," 145–46, 154–55; Trio Restaurant and Supper Club, 71–72; without Jim Ed, 113–16. *See also Louisiana Hayride*; recording sessions; road tours; *specific songs*
Bryant, Anita, 159, 290
Bryant, Boudleaux, 167, 290

Bryant, Felice, 167, 290
Bryant, Jimmy, 325
Buffalo, New York, 123
Bugs Bunny cartoons, 322
Bull Shoals Arkansas, 214–15
Burbank Recording Studios, 57
Burns, Jethro. *See* Homer and Jethro
Bus Fare to Kentucky (Davis), 294
Bush, George H.W., 311
Bush, George W., 311
business school, 33–34
Butler family, 4
"Butterfly," 251
Buttrey, Kenny, 226, 290
"Bye, Bye, Love," 290, 296

Caddo Hotel, 50, 55
"Cajun Stripper, The," 243
California adventures, 56–57, 81–85, 118, 164–65
Calloway Gardens, Georgia, 219
campaign trail, 104
Campbell, Archie, 161, 290
Campbell, Glen, 309
Canada, 175–76
cancer treatment, 220–21
Capital Records, 317
Caravan of Stars, 294
Carlisle, Clifford, 291
Carlisles, 97, 291
Carlisle, William (Jumpin' Bill), 291
carnival, 14–15
"Carroll County Accident, The," 324
Carson, Martha, 97, 291
Carter, A. P., 291
Carter Family, 91, 92, 103, 291
Carter, June, 103
Carter, Mother Maybelle, 103, 291
Carter, Sara 291
car troubles 29, 32–33, 59–61
Cartwright, Hoss, 114
car wreck, 193
Cashbox: and Austin, Bob, 176, 211; awards 135, 211, 284–86; background information, 291; "Old Lamplighter, The," 167; promotional photos, 151; song reviews,